The Art of Kabuki

The Art of Kabuki
FAMOUS PLAYS IN PERFORMANCE

translated, with commentary, by
Samuel L. Leiter

UNIVERSITY OF CALIFORNIA PRESS   BERKELEY • LOS ANGELES • LONDON

University of California Press
Berkeley and Los Angeles, California
University of California Press, Ltd.
London, England

ISBN: 0-520-03555-0

Library of Congress Catalog Card Number: 77-83107

Designed by Linda M. Robertson

Printed in the United States of America

PHOTO CREDITS: Figs. 1-14, 16-24, 26-27, 79-87, 94: Andrew T. Tsubaki; Figs. 15, 35, 38, 41, 66-67, 71-73, 76-77, 89-91, 93: *Engekikai;* Figs. 25, 53, 57: Shōchiku; Figs. 28-34, 36-37, 39-40, 42: Yūki; Figs. 43-52, 54-56, 58-65: Yoshida Chiaki; Figs. 68-70, 74-75, 78, 88, 92, 95-99, 103-107: National Theatre.

To Marcia

Contents

Preface

The Kabuki theater of Japan is now a form of theater acknowledged the world over as a major example of the high degree theatrical art can attain when it is nurtured by centuries of devoted artistry. Professional Kabuki troupes have toured Europe, China, and America on several occasions, playing to thousands of foreign spectators and enthralling them with the power and perfection of their skill. The jet-age shrinking of the globe has brought thousands more into the great Kabuki playhouses of Japan themselves. Fewer and fewer people confuse Kabuki with its theatrical predecessor, the Nō, and an audience for books and articles on Kabuki in Western languages has grown rapidly.

Probably the clearest sign that Kabuki holds a deep interest and fascination for many Westerners is the number of English language productions of Kabuki plays being put on at American colleges and universities. Such capable directors and scholars as Leonard Pronko, James Brandon, Earle Ernst, A. C. Scott, Shozō Satō, Andrew T. Tsubaki, and Onoe Kuroemon (himself originally a Kabuki actor from one of Kabuki's most outstanding families) have shown American audiences the delights to be gleaned from the presentation of Kabuki plays staged in the authentic manner. In two instances, Kabuki productions were selected as winners in the American Theatre Association's annual College Theatre Festival and were staged at the Kennedy Center in Washington, D.C., as part of the Festival proceedings. In New York, a professional group, the Institute for Advanced Studies in the Theatre Arts, did two very well-received Kabuki productions in the 1960s and brought famous Kabuki stars to New York to direct them on both occasions. These stars included Onoe Baikō VI, Matsumoto Kōshirō VIII, and Nakamura Matagorō. The presence of such stars is by no means unusual since even the colleges have employed their services both as directors and technical advisors or coaches.

It has long been recognized that the plays of the Kabuki theater, though never totally devoid of literary elements, subordinate their literary aspect in favor of theatrical effectiveness. That is, the plays are often cut and adapted to suit the tastes of the leading actors, who are more interested in putting on a good show than providing a lesson in classical literature. Yet, despite this fact, well understood by Western students of Kabuki as well as by the Japanese, the greater majority of Kabuki plays published in English translation up to now have given barely any attention to the theatrical aspect, concentrating instead on presenting the plot and dialogue as clearly as possible. Unfortunately, this approach does not go far enough in aiding the reader to envision what an actual performance is like. Except for the translations of James Brandon (whose recent *Kabuki: Five Classic Plays* [Cambridge, Mass., 1975] is excellent) and two plays translated in the early 1950s by A. C. Scott, Kabuki translations usually provide little in the way of detailed stage directions. Such an approach may well be acceptable to those interested in Kabuki primarily as literature, but, given Kabuki's unique theatrical qualities, it is a decidedly inferior approach to Kabuki translation.

Kabuki is, par excellence, a theater of visual and aural delight, a theater which must be seen to be appreciated. As with most forms of classical Asian theater, it is nearly impossible to get an idea of its sumptuous and thrilling theatricality from the bare bones of plot and dialogue. More than with the theater of the West, the reader is forced to imagine a world of incredibly vivid costumes, sets, and makeup, in a variety of styles ranging from the bizarrely grotesque to the semirealistic. Further, the plays are all performed on the basis of long-standing traditions and only a spectator with an understanding of the various theatrical conventions can truly comprehend the heart of what he is viewing or reading. It is for this reason that one of Japan's leading Kabuki scholars, Professor Gunji Masakatsu, has said that reading many Kabuki plays, which even in Japanese are published with only a minimum of stage directions, can be a tiresome thing.

There is, then, an obvious need for new and stageworthy translations of Kabuki plays.

The aim of such translations should be to make clear the stage movements, scenic appurtenances, types of costume and makeup used, acting styles, and so forth. I have attempted to provide such information in this book. As I have suggested, practically none of this information is to be found in the scripts themselves. In addition to research in written sources, the only way to gather data on stage production is to witness actual performances. The translations in this book are all supplemented by descriptions based on repeated visits to the plays in Japanese theaters between September 1974 and June 1975. My stay in Japan was made possible by a Research Grant awarded me by the Fulbright-Hays Commission, for which I am very grateful.

During the months that this book was in preparation, it became clear to me that merely to add stage directions and detailed descriptions of the visual and aural aspects of productions was not enough. Though Kabuki performance is based on tradition it is not based on one tradition. A description of one cast's version of a play is not necessarily the same as that of another's. This element of variations in the tradition has been almost completely overlooked in earlier translations.

Kabuki has been in existence since the early seventeenth century, and the classical plays staged today were written during the seventeenth, eighteenth, and nineteenth centuries. The major interpretations of the leading roles have been commented on frequently though such comments have rarely appeared in English. These comments derive from both actors and critics. It is my belief that such materials should be made available to the

English reader for with them his appreciation, not only of the plays but of Kabuki itself, will be immeasurably enhanced. Therefore, the present translations have been prepared with extensive introductions to each play. In addition to basic background material pertinent to the particular plays, a summation of the action is given with special attention paid to the critical commentary of actors and theater specialists. Almost all such critical material is performance-oriented rather than "literary" in nature. Many Western theater people who believe that Kabuki is merely a thing of beautiful outward form will be surprised to learn that Kabuki is not lacking an inner life conceived in the same rationalistic spirit that informs the theatrical approach of those trained in systems such as that of Stanislavski. The reader will come to understand that Kabuki, though considerably more ossified than in the past, always has been and continues to be a living form of theater with a variety of approaches to even the most conventional of its techniques.

A word is in order about the plays translated here. Kabuki plays are basically performed in one of two ways. Either a famous scene (or scenes) is performed from a much longer work or the full-length work is performed in its entirety. There are variations of this practice but, as a rule, these methods are the most frequent. Tokyo's Kabuki Theatre (Kabuki-za) traditionally produces programs made up of acts from the popular repertoire. The National Theatre (Kokuritsu Gekijō) normally produces full-length versions of the plays. Because of the horizontal or "scene-by-scene" style in which Kabuki plays are constructed one can appreciate a scene or act even

when performed out of the context of the play in its entirety. The scenes are normally self-contained and, in most cases, as with the plays included here, are virtual one-act dramas. Only a minimum of background, if that, is required to follow the action. Nevertheless, to make the action as clear as possible, each play has been provided with an introduction in which pertinent background details are filled in. These introductions are divided into three major sections: (1) Background to the Play, (2) Plot and *Kata,* and (3) The Playwright(s).

The translations in this book are all of famous scenes or acts in plays that are infrequently played in their full-length versions. If one were to see a production of these plays in Japan, the chances are that he would see them pretty much as they are printed here, though some differences deriving from an individual actor's preferences might be apparent. A number of such differences have been suggested in the introductions to the plays.

In translating the dialogue, I have attempted to capture the flavor of the original in terms of internal rhythms. As a result, many lines, at first glance, may seem overwritten and verbose. I hope that actors speaking these lines will be taught something of the rhythmical flow of Kabuki speech so they may impart a sense of the Japanese style to their delivery. In those cases where recordings of the original are available, companies preparing productions are urged to study these recordings closely if they wish to convey an aura of authenticity in performance.

Ultimately, the true test of the translations must come when they are acted. To date, the only play in this collection which I have had the opportunity to direct is *The Village School*. The process of actual production led me to make a good number of alterations in my original translation. These have been incorporated in the version given here. It may well be that production of the other plays would have led to alterations in their dialogue as well. However, I have gone over these translations very closely on the basis of my experience with *The Village School* and hope that they will prove not only readable but, even more important, worthy of being acted on the stage.

Note: all Japanese names in this book are printed in the Japanese order, family name first. Japanese words and names should be read with consonants as in English and vowels as in Italian. Thus, "a" is pronounced as in "corsage," "e" as in "neigh," and so on. Long vowels have a line over them except in city names such as Osaka, Kyoto, and Tokyo.

Acknowledgments

Without the friendship and advice of many people, I could not have completed this book. I wish to thank Mr. Sasaki Einosuke of the National Theatre of Japan and Professor Yamamoto Jirō of Waseda University in Tokyo for sponsoring my stay in Japan and offering their superb knowledge of Kabuki when needed. Mr. Faubion Bowers, Mr. Sugano of the Tōhō Producing Company, and Mr. Mogi of the Shōchiku Producing Company were very helpful in gaining me admittance to rehearsals where I was allowed to take photographs. Actors who were of service include Ichikawa Ebizō X, Onoe Shōroku II, and Nakamura Matagorō II. Mr. Chiaki Yoshida was kind enough to supply me with photographs of *The Village School*. Scholars whose advice was often essential include Professor Masakatsu Gunji, Professor Leonard Pronko, Mr. Nakamura Tetsurō, Professor James R. Brandon, Mr. Noma Seiichi, Mr. Hattori Yukio, and Professor Andrew Tsubaki. Professor Tsubaki was especially helpful with problems of translation. He also took many of the photographs printed in this book.

Others whose suggestions were helpful were Mr. Kawashima Atsumi of the National Theatre, Mr. Akita Minoru of the same institution, Mr. and Mrs. Futagawa Bungo, Mr. Shirakawa of the Waseda University Theatre Museum, Mr. Yano Hiroshi (Bandō Mitsuo, my dance teacher), Mr. Takao Tomono, Miss Okuda Akiko, Mrs. Okuda Natsuko, Mrs. Yamamoto Mariko, and Miss Matsumoto Yoshiko. For first introducing me to the world of Kabuki I must thank Professor Earle Ernst, whose book, *The Kabuki Theatre*, recently reissued by the University of Hawaii Press, is still the best in the field. My gratitude is extended to the excellent staff of the Tokyo office of the Fulbright-Hays Commission, presided over by the charming and efficient Mrs. Caroline A. Yang. I am sure I have forgotten someone on this extensive list; if so, I offer my apologies. But it will not do to forget my greatest aid and source of encouragement, my wife, Marcia.

Howard Beach, N.Y.   S. L. L.
Summer, 1977

Introduction

When a classical play, such as one of Shakespeare's, is produced in the Western theater, the production is as much the work of a stage director as it is that of the actors. Each director coming to a well-known text attempts to determine the play's special qualities and to bring these across to the audience in performance. Modern Western theater practice is often said to be director-centered and the enormous variety of interpretations brought to the production of familiar old plays by the many directors who stage them certainly helps to substantiate this viewpoint. The degree to which Western directors follow established traditions in their classical productions varies widely; some seek novelty at any price whereas others are more conservative. Still, it is the presence of the director and his vision which clearly distinguishes contemporary theater practice in the West.

Such a situation does not obtain in Japan's Kabuki theater, where the classical repertoire, dating back in some cases to the seventeenth century, continues to be produced today in a manner closely approximating the presentations of earlier years. Although the director is not unknown in today's Kabuki, his presence is something of an anomaly; Kabuki remains an actor-centered theater very much like that known in the West through the late nineteenth century. The leading Kabuki actors, familiar with specific traditions for the staging of the repertoire, assume a proto-directorial function in the rehearsal process, seeing to it that the other members of the cast perform the accepted business and that their own performances are the central feature of the production. Kabuki's traditional staging methods for the classical repertoire are so close to the actors, all of whom have been a part of the theater since their youth, that it is rare for a production to have more than a five- or six-day rehearsal period. The better known the play, the less rehearsal given to it.

In the West, there is also a fairly well-known body of traditions for the famous plays of the past. Yet, nowadays, these traditions are far more frequently honored in the breach than in the observance. In the late nineteenth century, the American star, Lawrence Barrett, could write:

> ...the so-called "business" of nearly all the commonly acted plays has been handed down through generations of actors, amended and corrected in many cases by each performer, but never radically changed. New readings of certain passages have been substituted

for old, but the traditional "points" have been preserved, personal characteristics and physical peculiarities finding ample expression within the old readings of the plays.[1]

The appearance on the scene of the director as the leading force in the staging of plays has changed all that and respect for the old stage business has gradually withered and practically disappeared.

In Japan, of course, the idea of artistic tradition is still thriving, though it does so side by side with a flourishing interest in the new and experimental. Japan manages to stand, like the Colossus of Rhodes, with one muscular foot in the modern world and the other firmly planted in the past. Kabuki is a theater of traditions. For a theatergoer to truly appreciate a Kabuki performance, awareness and understanding of these traditions is essential. For this reason, it is said that the best way to develop a firm grasp of Kabuki's fundamental qualities is to study the same play over and over again, not on the page but on the stage. The theatergoer wishing to delve into the heart of Kabuki is urged to attend the same production of a play as many times within its month-long run as possible.[2] Gradually, the finer points in the staging will become clear. At first, one's attention will be mainly concentrated on the intricacies of the plot and character relationships. Repeated visits, however, will change the focus to those aural and visual elements that compose the *mise-en-scène* and which, in this performance-dominated theater, take precedence over the play's existence as "dramatic literature." Constant attention to the performance will bring out all the nuances established by the many actors of the past whose interpretive inventions live on in ever more polished form in the artistry of today's performers. When the spectator has become as familiar as he can with the approach of one set of actors he should then see the same play as done by others. This procedure will help him to perceive the fascinating differences in the traditions as they have been transmitted down the years in the various acting families. These differences are often subtle, yet they may also be rather bold. Exposure to them is a prerequisite for full enjoyment and appreciation of Kabuki technique. Only when the spectator can distinguish between the variances in tradition or the difference in the execution of the same tradition will he be in a position to adequately judge the quality of a performance. The introductions to the plays in this book provide the reader with a thorough background for understanding the principal traditions associated with the performance of several outstandingly popular plays. They are intended to be an avenue to the enhancement of Kabuki appreciation.

When a Japanese theatergoer speaks of the traditional methods of Kabuki he uses a single word which has rather broad implications. This word, *kata,* or "form," may be used to refer to all aspects of a production, from the costumes, wigs, and makeup, to the music, sets, and properties. Most often, it is used with reference to the differences in the acting interpretations of the leading roles. At

1. *Edwin Forrest* (New York, 1969; first published 1881), p. 3.
2. Kabuki programs generally run from the second or third of the month to the twenty-sixth or twenty-seventh. The week or so between programs is given over to rehearsals.

the climax of *The Village School* (*Terakoya*) Matsuō, the chief character, must identify a decapitated head presented to him in a closed box. He has reason to believe the head in the box is that of his own beloved son; the moments before he raises the lid are, naturally, charged with great emotional tension. Actors playing Matsuō have developed a number of interesting variations on his behavior as he prepares to remove the lid.[3] Each of these interpretive approaches has been established as a kata; the actor playing Matsuō performs the kata he has learned as part of his own family's traditions. Ichikawa Ebizō will perform the kata of his father, Danjūrō XI, just as Matsumoto Kōshirō will do that of his master, Nakamura Kichiemon I.

In this sense, the performance of traditional stage business in the West differs from that of Kabuki. In general, the Shakespearean tradition refers to interpretive business which is not aligned with any particular family or notion of hereditary continuity. If a director wishes to motivate Hamlet's sudden line to Ophelia, "Where's your father?" he may have Hamlet catch a glimpse of an eavesdropping Polonius, thus drawing on a tradition going back many years. Conceptually, the motivation may be considered a kata; in terms of execution it is not, as the actor and director may choose from an infinite variety of possibilities in deciding precisely how the actual performance of the moment is to be arranged. The actor is not restricted, as in Kabuki, to a presentation of the kata in precise physical terms. In fact, the Western actor's business usually proceeds from an idea, an intellectualized rationale, a need to find an appropriate reason for his behavior. Some such drive undoubtedly propelled the actor who created the original Kabuki kata in the distant past; however, the modern actor, especially one performing a role relatively new to him, may not even be fully aware of the reason for his kata; he performs it as he has learned it and may, at first, worry more over his technical precision than his subtextual interiorization.

Kabuki's emphasis on the preservation of effective kata is actually a phenomenon of the relatively recent past. Kata have been important in Kabuki since the late seventeenth century but for many years actors enjoyed great creative freedom in the handling of their roles. They were far freer than are their modern counterparts in choosing from the reservoir of kata available and in creating their own new kata. The tendency to classicalize the kata and set them in the formaldehyde of tradition evolved in the second half of the nineteenth century. As a consequence, a disproportionate number of today's respected kata were first evolved by the two greatest actors of the Meiji period (1868-1912), Danjūrō IX and Kikugorō V. When one of today's stars decides to experiment with the traditions, he frequently researches the kata of pre-Meiji actors and performs them instead of those that are more familiar to contemporary audiences. It is more common for an actor to investigate and present kata that have fallen into disuse than it is for him to generate entirely new kata with no basis in tradition.

Kata are learned by the actor today in essentially the same way as in the past. This is by the simple method of observation and imi-

3. These are described in the introduction to *The Village School.*

tation. Kata are also transmitted by word of mouth and in the written descriptions left to posterity by the actors themselves and their contemporaries. Occasionally, these written sources reveal fascinating insights into the reasons behind certain kata, as will be seen in the introductions to the plays in this book. An actor grows up in the theater and watches his seniors day in and day out, from early childhood on, storing the numerous kata in his memory against the day when he will be called on to perform the roles he has learned. He also takes lessons from master actors, an aspect that has become even more important in recent years as actors' children have taken to attending school for the purpose of gaining a general education. The number of college-educated Kabuki actors is growing though there are those who complain that the time spent in college is a waste for the Kabuki actor who aspires to greatness.

Certain unwritten rules must be observed when learning the kata. One is that the first performances of a role must be done precisely as the actor has learned it. When the actor doing the teaching is the equal in status of the actor learning, the teacher will carefully observe the temperamental and physical qualities of the student; a tacit understanding exists that, should some difficulty arise, the learner may request whatever variations he deems suitable, providing his suggestions are reasonable. Similarly, younger actors are often allowed minor variations by the teacher when the latter feels that physical and temperamental factors justify them. An actor who often altered the kata so as to suit his rather thick physique was the famous female impersonator, Onoe Kikugorō VI. Kikugorō sought to make himself appear thinner on stage by performing most of his actions while standing at a three-quarters angle to the audience.

Many respected kata were first produced when actors such as Kikugorō sought to find a method by which their personal appearance could be enhanced. Later actors often follow such kata though their own physiques require different approaches. An actor often lays himself open to critical attack for blindly following kata that are not especially suitable for his own qualities. Some serious actors, like the popular young female impersonator, Bandō Tamasaburō, earnestly study the techniques of earlier actors, whose physical appearance is said to have been similar to theirs, in order to make the most of their unique features. Tamasaburō has been applauded for his effective employment of old kata that show off his tall, willowy looks to their best advantage.

The kata learned by an actor are considered treasured possessions, especially when they are revered by his own family. An actor will adhere strictly to the traditions he has been taught though he may, after achieving acclaim as a master-actor (a position he will not normally reach until he is in his forties), add personal interpretations of his own which may then become a part of the tradition themselves. Some major actors, however, have incorporated new interpretations only to abandon them on their next outing in a role.

In the past, actors often faced the danger of losing the support of their late parents' patron, who always felt a sentimental attachment to the dead actor. If he felt the son was even slightly inferior in his performance of the kata the patron may have criticized the actor sharply or even have gone so far as to withdraw his support. This system forced the young actor to preserve his father's or master's kata intact until powerful enough to alter them on his own terms. Though dying out, vestiges of this system still remain.

An actor playing the traditional kata may, through his recreative ability, resuscitate the energy first infused into the form. One may actually catch a glimpse of the role's original performer, long since dead. In the West, theater is often described as a transient art, a mode of expression that cannot be retained except in the vague hallways of memory. Despite the relative permanence of film art, the notion still has validity with regard to the chemistry of the living stage. Japanese theater, existing paradoxically in a world where transience is venerated almost as a mode of life, has overcome the merely ephemeral quality of live stage performance by the employment of kata. Despite the obvious distinctions that, over the years, have insinuated themselves into the manner of performing a particular role or play, the original impetus and interpretive afflatus may still be largely discerned beneath the layers of refinement and polish. We may not be able to recreate the performance of Burbage or Garrick in the role of Hamlet, despite the existence of a so-called tradition, but the equivalent task in Kabuki is surely within the grasp of the kata-trained player.

Despite the externally vivid dynamics of Kabuki performance, everything seen or heard on the stage is the result of a meaningful inner dynamic. Kabuki's kata were not created from an art for art's sake aesthetic; they are instead the outcome of a need on the part of their creators for externalization of a hidden idea or emotion. Concepts which words are often incapable of expressing may be conveyed through the performance of highly polished kata which present quintessential elements of reality in terms both immediate and compelling. There is a scene in *Scarface Yosa* (*Kirare Yosa*), for instance, where Yosaburō is walking along the beach when his eyes come to light on the beautiful Otomi. The actor playing Yosaburō performs a kata in which he stops, stares, and in a charmingly abstracted way, allows his overjacket to slip slowly from his shoulders to the ground. This kata establishes far more succinctly than mere words could the inner meaning of love-at-first-sight.

Perhaps the most impressive example of kata that externalize a character's feelings are those generically termed *mie*. These are those exciting moments in the course of a performance when the actor strikes an aggressive and somewhat exaggerated pose, usually in time to the beating by a stagehand of two sticks of wood on a flat board situated on the floor at stage left. These concentrated poses are similar in effect to the use of a zoom lens close-up in the cinema. In *The Village School*, Matsuō's son is offstage where he is about to be decapitated. Matsuō, on stage, knows this, but cannot reveal to the others in the scene that the boy is his son. When he hears the offstage sound of the blade striking flesh, he moves toward center stage almost involuntarily. Suddenly, he bumps into Tonami, the wife of the man ordered to kill the boy. He quickly straightens up, shouts "Brazen woman!" and performs one of Kabuki's most intense and devastatingly dramatic mie.

Everything stops and all eyes immediately focus on the distraught yet domineering figure of this emotionally ravaged father. Matsuō must display an attitude of scorn to conceal the unspeakable grief he suffers as a man whose son has just been slain. The kata created by the various actors of the past for this moment, like so many others, demonstrate conclusively how dependent the Kabuki theater is on the supraliterary qualities of performance.

In spite of Kabuki's inner life, the actor is not commonly taught to justify or motivate his stage activity (several modern actors, influenced by contemporary theory, attempt on their own consciously to do so). Typically, however, numerous repetitions lead the actor to an appreciation of the interior truth behind his physical exertions in the role. He gradually comes to recognize the reason for the kata's original creation. In a sense, the Kabuki actor who learns to justify his performance only after having had it imposed on him from without is like the Western actor influenced by the later ideas of Stanislavski. Stanislavski, toward the end of his long career, came to the conclusion that an actor's inner life as a character would be hampered by conscious attempts at the creation of emotion. Shifting his ground from ideas he propounded earlier, Stanislavski felt that the actor should shun such tricks as evoking emotion by recalling moments from his life which parallel those of his character; instead, the actor must employ the "method of physical actions" by which he makes conscious choices as to how the character will relate physically to his "given circumstances." Once the ap-

propriate choices have been made, the actor will find that the proper emotional responses will arise within him naturally, without forcing. This process works for the Kabuki actor, too, the difference being that his choices have been made for him by his predecessors in the role. Eventually, then, the sensitive and talented Kabuki actor will find the truth behind his actions from the ongoing process of performing them.

Kata are not static but continually undergoing change and development, though this process is no longer as free and unrestrained as it once was. Nevertheless, despite the tendency in modern times to classicalize the kata, today's actors continue to polish, perfect, and reinterpret the conventions they have inherited. This may be most strongly remarked in the work of the progressive, leftist-oriented theater company, the Zenshin-za, which produces both Kabuki and modern drama. The Zenshin-za never does a Kabuki play without first reexamining the traditional kata and determining if these may not be freshened up on the basis of a politically progressive viewpoint. This group always employs a director for the revival of Kabuki plays, and their work, as a result, generally displays a cohesiveness lacking in the star-dominated world of the better-known Kabuki productions. *Shunkan* is a play that normally ends on a gloomy, almost tragic note as the title character sadly confronts the loneliness to which he has purposely condemned himself. The final curtain of the Zenshin-za production, however, sounds a note of optimism as Shunkan, glowing with a sense of love for his fellow man, allows a smile to steal over his face. Changes such as those of the Zenshin-za demonstrate how kata may be influenced by modifications in the outlook of an age.

Kata, then, are the very bones of Kabuki performance. They are the building blocks of which every production is constructed. They exist in all forms of traditional Japanese theater but in none do they possess as much interest for theatergoers as in Kabuki, which has long been the mainstay of Japan's performing arts. Study of Kabuki kata often permits one to understand both the nature of the actors who created them and the differences in the actors who have followed their leads.

Benten Kozō

(*Benten Musume Meono Shiranami*)
A Kabuki Play by
Kawatake Mokuami
The Hamamatsu-ya Scene (*Hamamatsu-ya no ba*)
The Mustering Scene (*Seizoroi no ba*)

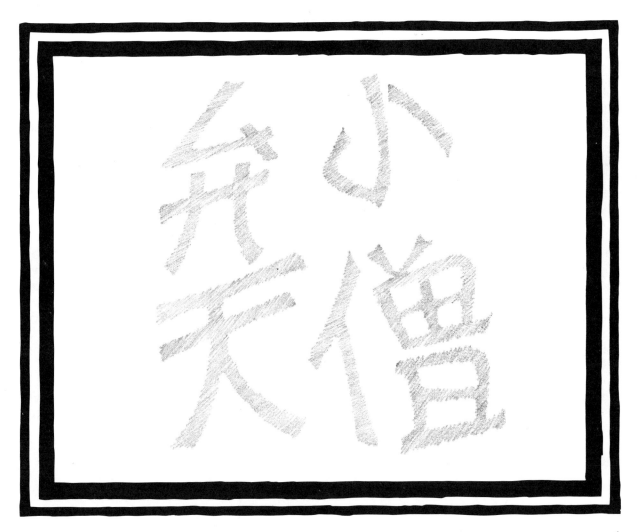

BACKGROUND TO THE PLAY

Benten Kozō was first performed in March 1862 at Edo's Ichimura Theatre (Ichimura-za). Its title role was acted by the nineteen-year-old Ichimura Uzaemon XIII (1884-1904), who later became one of the three outstanding stars of late nineteenth-century Kabuki under the name of Onoe Kikugorō V. Nakamura Shikan IV (1830-1899), a very popular performer, played Nango Rikimaru, Kawarazaki Gonjūrō (1838-1903; later to become renowned as Ichikawa Danjūrō IX) was Tadanobu Rihei, Seki Sanjūrō III (1805-1870) was Nippon Daemon, Ichikawa Danzō VII (1800-1871) acted Kōbei, and Iwai Kumesaburō (1829-1882; later Iwai Hanshirō VIII) played Akaboshi Jūzaburō. This was an all-star cast. The play became a specialty of Kikugorō's and has been handed down as one of the favorite works of the Onoe family of actors.

Benten Kozō is only one of a number of titles by which the play is known. Its author, Kawatake Mokuami (1816-1893), called it *The Glorious Picture Book of Aoto's Exploits* (*Aoto Zōshi Hana no Nishikie*). This peculiar title refers to Aoto Saemon Fujitsuna, a Shogunate vassal during the Kamakura era (1185-1333) who was the subject of a popular ten-volume series of story books published in 1812. Though this series was the basis for several earlier plays, Aoto barely figures in the present work, appearing only briefly in the final scene. The reference in the title to woodblock prints (*nishikie*) is apt, as Mokuami is said to have been inspired to write the play by a series of prints produced by Utagawa Toyokuni III.

Other well-known titles are *The Five Bandits* (*Shiranami Gonin Otoko*), *Miss Benten, The Male/Female Bandit* (*Benten Musume Meono Shiranami*), *A Chrysanthemum Boy From Enoshima* (*Enoshima Sodachi Neoi no Chigogiku*), and *The Kikugorō Line's Benten Kozō* (*Otonikiku Benten Kozō*). Any one of the first three titles may still be used to advertise the play; the latter two are not as well known today. *Benten Musume Meono Shiranami* is the title used most frequently when only the Hamamatsu-ya and Inase River scenes are performed.

Scholars dispute the actual source of the play and several explanations have been offered. According to the memoirs of Kikugorō V, this actor came across a set of Toyokuni's prints depicting him and several other popular actors of the time in the guise of members of a bandit gang. Struck by the character in which Toyokuni depicted him, Kikugorō says he went right to Mokuami and begged him to write a play for him in which he could act this character. Another story has it that Mokuami asked Toyokuni to create his prints as a sort of "feeler" for public reaction. Seeing the success of the prints, Mokuami is said to have sat down to pen his drama. Yet another version has it that Mokuami based his chief character on a man he encountered crossing Ryōgoku Bridge in Edo one evening. This man, dressed in a girl's kimono and resembling Kikugorō, intrigued the playwright so that he described it to Toyokuni, who created his "Five Bandits" print series, following which Mokuami put his experience into dramatic form.

Whatever the truth, it is well known that a close relationship had long existed between the art of woodblock prints and Kabuki. Such prints were often used in illustrating story books (*sōshi*). Mokuami attempted to combine these three genres in *Benten Kozō*—to put on stage a work that suggested the fantastic world of the illustrated books through a succession of impressive and colorfully exaggerated scenes.

As a result, the play combines several Kabuki styles. Since it alternates history play (*jidaimono*) scenes with domestic play (*sewamono*) scenes, the play is classed as a *jidaisewamono*. The Hamamatsu-ya scene is a sewamono. Some critics have considered it an example of the *kizewamono* genre because of its depiction of such lower-class types as Benten and Nango. *Kizewamono* ("living" or "raw" domestic plays) usually deal with the seamier side of contemporary urban life. The scene is also famous as an example of the *yusuriba* or "blackmail scene." Blackmail scenes frequently appeared in mid-nineteenth-century Kabuki domestic plays; the present one is considered representative of the genre. The Inase River Mustering scene differs from the blackmail scene in a marked way: it is played in the rather formalistic jidaimono manner. It contains a brief but interesting example of *tachimawari* (stage battles). These two scenes are by far the most popular in the play and are among the most frequently performed in the Kabuki repertoire. The full-length play from which these scenes are drawn is in five acts, eight scenes. Act III, scene i corresponds to the Hamamatsu-ya scene, whereas Act IV would be the Inase River scene.

PLOT AND KATA

Benten Kozō tells the story of how the five thieves, Benten Kozō, Nango Rikimaru, Nippon Daemon, Akaboshi Juzaburō, and Tada-nobu Rihei banded together and of their ultimate fate. In the scenes prior to those translated here, we see Benten display his nihilistic character as a young man who will go to any lengths to obtain what he wants, which is usually money. Despite his callousness, he has a certain charm and we watch with interest as he joins up with a band of brigands led by Nippon Daemon.[1]

The Hamamatsu-ya scene takes place at a better-class textile shop by that name in Kamakura's Yukinoshita section. Contemporary audiences were aware, though, that the scene was actually meant to be a shop in the Nihonbashi district of Edo. When the curtain opens three or four clerks (some productions use seven or eight) are seen going about their business. Soon, a rough-looking character, Arajirō, comes to the shop and demands that five kimono he ordered dyed be ready when he returns. These kimono are later worn by the five thieves in the Mustering scene. After he departs a beautiful young lady (Benten in disguise) and her samurai attendant (Nango in disguise) appear on the *hanamichi* runway. The chrysanthemum patterns on Benten's kimono are an immediate signal to the audience of the role's connection with the Kikugorō line of actors, as *kiku* is the Japanese word for chrysanthemum.

On Acting the Role of Benten. According to the respected critic, Miyake Saburō, two major ways of playing Benten have been handed down. The play, he says, is

---

1. The name Nippon signifies Japan. The first syllable in Daemon is a pun on the word *"dai"* or *"great."* By means of an inverted pun, then, the character's name suggests "greatest in Japan." Faubion Bowers informs me that he learned this from Matsumoto Kōshirō VII.

really a bit different from the true kize-wamono, in which genre it is classed, in its attention to colorful and stylized details. Its overtly realistic qualities, however, cannot be denied. Therefore,

> The acting style for Benten stresses his style and form more than his realistic basis. The acting veers toward the showy and formalistic and there are a number of acting highlights. One of the two traditions handed down for playing Benten follows the way of Kikugorō VI and it emphasizes numerous realistic details in a finely wrought interpretation. This is fine but there is also the tradition originated by Ichimura Uzaemon XV (1874-1945), a high-pitched, clear-cut, 'romantic' approach, which is surely the best.[2]

In the 1950s and 1960s two of the chief players of Benten were Ichikawa Danjūrō XI (1909-1965) and Nakamura Kanzaburō (1909-). Kanzaburō acted the role in Kikugorō's style. Ichikawa Somegorō, upon whom the stage directions in the text are based, learned the role from Kanzaburō. Danjūrō is said to have followed the Uzaemon style, but he himself put it this way:

> When I first acted the part, Kikugorō VI had been dead for a brief time so I wasn't instructed by him personally but I asked a good many questions concerning his performance. In addition, I had seen Uzaemon XV play the role, having played Sonosuke in one of his productions, so I learned a good deal from watching him. Therefore, I came to perform the role on the basis of having studied both styles. The kata of these two stars were, whether one talks in general or in detail, quite different. For example, they differed even in the detail of whether they wore their hair ornament on the left or the right.[3]

Danjūrō goes on to say that he compared their kata and chose those he felt best for himself. Since Danjūrō was from a family without a very strong tradition for the role of Benten, he had more freedom in developing his performance than would an actor in the Onoe family or one with close ties to it.

After a brief exchange on the hanamichi, Benten and Nango move on to the doorway of the Hamamatsu-ya, where they are received with much enthusiasm by the shop-clerks and their chief, Yokurō. A definite undertone of sexual byplay runs through the following scene as the apparently lecherous clerks eye the attractive Benten and comically fawn on him. Benten and Nango pretend to be shopping for kimono materials so the clerks go off and bring back several boxfuls for their inspection.

2. *Kabuki o Mirume* (*An Eye for Kabuki*) (Tokyo, 1956), p. 58.

3. "Geidan: Shiranami Gonin Otoko" ("Chat on Art: The Five Thieves"), *Engekikai*, no. 4 (1957), p. 94.

A "Crippled" Benten. An interesting performance variation to that described in the text occurred here when Kikugorō gave his final performance as Benten in 1902. This was also his final appearance on the stage. He had suffered a cerebral hemorrhage and could barely walk, his left leg being paralyzed. The performance was therefore arranged to suit his disability. When the curtain opened his red thonged sandals and those of Nango were seen at the entry to the shop. The opening business with Arajirō was performed, followed by the entrance of Nippon Daemon disguised as Tamashima Ittō, a high-ranking samurai. Nippon was accompanied by an accomplice. This entrance is in the original script but is rarely performed nowadays. It would, of course, make Nippon's later entrance in the scene more logical. Nippon and his accomplice were led off by the proprietor, Kōbei, so as to make them more comfortable while selecting gifts, their ostensible reason for being there. The stage was cleared, music played, and the stage made a half-revolve, changing to a scene in the tatami mat room of the firm's storehouse where Benten, Nango, and Yokurō were discovered in the midst of examining various textiles. The sandals placed at the door in the opening scene justified Benten and Nango's presence in this scene and eliminated the need for the crippled Kikugorō to make the long entry on the hanamichi.[4]

In the interval during which the clerks are off the stage, Yokurō banters with Benten and Nango about their playgoing experiences. During this chatter, the names of the actors playing the roles of Benten, Nango, and Yokurō are mentioned.

Kabuki "Charm." The comic use of anachronisms is a common Kabuki technique. The device is called *aikyō* or *goaikyō,* literally meaning "charm." The use of actors' names on stage is a reminder of the days of Kabuki's glory, during the Edo era, when actors and audiences enjoyed a very close relationship. In the original production, for instance, Nango was played by the very popular Nakamura Shikan. Shikan's lines included a passage where he said of himself: "He (Shikan) hates to drink, doesn't care to philander, and scorns gambling. Moreover, he can't stand learning his lines." It is said that Shikan was hit on the head when young, resulting in a weak memory. Thus, his line about the difficulty of learning lines got a big laugh. Shikan was notorious for forgetting his words and always had to have a stage assistant feed him his lines *soto voce.*[5]

As Nango and Benten are examining the materials placed before them by the clerks, Benten slips a piece of scarlet crepe into his kimono. He has actually brought this with him but wants it to look as though he has stolen it from the pile before him.

---

4. Suzuki Shunbō, *Kabuki no Kata* (*Kabuki's Kata*) (Tokyo, 1927), pp. 358-383, has a full account of this production.

5. Kawatake Shigetoshi, ed., *Kabuki Meisakushū* (*Collection of Kabuki Masterpieces*), Vol. II (Tokyo, 1956).

A Difficult Kata. This moment is considered very difficult to perform. As Atsumi notes, "It must be seen by the clerks so it may be done openly but if it is too open it will create misgivings in those spectators seeing it for the first time. Thus, the proper degree of exposure must be found."[6]

As Benten had hoped a clerk spots the "theft" and creates a commotion about it. A fireman, Seiji, employed by the establishment as a guard, is called in and reprimands Benten who, together with Nango, acts as if he is completely innocent. Yokurō takes the cloth from Benten and strikes him on the forehead with his abacus as the clerks mill about threateningly.

A Rule for Nango. The actor, Ichimura Uzaemon XVII (1916-), has noted that a cardinal rule for players of Nango is to watch the action of the clerks carefully when Benten is struck. Since a lot of action is occurring at the moment, some audience members are likely to miss the act of Benten's being struck so Nango's gaze helps focus attention on the action.[7]

Sonosuke, son of the owner of the shop, enters hurriedly and tries to find out what has occurred. Nango angrily decries the accusations leveled at his "young mistress" and disproves them by producing a receipt for the cloth from another shop. He also points to

the other shop's trademark on the cloth. The clerks and Sonosuke are abashed at the terrible error that they seem to have committed. Sonosuke begs Benten and Nango's pardon.

Switching Wigs. During this scene Benten changes his wig and fixes his makeup with the aid of a stage assistant. This wig-switching is a recent development. In former days the actor and stage assistant undid the topknot of the original wig, loosened the red cloth at the rear of the wig, and mussed the hair in front, removing the comb placed there. It was a kata of Kikugorō V's to make a change of makeup, too. The length of Benten's eyeline was adjusted and his lipstick wiped off with a wad of tissue paper. Kikugorō VI and his son, the present Baikō VII (1915-), are among the actors who make the wig-switch whereas others, such as Uzaemon XV, preferred to wear the same wig throughout.

Nango is furious and will accept no apologies. The master himself, Kōbei, enters to settle the matter. Nango shows Kōbei the scar inflicted on Benten by Yokurō.

Kōbei's Entrance and Benten's Scar. Kōbei usually enters by first saying his line, "I will be with you in a moment" offstage and then opening the upstage sliding doors. However, when Nakamura Nakazō III (1800-1886) played the role, he interpreted it as if Kōbei, having heard the commotion out front, was worried over what was going on. He therefore said his "Yes, yes" offstage, then opened

6. Atsumi Seitarō, "*Benten Kozō* Kanshō" ("Appreciation of *Benten Kozō*"), *Engekikai,* no. 6 (1949), p. 43.
7. "Geidan: Shiranami Gonin Otoko," p. 95.

the door a bit and said, "I will be with you in a moment" and came in while speaking. Opening the sliding doors in this way is considered appropriate for history-style plays (jidaimono) but should not be used in domestic plays.[8]

Benten's scar is now produced by attaching a small half-moon shaped piece of red cloth to the forehead. Originally, Kikugorō V dabbed red makeup on his forehead to simulate the wound. Another trick often used by actors in the past was to have a bit of red makeup smeared in a spot behind an ear, where it could not be seen by the audience. At the appropriate moment, the actor would secretly touch his middle finger to this makeup and then apply the red color to his forehead, simulating the shape of a wound.

Nango threatens to kill everyone there unless the matter can be suitably adjusted. Seiji, the fireman, now intervenes with Kōbei.

Seiji's Business. Seiji has been sitting near Nango at stage right. Kōbei is across from them at stage left. Many productions have Seiji cross quickly to Kōbei at this point, confer with him briefly, and then cross back to the right. This stage direction is in the original script as well. The production described in the present translation, though, omits the movement. When asked the reason for this ap-

proach, Nakamura Matagorō II (1914-), the actor playing the role, revealed that the omission was owing to a personal interpretation. He feels Seiji has often done similar favors for Kōbei in the past and would not need his permission before broaching his plan.

When Nango is given only ten *ryō* as compensation, he refuses to accept them. (This sum was ten ryō when the play was first produced, later was twenty ryō, and even went as high as thirty ryō. Today's performances usually revert to the original sum.) This refusal angers Seiji who, about to begin a brawl, is hustled out of the shop, throwing his hand towel (*tenugui*) at Benten as he goes.

"The Towel Kata." The towel is used by Benten later for a number of gestures. The business of throwing the towel was not included in early productions of the play. When Benten, later in the play, had to use a towel, one was handed him by a stage assistant. An actor, Sawamura Gennosuke IV (1859-1936), added this kata to justify the towel's presence later in the scene. Some critics have criticized the kata for smacking too much of the methods of modern realism.

Kōbei agrees to Nango's demands for one hundred ryō and hands them over to him. Nango and Benten begin to leave but are stopped in their tracks by the entrance (from within the shop) of an imposing-looking samurai, Tamashima Ittō, actually Nippon Daemon in disguise.

8. Tomita Tetsunosuke, "*Aoto Zōshi Hana no Nishikie Saiken*" ("A Close Look at *The Glorious Picture Book of Aoto's Exploits*"), *Kabuki*, III (1968), 133.

Nippon's Turban. An unusual part of Nippon's costume is a black turbanlike head covering. It is only in this scene that Nippon wears this item and the reason for its being worn is not revealed during the present action. In the warehouse scene (not translated here) he removes it to reveal a bushy wig of the type known as *gojunichi* (fifty days), signifying his neglect of the barber's razor as the result of a lingering illness. In the Hamamatsu-ya scene he is passing himself off as someone else so, as Atsumi Seitarō suggests, the turban is not really necessary. Thus, some actors, such as Danjūrō IX, Kōshirō VII (1870-1949), and Sadanji III (1898-1969), appeared with a normal hairdo of shaved crown and lacquered side-locks in the present scene though they wore the "fifty day" wig in the Mustering scene. This was done even though the Mustering scene supposedly takes place shortly after the action of the present scene. Kōshirō VII appears to be the only actor ever to have appeared without the bushy wig in the Mustering scene but, as is common in Kabuki, tradition proved stronger than innovation, and he soon gave up the new approach. Kabuki's conventions allow a sudden change in a character's appearance from one scene to another though modern actors often disdain such an unrealistic procedure and seek out more "believable" techniques.

Benten and Nango sit down again. Confronted by Nippon's accusations, Benten reveals his true male identity.

Benten's "Sex Change." Benten's acting as he decides to give up his hoax and switch from female impersonation to masculine behavior is very difficult. As the audience waits to see his reaction, the white paper in his hand flutters rapidly. The business of fluttering the paper is an Uzaemon XV kata. This actor would make his right hand, holding the paper, tremble, then grit his teeth, crumple his body, and show an expression of deepest chagrin and mortification at having been thus cornered. His beautiful and sharply chiseled features (his father was French) are said to have looked splendid at this moment. As Benten switches from a female to a male acting style, a rosette in his wig is removed. Uzaemon and others removed the rosette by hand but Kiku-gorō VI, wanting it to look as though it fell out of its own accord, attached a thread to it which he pulled at the right moment.

As previously noted, Kikugorō V removed his lipstick and changed his eyeline during the section when his back was to the audience. He did this so as to make the sudden change to a man more believable. He used the tissue paper in his hand to wipe off the lipstick. When he later revealed the paper to the audience the red color on it appeared to be from the blood supposedly oozing from his wound. Though this kata is no longer performed (the lipstick remains the same and a stage assistant provides Benten with the red-stained tissue paper) it was considered a stroke of genius when first created by the then nineteen-year-old Kikugorō.

Now that he can be himself, Benten begins to make himself comfortable. He opens his kimono and sits cross-legged with his obi-less kimono draped loosely over his shoulders. This brazen posture has a delightfully erotic flavor to it in view of Benten's decidedly feminine appearance. He begins to describe the reasons for his extortion attempt. The highlight of the play comes when he delivers one of Kabuki's most famous speeches, describing himself and his past. The technique is called *yakuharai*. During the speech he makes reference to a period spent as a temple page, a position tantamount to his having served as a catamite because of his youthful beauty. At another point (in the original) he mentions that he learned how to use his voice to act "extortion scenes" by listening, as a child, to his grandfather at Terajima. This is a veiled reference to Kikugorō V's grandfather, Kikugorō III (1784-1849), who lived at Terajima Village. Terajima came to be the family name of Kikugorō's descendants, such as the present Kikugorō VII (1942-). Kikugorō III was well known for his acting of extortion scenes in Kabuki's domestic plays. The old-time audiences recognized the allusion, of course, and delighted in it as part of Kabuki's special charm.

Toward the end of the speech, Benten taps his pipe on a charcoal brazier to remove its tobacco. This is an important gesture since he slams the pipe down at his right in a moment and, as Kikugorō V pointed out, the audience would laugh if a burning ball of tobacco rolled out. He ends the speech by stating his name and performing a powerful mie pose, revealing a tattooed arm and shoulder.

Nango then proceeds to give a similar speech about himself. Nango's speech is spoken more conservatively than Benten's as his role in the scene is secondary. The actor must labor to set Benten off and not himself.

The extortionists return the hundred ryō and brazenly tell Kōbei to call the police and have them arrested. Nippon appears angered by their brashness and threatens to do them violence but Benten mocks him, calling him an amateur executioner. Kawatake suggests that Benten's irony here is intended to imply his "gratitude" at being decapitated by an amateur samurai executioner, rather than by one of the members of the outcast groups (*hinin*) who were entrusted with the odious task of executing criminals.[9]

Kōbei, unwilling to make a fuss because of the fear of scandal, hopes to convince them to leave but they refuse to do so unless given some compensation for their troubles. Kōbei offers them twenty ryō which, after some squabbling, they accept. Benten and Nango prepare to leave. As they go, Yokurō makes a nasty remark and is struck sharply by Benten. The pair move to the hanamichi where they enact a humorous scene centering around a game they play to determine who will carry their bundle.

Kikugorō's Exit Kata. As previously mentioned, Kikugorō V had to make a number of changes in his final performance of this play, due to his being crippled by a stroke. Having cut Benten's hanamichi entrance, he also was forced to cut the play's famous hanamichi exit. This was done by leaving the warehouse (where the scene had been played for this production) and having the stage begin a

9. *Kabuki Meisakushū*, II, 610.

slow resolve. As Nango and Benten walked in place the stage revolved beneath them until the side of the Hamamatsu-ya was at stage left and a board fence was seen running across the rear of the stage. The set was much like that used in *Scarface Yosa* (*Kirare Yosa*), which was appropriate, since the action at this point closely resembles a well-known scene in that play. The scene was supposed to be taking place at evening-time with a girl seen returning from the baths, a husband and wife strolling by, etc. The same basic business as in a traditional performance was enacted but it took place on the main stage as the actors slowly made their way off at the right.

During the exit Benten has a moment when he sings a verse in the musical style called *shinnai bushi*. This verse, "*amari doyoku na, mada mada*," contains a pun on the word *amma* (masseur) and *amari* (too much, excess). The line may be literally rendered as "Too much heartlessness, cruelty, and greed, more and more...."

Benten's Singing. As Benten sang, the actor playing Nango used to accompany him with a vocal shamisen imitation but this is no longer performed. Some actors, embarrassed at their poor singing ability, relegated the singing to an unseen performer in the *geza* music room. Uzaemon XV and Danjūrō XI were among the actors whose singing was "dubbed." There is an anecdote that informs us that when Kikugorō VI, then called Kikunosuke, played Benten Kozō, his father Ki-

kugorō V played the role of Yokurō, the chief clerk. Since the young Kikunosuke was ashamed of his voice, he did not sing the shinnai; instead his father sang it for him from the main stage. This was a playful violation of theatrical convention. When the song was over, Kikunosuke suddenly turned to the stage and said, "Dad, thanks for the favor."[10]

In the following scene, not included here, Nippon Daemon reveals his true identity to Kōbei and calls in the other members of his gang to help him rob the shop. Benten and Nango return to participate in this action. Nippon had assumed the guise of Tamashima Ittō as a ruse to get him into the good graces of Kōbei and Sonosuke. It turns out, however, that Kōbei is Benten's long-lost father and that Sonosuke is the long-lost son of Nippon. An emotional scene of reunion is interrupted by news that the police are closing in.

The next scene is that which follows the Hamamatsu-ya scene in this book, that is, the mustering of the thieves. The scene begins with a group of policemen in disguise searching for the bandits along an embankment of Kamakura's Inase River. Edoites were aware that the scene was, in actuality, meant to be at Edo's own Sumida River. After the policemen leave, the five thieves enter one at a time on the hanamichi where they line up, displaying their gorgeous new kimono and carrying paper umbrellas. As they enter, special music evocative of each thief's character is played

10. Watanabe Tamotsu, "Shiranami Gonin Otoko," *Engekikai*, no. 7 (1974), p. 98.

and sung. Much of the meaning of these verses is rather obscure, being aimed more at the creation of mood than literal description.

The Original Entrance Kata. In the original production of this scene, the actors entered in a boat which appeared on the upstage side of the embankment. They then stepped onto the embankment platform where they lined up in a row. There is also supposed to have been an arrangement where they entered one at a time on stage traps.

Once all the thieves are lined up on the hanamichi they recite a sequence of pass-along dialogue (*watarizerifu*). Each speaks a verse that leads into a verse spoken by the next, and so on, with the final verse spoken by all in unison. They then walk to the stage proper where they line up across it with their backs to the audience as eight to ten policemen rush on to the upstage platform and face the thieves, below them.

Entrance of the Policemen. In early productions eight policemen, dressed as if members of a lost-child search party and beating hand drums and gongs, entered from stage right, calling ''Lost child! Lost child!'' They passed by the five thieves, there was some movement and shifting of positions as they recognized the gang, and the policemen with drums climbed to the top of the platform and beat their drums very rapidly. At this cue, all the police removed their hats, revealed their police uniforms, and surrounded the gang at left and right. To-

day's staging of the scene, described in the text, differs markedly from this old approach.

The policemen now challenge the thieves who respond by giving a stylized series of speeches in which each recites his background and name. As each thief finishes his speech, he performs a dramatic mie pose. This convention of reciting one's name and background was introduced in the Hamamatsu-ya scene as well. As noted, it is called yakuharai but may also be termed *tsurane* (self-introduction). At the end of these speeches the thieves engage in another sequence of pass-along speech in which each line contains an untranslatable pun on the names of the members of an old gang (the Karigane) that was active in Osaka during the Genroku era (1688-1703).[11] Following this sequence the thieves and policemen engage in a final tableau with each thief holding down one or more policemen as the curtain closes.

How the Fight Scene Used to Be Played. In nineteenth-century productions of this scene, the thieves performed a mie soon after the fight sequence began and a black curtain hanging at the rear of the stage suddenly dropped, displaying a river landscape such as is seen through-

11. The puns revolve around the first names of the gang members. For example, Benten's line, *An ni soi no kaobure, tare shiranami no goninzure* ("And though it may surprise you, the five thieves lined up here....") turns on the word *an*, a reference to An Hyoei, just as Tadanobu's line, which follows, points to Kaminari Shōkurō, by including the word *kaminari* or "thunder." These are followed by references to the names Gokuin (the stamp impressed on gold and silver coins) and Hotei (a Chinese god of good fortune). The leader of the gang was Karigane Bunshichi.

out the scene as produced today. The first part of the fight was with umbrellas only, as today, and was highly stylized and colorful, but the next portion switched to a battle with swords and the tone became more serious and intense. After driving the police off to left and right, the thieves posed in a tableau and continued with a few minutes of dialogue. Then Nango and Benten exited on the main hanamichi, Tadanobu and Akaboshi on the temporary hanamichi set up for the scene, and Nippon remained on the stage holding two policemen down while looking off at his departing comrades. A moment or two later, the curtain closed.

In the play's closing scenes, not given here, Benten commits suicide as repentance for his crimes and the rest of the gang are captured by the authorities.

THE PLAYWRIGHT

Kawatake Mokuami, whose real name was Yoshimura Shinshichi, took the former name after his retirement though it is the name by which he is best known today. He was Kabuki's most prolific playwright and wrote plays in every style though he was popularly called the "bandit play" dramatist because of his great success with plays whose chief charac-

ters were thieves and blackmailers. The star actor in many of these works was often Ichikawa Kodanji IV (1812-1866). Mokuami's most popular works were those in which he skillfully depicted the decadence of the late Edo era. In his later years he was Kabuki's major playwright and wrote many plays for the leading actor of the age, Danjūrō IX. Another of Mokuami's bandit plays, *Naozamurai,* is included in this collection.

The translation of *Benten Kozō* is based mainly on an acting script provided by the Tōhō Producing Company. The script was that used for the production at Tokyo's Imperial Theatre (Teikoku Gekijō), December, 1974, starring Ichikawa Somegorō VI (1942-) as Benten (this was his first appearance in the role), Nakamura Kichiemon II (1944-) as Nango, and Matsumoto Kōshirō VIII (1910-) as Nippon. Kōshirō is the father of Somegorō and Kichiemon. Most of the stage directions given here were taken from that production.

Other texts consulted were those in *Meisaku Kabuki Zenshū (Complete Collection of Kabuki Masterpieces)*, Vol. XI, Tokyo, 1969, and Kawatake Shigetoshi, ed., *Kabuki Meisakushū (Collection of Kabuki Masterpieces)*, Vol. II, Tokyo, 1936.

A recording of *Benten Kozō* is available on Japan Victor, JL-102. The performance featured is that of Kikugorō VI but, unfortunately, there are some cuts that make it fairly incomplete. Both the Hamamatsu-ya and Mustering scenes are included.

THE HAMAMATSU-YA SCENE

(For several minutes before the curtain opens, the audience hears the sound of wooden clappers [ki] *being struck at intervals of anywhere from twenty-five to forty seconds. About forty-five seconds before the curtain opens, two beats of the clappers are heard and the old popular* nagauta-*style tune known as* Echigo Jishi [*The Lion of Echigo*] *begins to be played on the* taiko *drum and sung within the* geza *room at stage right. Soon, another double clap of the ki is heard and they begin to beat faster and faster until the curtain is pulled across the stage, from right to left, by a stage assistant in black* [kurogo]. *The scene is set in the Hamamatsu-ya, a prosperous textile-goods shop in the Yukinoshita section of Kamakura. The audience can see both the shop interior and the area outside the shop's entrance, located at stage right. The shop interior occupies most of the stage area. Upstage is a platformed area, about 18 inches high. A single step is placed up center against the platform. To the stage left side of the platform is a small room* [shōji yatai] *enclosed with shōji screens. Sliding paper doors are at upstage center, at the rear of the platform. To the right of the upstage doors is an area about six feet in width with three shelves laden with dry-goods, mainly bolts of cloth. On the vertical beam separating these shelves from the sliding doors is a long, narrow, three-compartment wooden note holder, stuffed with bills. The area directly before the shelves contains a low lattice-work screen* [kōshi] *which denotes the area's use as an office. A large old-fashioned abacus and several account books are placed here. The wall to the left of the sliding doors varies in design but usually shows some sort of sliding panels painted on its upper half. The lower half may contain a chest of drawers set flush with the wall. Immediately downstage of the platform, on the stage proper, are three strips of thin, woven bamboo matting running lengthwise across the stage. Adjoining the shop on stage right is a small tea shop run by the Hamamatsu-ya for the convenience of its customers. A navy blue curtain* [noren] *fills its upstage doorway. The downstage doorway is half-filled by another such curtain kept from flapping in the wind by the weights attached to its two lower corners. Both curtains bear the shop's emblem, the character for kō* [good fortune] *—the initial of the proprietor, Kōbei— under a mountain shape, i.e.,* 峯 *. The downstage tea shop curtain also has the word "Hamamatsu-ya" written on it. A long narrow curtain runs like a border across the entire width of the shop at the front. It too bears the shop emblem, at the center, and the word "Hamamatsu-ya" is written in small characters on either side. A large wooden charcoal brazier* [hibachi] *is situated downstage left center. In addition, several small braziers* [tabako bon], *used for smoking, are arranged on stage. A small one is upstage left, on the platform, and a medium-sized one is at right center. Real charcoal is burning in these. A square cushion is up-*

stage left, on the platform. At stage right, outside the shop, the outer walls of several houses may be seen painted on a backdrop at the rear. Seated up right, behind the low lattice-work screen, is the officious chief clerk, Yokurō, who is going over business accounts in his ledger. He wears a simple brown kimono, a navy blue apron, tied around his waist and covering his kimono from the waist to slightly below the knees, and white Japanese socks [tabi]. He is acted in the semicomical tradition of the clerk-villain [tedai gataki]. Kneeling beside him, to his left, is a lesser clerk, Sensuke. Below them are three customers, two women, and a man, who are kneeling at the shop's entrance where they are being waited on by three other clerks, Tasuke, Sahe, and Kichizo. The clerks all wear simple gray kimonō and white tabi; all wear an apron like Yokurō's. Tasuke hands one of the ladies a package which he has just brought over. The following occurs quite rapidly, and immediately sets the tone of a lively, bustling shop. Some ad-libbing is permissable here.)

TASUKE: Here you are, sorry to have kept you waiting.

LADY: *(Taking package and rising)* Thank you. My husband will take care of the bill, of course.

TASUKE: *(Bowing, as do the other clerks)* Certainly, certainly. Thank you and please come again.

(The customers exit stage right and, as they leave, a suspicious-looking charac-ter, Arajirō, enters. He wears a bold, checkerboard-patterned kimono tucked up at the rear to free his legs for walking. He is actually a thug in the employ of the master bandit, Nippon Daemon, but this fact is not brought out in the scene as now performed. He sits down, cross-legged, at the entrance to the shop and looks around cautiously as he speaks. His manner is rather rough.)

ARAJIRŌ: Excuse me.

SAHE: *(Bowing slightly)* Welcome, sir.

ARAJIRŌ: Are the five kimono I ordered dyed this month done yet?

(Meanwhile, Kichizō and Tasuke have returned materials they were showing the previous group to the upstage right shelves and have come down to the lower area where they sit at right center.)

SAHE: I'm really very sorry but they are not quite ready yet.

ARAJIRŌ: Not ready yet? Why the hell not? Haven't I waited long enough?

SAHE: Well, you know *(rapidly)* the weather has been pretty bad and the kind of dyeing you ordered requires good weather if the pattern is to take. I realize that we are rather behind but we would greatly appreciate it if you would be kind enough to wait until this evening.

ARAJIRŌ: Well, I'll come back tonight but it better be ready like you said.

(He looks here and there about him, then rises and exits right.)

TASUKE: Who is that guy? He comes and demands his goods and then looks around the place as if someone were after him.

SAHE: He looks pretty creepy to me.

SENSUKE: Hey, Yokurō, it really has been busy today, hasn't it?

YOKURŌ: (*As the music fades*) I'm not concerned about how busy it is. What bothers me is this endless rain which is causing us to fall so far behind in our orders that we have to be scolded by customers. However, we'll make up for it this time with some really eye-opening goods, won't we?

(*He rises and crosses to the large brazier at left center. The nagauta music from the dance play,* Sagi Musume [The Heron Girl], *is heard from the geza. The sound of the* agemaku *curtain, at the rear end of the hanamichi runway through the audience, being swished aside, signals the entrance of Benten Kozō and Nango Rikimaru. Benten, actually a man, is dressed as a samurai's daughter in a long-sleeved black kimono* [furisode] *with a pattern of chrysanthemums and woven bamboo on its lower portion and sleeves. Two chrysanthemums decorate the breast portion as small crests* [mon]. *He wears the* bunkin-takashimada-*style wig. A piece of red crepe is tied to its topknot at the rear and a red and white decorative rosette with a hanging fringe is placed in the left front portion near a comb used to hold the hair in place. Underneath his outer kimono, Benten wears a pale-blue and red patchwork-design under-kimono* [juban]: *another juban is worn beneath this; it is a long red crepe garment and both it and the patchwork juban play an important role later in the scene. The obi is a red one of cotton on which chrysanthemums are embroidered. His straw sandals* [zori] *have red thongs. Benten's acting does nothing to reveal he is a man until later in the scene. He is accompanied by Nango Rikimaru, a fellow thief and extortionist, disguised as Benten's samurai man-servant, Yosohachi. Nango wears a striped silk jacket* [haori] *over his brown kimono and culotte-type Japanese trousers* [hakama]; *the latter are tucked up so that his legs are exposed to the thighs. He wears two swords, a long one and a shorter one, tucked samurai-style into his obi at the left. Whenever he sits, he places the long sword on the ground at his left, hilt facing forward. If he moves to a new position, he always moves the swords as well. This also holds true for Nippon Daemon, who enters later, disguised as a samurai. Benten precedes Nango on the hanamichi and holds a white fan before him with which he gestures demurely. When they reach an area about seven-tenths of the way from the rear of the hanamichi to the stage* [the spot called the shichi-san], *they stop and Benten speaks, using the falsetto tones of a female impersonator.*)

BENTEN: Yosohachi, where is the Hamamatsu-ya textile shop?

NANGO: (*Speaking in a deep, powerful voice and in a very formal, self-important manner*) It's right ahead, miss.

BENTEN: Now, remember, you must not mention that I am shopping for my wedding robes.

NANGO: Why not, miss?

BENTEN: (*Shyly, hiding his face with his fan*) Because I'm so embarrassed.

NANGO: In that case, I won't say a word about it. Let's move on.

(*They continue walking until they reach the shop entrance. Shamisen music plays softly in the background. Nango stands at the entrance while Benten turns his back to the audience and faces the tea shop entrance.*)

Pardon me!

(*The clerks look up and see Nango and, behind him, Benten. They stumble over each other in their eagerness to wait on this impressive pair. Some ad-libbing is acceptable.*)

SAHE: Welcome!

TASUKE: Please come this way!

YOKURŌ: Here, here! Please come right in, miss.

SAHE: No, no. This way, this way.

(*There is a good deal of overlapping of these lines to create the effect of humorous confusion. The voices rise to a fast crescendo capped by Nango's lines.*)

NANGO: Ah, now, now! Will you please be quiet? You'll drive me out of my mind!

YOKURŌ: (*Rising and coming over to chase the clerks away with a yardstick*) That's right, will you all shut up? (*To Nango, officiously*) Well, now, we've got beautiful, really beautiful goods in stock. But first, please step into our shop.

(*Benten and Nango remove their sandals at the entrance and enter the shop. Yokurō sits left of center, Nango sits at right center, and Benten sits at center. After they have entered the shop, a boy wearing an apron comes out of the tea shop and arranges their sandals neatly. He does this whenever someone enters the shop from outside.*)

Fine weather we're having today, eh?

(*Shouting in the direction of the tea shop.*)

Let's have some tea here!

SHOP BOY: (*Holding the vowel until the tea is served*) Y-e-e-e-s!

(*He enters immediately, carrying two cups of tea on a small black lacquer tray. He puts one cup by Benten and one by Nango, then sits at Nango's right side.*)

YOKURŌ: Now, what would you like to look at?

NANGO: Please show us some Kyoto-style woolen brocade obi material, some scarlet crepe for undergarments, and some scarlet dappled material as well.

YOKURŌ: Certainly, certainly.

(*Practically singing this out in a rapid manner and holding the last word*)

Clerks, bring out the Kyoto-style woolen brocade, scarlet crepe, and scarlet dappled material as well.

CLERKS: Y-e-e-e-s!

(*This is spoken in unison as the clerks rush to the doors up center and exit.*)

YOKURŌ: The materials will be here in a minute. (*Pause*) They say the Kabuki is really booming these days. Do you go to the theater, miss?

BENTEN: (*Shyly*) Yes, I do. I recently saw a play at (*name of theater where present production is being given*).

YOKURŌ: (*Delighting in the exchange, he rubs his hands in glee.*) You did, did you? Do you have any special favorite among the actors I mean? Let's see if I can guess who it is. I'll bet it's that young star who steals all the girl's hearts, (*name of actor playing Benten*), isn't it?

BENTEN: (*Still shy*) No, I hate that actor with a passion.

YOKURŌ: (*Undaunted*) Wrong, huh? Then it must be (*name of actor playing Nango*), right?

BENTEN: (*Embarrassed*) Yes.

NANGO: But *I* hate that actor with all my heart! You really are a theater buff, aren't you? I'll bet you have a favorite actor, too.

YOKURŌ: I sure do. (*Names himself*) I enjoy the theater more than my daily meals.

(*Calls the clerks in singsong fashion*)

Let's have those goods here, on the double!

CLERKS: (*In unison*) Here we come!

(*The clerks enter up center carrying bolts of cloth and open boxes filled with piece-goods. They place the materials near Benten. One of them carries two tall floor lanterns with the word Hamamatsu-ya on each and places them at either end of the upstage platform. Four shallow boxes are stacked unevenly on top of one another and placed in front of Benten. The clerks busily take materials and hand them to Benten for his examination. He shows those he likes to Nango who also examines them.*)

YOKURŌ: Sorry to have kept you waiting.

(*The clerks appear to be ad-libbing with one another though we don't hear what they are saying.*)

BENTEN: Which one of the dappled materials do you like, Yosohachi?

NANGO: Whatever pleases you is fine with me.

BENTEN: I do like this one with the hemp-leaf design.

NANGO: We should select one with an auspicious design since it is for your wedding, after all.

YOKURŌ: Ah, it's for a wedding, is it?

BENTEN: (*Slowly, to Nango, as if embarrassed*) Oh. Now didn't I tell you not to mention that?

NANGO: Well, it slipped out.

YOKURŌ: (*Figuring all the while on his abacus*) These materials would come to...

(*Benten stealthily slips a piece of scarlet crepe out of his sleeve and drops it in the materials before him, mixes it in with the others, and then removes it, tucking it into his kimono at the breast.*)

SAHE: (*Leaning over to Yokurō, just prior to Benten's action*) Hey, Yokurō-san, she really makes me drool.

YOKURŌ: Now that's uncalled for...

(*The clerk to Yokurō's left has noticed Benten's deliberate actions and, aghast, is tapping Yokurō and whispering to him fiercely. Yokurō motions to the clerks and they instantly gather up all the materials and run inside. The shop boy takes the empty tea cups and returns to the tea shop. One clerk runs to the tea shop to summon a fireman, Seiji, who is there. This clerk runs back to the textile shop to join the other clerks who emerge from up center and take up positions standing in a row at upstage left. Benten and Nango have acted as though nothing were happening. The previously light and buoyant mood has suddenly changed to one charged with tension.*)

NANGO: (*Casually*) We'll take two bolts of the patterned material and three of the woolen brocade obi materials as well as the scarlet crepe. Please figure out what it all comes to. We're going to visit the Hachiman shrine and will pick up everything on our way back.

(*Benten and Nango rise to leave, Nango replacing his sword in his obi, but Yokurō stops them with his voice.*)

YOKURŌ: Please hold on for a moment.

NANGO: What should we wait for?

YOKURŌ: You haven't been joking with us, have you?

NANGO: What do you mean, "joking"?

YOKURŌ: Please hand over the scarlet crepe you stole.

(*The fireman, Seiji, has entered from the tea shop and stands at stage right, barring the way. He wears a fireman's leather* happi *coat over his kimono, as well as tight leggings and dark tabi. The music fades.*)

SEIJI: (*Nasty*) Don't tell me a fine-looking young lady like yourself has been caught trying to steal?

CLERKS: It's a dishonest world we live in, eh, Seiji?

NANGO: What is this? My young mistress a thief? (*Slowly*) You'll be sorry you had such careless tongues in your heads!

YOKURŌ: We do business all year long and are never mistaken.

SAHE: If you say you're innocent we'll simply take off your clothes and search you.

TASUKE: You'd better hand it over...

CLERKS: Before something unpleasant happens to you!

SEIJI: Don't think you're going anywhere. Sit down. I say, SIT DOWN!

(*He pushes Nango down by pressing on his right shoulder. The* tsuke *is beaten sharply to emphasize the movement.*)

BENTEN: (*Plaintively*) Oh, Yosohachi, what shall we do now?

NANGO: There's nothing to worry about. These beasts called you a thief but I will not leave until your name is cleared.

YOKURŌ: What? You won't leave till her name is cleared? You seem pretty good at saying such things.

NANGO: As you are at calling people thieves.

YOKURŌ: Still holding to that line, are you? Well, you'll change your tune now.

(*He crosses to Benten and pulls the cloth from his breast. The* tsuke *beat at each strong movement now.*)

Where did you get this from? You're going to get it!

(*Echigo Jishi music begins again as the clerks rush over to thrash Benten. Seiji holds Nango back. Yokurō strikes Benten on the forehead with his abacus and the fireman and clerks force Benten and Nango into a position near the upstage platform where they form a wall around* them. *Yokurō stands at the up center position making as if he were flailing Benten with his abacus. These blows are only suggested, of course. Sonosuke, son of the shop's owner, enters from the right hurriedly, tries to see what the commotion is about, and moves to center. He is dressed in a fine light-blue kimono with a three-quarter-length haori jacket over it. His is the delicate manner of the* waka-shu [*young male role*] *or* wakadanna [*young master*]. *His wig bears the forelock of an adolescent and he speaks in a rather high-pitched voice. During the beating of Benten a stage assistant dressed in black enters to help Benten with makeup and wig adjustments.*)

SONOSUKE: What is going on here? What is all the fuss about?

YOKURŌ: (*Joining him at center*) Don't get upset now but we caught these two in the act of stealing.

SONOSUKE: What? Thieves in this shop? What did they steal?

YOKURŌ: A piece of scarlet crepe material.

(*Turns to the others*)

Beat them good!

(*The others are scarcely moving so as not to distract from the other stage action. At this cue they begin to ad-lib and make threatening movements. The next line is heard above the din and must be held and greatly emphasized to bring the moment to a rhythmic climax.*)

NANGO: (*He strikes a pose on one knee; the tsuke accentuate the moment. He thrusts his hands out to either side as if parting a wall, palms outward, fingers stretched backward.*) Hold on, hold on, H-O-L-D O-N!

(*Two clerks have moved up right and two up left. Benten remains at center, just below the platform, where he crouches low, keeping his back to the audience and covering his forehead with a piece of white Japanese tissue paper.*)

You insist on calling us thieves, do you? Is that the cloth you say we have stolen?

(*He points to where Yokurō has dropped it on the floor.*)

YOKURŌ: Don't play dumb.

NANGO: We bought that cloth at the Yamagata shop. If you look at it carefully you'll see that their mark is on it.

YOKURŌ: (*Looking at the cloth and realizing his error*) Ahhh! The mark is that of the Yamagata, a mountain drawn inside a circle. This really is from their shop.

SAHE: We called them thieves...

TASUKE: But it was something from another shop.

CLERKS: Yes, yes, yes.

(*Pause*)

NANGO: Furthermore, Mr. Chief Clerk, I have proof of the sale right here.

(*He withdraws a receipt from his breast and holds it in his left hand, pointing to it with the right. Drawing out his words with great emphasis, he continues.*)

Now, do you still insist on calling us thieves?

YOKURŌ: (*Staring at the receipt*) I don't know what to say.

NANGO: Let's have an end to this thief business (*with emphasis*), shall we?

TASKUKE: Surely.

(*Pause. All the clerks and Sonosuke now kneel and bow low in apology. Seiji, however, merely lowers his eyes and does not prostrate himself. The stage assistant has helped Benten to change his wig, though the audience does not see the switch. The new wig has only the rosette decoration inserted in the forelock. The topknot is made to look somewhat awry. Shamisen music begins to play softly in the background and continues throughout most of the scene, highlighting the action.*)

SONOSUKE: My name is Sonosuke and I am the son of the owner of this shop. The clerks appear to have made a dreadful error and to have treated you very badly so I must beg you on hands and knees to accept my deepest apologies. Please find it in your hearts to forgive us.

CLERKS: (*Bowing low*) We beg of you to do so.

NANGO: What? (*Angry*) Now everyone is begging for forgiveness. It was easy enough for you to accuse innocent people of being crooks, wasn't it?

SONOSUKE: What you say is perfectly justified, sir, but please have pity and forgive us.

(*He rattles on, ad-libbing phrases begging forgiveness, overlapping with Nango's next line.*)

NANGO: Shut up, shut up, SHUT UP! To speak frankly, my mistress here is the daughter of Hayase Mondo, vassal of Nikaidō, Lord of Shinano. She is betrothed to a member of the powerful Akita family and will soon be married; do you think you can simply brand her a thief and let it go at that?

SONOSUKE: We are deeply mortified at our mistake, sir.

NANGO: You fools don't understand a thing. Call your master. I said, call your master. CALL YOUR MASTER!

KŌBEI: (*Offstage*) Yes, yes. I will be with you in a moment.

(*Offstage accompaniment called* tada ai [*"be right with you" music*] *begins to play as Kōbei enters and crosses down to left of center. He gestures to Sonosuke, who moves over for him, that he will handle the situation. He bows low to Nango.*)

NANGO: Well! I guess you must be the master himself, eh?

KŌBEI: I am Kōbei, the owner of this establishment. I overheard what happened and am at a loss as to how I can make amends for the rash behavior of my clerks. Please think of some way with which I can gain your pardon.

NANGO: If it were up to me I might accept your apology, since it comes from the master of the house.

(*Slowly and seriously*)

But I'm afraid...

KŌBEI: I beg you to tell me how I can make this up to you.

NANGO: I can do nothing.

(*Brings Benten to his side; slowly*)

Here master! Take a good look at this scar.

(*He has Benten raise his face revealing a deep scar on his forehead. All are astonished at the sight. Kōbei points to Benten while looking at the clerks.*)

KŌBEI: Ahhh! You've scarred this young lady's face!

CLERKS: (*Perplexed*) Yaa, yaa, yaa!

NANGO: As I've just said, my mistress is engaged to be married but I can hardly bring her home with a gash on her face. It's unfortunate, I know, but I seem to have no alternative than to sever the head of each and every one of you and then commit ritual suicide right here.

(*He raises his sword and holds it perpendicular to the ground at his left.*)

Prepare yourselves!

BENTEN: (*Bent over with his hand to his head; slowly*) Yosohachi, isn't there some less violent way to settle this affair?

(*Nango puts his sword down.*)

NANGO: There's nothing that can be done. If we settle this peaceably news of it will leak out one day and what excuse can I offer for my behavior then?

SEIJI: (*Ingratiatingly*) Beg pardon, Mr. Samurai, but would you mind stepping over here?

NANGO: Here I am.

(*Crosses right to Seiji*)

SEIJI: It will only take a minute.

NANGO: Well, what is it?

SEIJI: From what I gather that clerk made a rather serious error. There's really no excuse for what he's done. But what purpose would there be in lopping off our heads like a bunch of pumpkins? You can make up some excuse like your mistress fell on her way home or something fell off a roof and hit her or something else like that, can't you? In return, we'll be glad to give you something nice for your troubles. Can we call it a deal?

NANGO: Wait a moment.

(*Turns to Benten*)

Shall I accept his offer, miss?

BENTEN: (*Quietly*) I suppose it's only right that we should.

(*He seems to be weeping.*)

NANGO: (*Pause*) Since it is your will, I'll accept.

SEIJI: (*Hearing this*) You will forgive us? Thank you very much.

(*Bows slightly*)

Please wait a moment.

NANGO: My mistress has been hurt and I have been struck so . . .

(*These words are spoken as Seiji rises and crosses quickly to Kōbei, left, where he kneels. He looks at Kōbei meaningfully and the latter reaches into his kimono to withdraw his wallet. He also takes the wad of paper from the breast fold of his kimono and, removing one sheet of paper, begins to wrap some coins from his wallet in it.*)

SEIJI: Hey, chief clerk, you'd better be more careful from now on. (*To Kōbei*) And you'd better keep a close watch on these clerks of yours.

(*Kōbei hands a packet with ten ryō in it to Seiji. Seiji returns with the money to stage right.*)

Sorry to have kept you waiting.

(*He places the money down by Nango.*)

I realize this isn't much but please take it and leave us be.

NANGO: (*Picks up money, holds it in his right hand as if weighing it, opens the paper, and looks at it. Then, menacingly*) You said there'd be something worth our while; is ten ryō (*the vowels are prolonged for emphasis*) what you meant?

SEIJI: (*Getting steamed up*) I sure did. I sure did! What's wrong with ten ryō?

NANGO: I thought we could settle this matter privately but (*growing angry*) if my master should hear of it, it could prove fatal to me!

(*Puts the money down*)

SEIJI: We've given you ten ryō. If you're not happy you can leave without it.

NANGO: I'm not leaving, so what do you propose to do? I'm not selling my life for pocket money. I'll take (*stretching the words*) one hundred ryō (*pause*) or (*quickly*) I'll take nothing!

SEIJI: What the...You won't sell? You won't sell? Well, we won't buy! Get out!

(*Turns to the clerk seated nearest him*)

Tasuke, give this money back to your master.

(*Tasuke takes the packet and quickly crosses to Kōbei with it, then returns to his seat at right, above Nango.*)

Well, you just said you were going to lop off our heads, right? You think you're tough because you carry two swords, huh? I'll tell you what! You can begin with me! Go ahead! Start chopping! Start chopping!

(*This has been spoken quite rapidly. Toward the end of the speech, the fireman stands, throws off his jacket, pulls back the lower flaps of his kimono revealing black leggings, and squats cross-legged on the ground in a position of defiance.*)

NANGO: (*Reaching for his sword*) If that's what you want...

(*The clerks rush over and hustle Seiji out right, into the tea shop. As they do so, Seiji throws his pocket towel which has blue polka-dots on a white ground, at Nango's feet. It stays there until picked up and used later by Benten. The following lines, spoken as the fireman is being pushed out, can be mingled with ad-libs.*)

YOKURŌ: Control yourself, Seiji!

CLERKS: Hold it, will you? Hold it!

(*When the clerks come back into the shop from the tea shop they each quickly wipe off the soles of their tabi with their pocket towels.*)

NANGO: (*Standing, ready to draw his sword*) Now that I have had one disgrace heaped upon another, I cannot leave without drawing blood. Get ready to lose your heads!

KŌBEI: (*Placating*) Please, please wait a moment.

(*Pause*)

A little while ago you said we hadn't given you enough money to make up for what has happened to you here. Money cannot buy a man's life but somehow it may heal the wounds you have suffered. Well, well, please wait a second.

(*He turns to Sonosuke and makes a gesture; Sonosuke nods and takes a packet of one hundred ryō out of his breast fold which he hands to Kōbei. Kōbei then places this by Nango who is kneeling at center.*)

Please forgive us.

NANGO: (*Opens and looks at the money, smiling*) It's not easy to forgive you but since you are resigned to your fate I'll accept these one hundred ryō.

(*The shop people are all bowing low.*)

KŌBEI: Then we may bring this matter to a close?

NANGO: As you wish.

KŌBEI: Then we can all...

CLERKS: Breathe a sigh of relief.

NANGO: We've stayed longer than we expected...

BENTEN: But the matter has been settled without incident...

NANGO: So let us be off at once.

KŌBEI: Farewell to the both of you.

NANGO: Thanks (*pause*) for everything.

(*The pair rise and begin to leave, Nango holding Benten's hand. Just then, Nippon Daemon enters at the upstage doors where he speaks, stopping Benten and Nango in their tracks. His is a bold and powerful presence. He wears a hakama and a haori jacket over his kimono. His headpiece of black cloth is rather unusual for a Kabuki character. Since he is disguised as a samurai he carries two swords, one of which he places at his side on the floor when he sits down. He holds a closed fan in one hand.*)

NIPPON: Wait a minute, samurai. Wait *one* minute, please.

(*A clerk moves a pillow for Nippon to sit on to up left center and places a small tobacco box near him. The clerk then rejoins his fellows who are sitting stage left.*)

NANGO: (*To Benten but barely turning to look upstage*) He's a pretty impressive samurai. (*To Nippon*) Do you have some business with me that you ask me to wait?

NIPPON: I do.

NANGO: And that business is...?

NIPPON: (*Meaningfully*) Well, well. Please take a seat.

(*Benten and Nango sit down, puzzled.*)

I heard everything that's been going on here and you are to be commended for your generous act of pardoning these people.

NANGO: It was not easy to forgive them but as I am in the company of my young mistress here...

NIPPON: All the more why this shop has been fortunate. It appears that I have unexpectedly run across a strange relation; you did say you are a member of the Nikaidō clan (*pause*), didn't you?

NANGO: Correct! This lady is the daughter of Hayase Mondo, vassal to Nikaidō, Lord of Shinano.

NIPPON: (*Louder*) Are you quite sure of that?

NANGO: (*Suspicious*) Why all these questions...?

NIPPON: (*Angry*) Because you're an imposter!

NANGO: What did you say?

(*Shamisen music begins to play in the background.*)

NIPPON: I happen to be steward to Nikaidō, Lord of Shinano. My name is Tamashima Ittō. I know of no one called Hayase Mondo in our family (*pause*) and this fair young lady who says she is engaged is clearly a man.

BENTEN: Eh?

(*This is accidentally spoken in a male voice but Benten immediately resumes his female voice.*)

Why, how can you say that I am a man?

(*He has been bent low at center all this while pressing his forehead with a piece of paper. He remains so for the following dialogue.*)

NIPPON: Even though you say you're a woman and are quite good looking, I caught a glimpse of tattooing all over both your arms.

BENTEN: Oh!

NIPPON: (*Sure of himself*) You are a man, aren't you?

BENTEN: Well, well, I...

(*The vowels are extended considerably.*)

NIPPON: If you insist you're a woman how would you like us to examine your breasts?

(*The present section should build in intensity and speed with some overlapping of lines at the end. It is a major climax of the scene.*)

BENTEN: Well, well, I...

NIPPON: Tell us who you are!

(*The music fades out.*)

BENTEN: (*The following sequence is in the style called* kuriage *and is a common Kabuki device for building an emotional climax, as one voice overpowers the other until they join together in chorus.*) Saa, saa...

NIPPON: Saa, saa, saa...

BOTH: Saa, saa, saa!

NIPPON: You fake! Answer me!

(*He holds the final vowel. Nippon slaps his fan to the floor to emphasize the moment. Pause. Benten has practically collapsed. He is now the center of attention as the audience waits to see what he will do. Slowly, very slowly, he raises his face to the audience. This section before he speaks may take as long as ten seconds or more. He is struggling with his emotions, it seems. The white paper in his right hand flutters rapidly. As he leans over his decorative rosette falls out of his hair to the ground. When he finally speaks, his manner is completely changed to that of the brash, arrogant young "son of Edo" [Edokko]. The contrast with his previous impersonation is striking.*)

BENTEN: Well, Nango (*pause*), no need for these disguises anymore. They've caught on to our game.

NANGO: (*To Nippon*) You're an impatient son-of-a-bitch, aren't you? Couldn't you have waited a little longer?

BENTEN: What an ass I am! They know I'm a man so why do I have to stand on ceremony? Mr. Samurai here has guessed my true sex so...(*pause, and with a derisive gesture of flipping the right hand*) I beg your pardons.

(*He begins to untie his obi cords and to loosen his cramped costume. Nango, too, starts to change his appearance. A stage assistant enters and crouches behind Benten to help him. The actor must create the impression of delight in the feeling of being unbound from the extremely restricting female kimono. He opens the cord holding his long red under-kimono in place and, stretching in a great yawn, for a moment reveals his male body underneath. Beneath his undergarments Benten wears a white loincloth and belly-band [haramaki]. He fans himself with his kimono folds and shakes his cramped legs. The business is accompanied by a good deal of humorous ad-libbing between Benten and Nango. Benten then sits down, cross-legged, at center. Nango has taken off his swords, his haori, and his hakama. He wears only a rather seedy-looking light brown kimono. His topknot has been pushed to the side to look disheveled.*)

Hey, chief clerk, how about a pipe and some tobacco over here?

(*The frightened Yokurō brings a pipe and a small box of tobacco taken from behind the large brazier stage left and places it by Benten cautiously, then scoots away left quickly.*)

YOKURŌ: (*At left, shocked*) I thought he was a woman, but he was only an imposter!

CLERKS: Yaa, yaa, yaa.

(*Benten has removed the sleeve of his outer kimono from his left shoulder leaving only the patchwork-patterned under-kimono visible on his left arm and shoulder. The stage assistant adjusts the folds of his disheveled kimono on the ground around him, making a pleasing arrangement of the materials. Benten picks up a pipe and the polka-dot pocket towel thrown down earlier by Seiji. His pipe is of the long-stemmed, small-bowled Japanese variety and can only be used for one or two puffs at a time before having to be emptied and refilled. The bowl is stuffed with a small ball of tobacco and then placed in the charcoal ashes to get it lighted; once lit it is brought to the mouth and smoked. Benten performs this action during the following lines and Nango, seated stage right and slightly upstage of Benten, does likewise. Nango has his own pipe and tobacco with him. The pipe is used for a great deal of gesturing by these characters, especially by Benten. To remove the loose tobacco the pipe must be tapped sharply on the bamboo ash receptacle on the brazier. Benten speaks with a very nasty, biting, arrogant tone, lengthening his vowels for effect. Shamisen background music begins.*)

BENTEN: As you know, I came here disguised as a woman to wring some money out of you. I was down on my luck and didn't even have a penny for a cup of soup, so, thinking to earn myself a lousy ten ryō, I rented this woman's getup. I get by pretty good as a woman so things would have gone nice and smooth if my cover hadn't been blown. This all ought to give you a good belly laugh.

(*Smokes his pipe*)

YOKURŌ: No matter how I look at him I keep seeing the young lady. Well, you sure are a brazen...

CLERKS: Character, aren't you?

BENTEN: Anyway, I came here in disguise. My neck is slender but my nerve is thick.

NANGO: Hey, what's all this chatter about thick and thin, anyway? You sound like you're selling potatoes.

BENTEN: Right. And you can take your pick.

NIPPON: Even though your disguise has been seen through, you carry on as though nothing had happened. You must be the greatest con-man of them all!

(*The music fades.*)

BENTEN: Hmm. You still don't know who we really are, do you?

YOKURŌ: You're obviously some no-good bum...

CLERKS: But we don't know who you are.

BENTEN: (*Boldly and with dramatic emphasis*) If you still don't know (*slight pause*), then lend me your ears.

(Pause. This is the most famous speech in the play, known to many Japanese by heart. Benten performs a wide variety of gestures with his pipe during its delivery. First, to get the audiences's attention, he taps the pipe sharply on the brazier. This is said to be a trick borrowed from the storytellers who always rapped on their stands with their fans before beginning their tales. Satsuma bushi, *a kind of shamisen accompaniment normally found in history plays, begins to play in the background. Meanwhile, Nango, having dropped his disguise, sits arrogantly smoking with his right hand while he keeps his left in the pocket of his right sleeve. Benten begins to speak while twirling his pipe round and round on the finger tips of his right hand, a trick requiring a good deal of manual dexterity, though he does it quite casually. His voice rises and falls regularly during this stylized speech written in 7-5 meter* [shichigo]. *Shichigo has not been used in the present translation. The last line culminates in a famous stylized pose* [mie].)

In the words of the notorious bandit,
Ishikawa Goemon, we thieves are
As countless as the sands of
    Shichigahama.

(Pause)

I began my career as a denizen
Of the night while serving as a page
At the Enoshima Temple where I
Gambled freely with the pennies
    offered

To the Buddha (gestures with pipe)
    by the pilgrim groups from Edo.

(Gestures with pipe)

I grew bolder and my take grew
    bigger.

(Gestures with pipe)

My crimes increased as I took to
    grabbing
The cash piled up in offertory boxes.

(Gestures with pipe)

Time and again I robbed the sleeping
    pilgrims
At the Iwamoto Temple until
Finally, things got too hot for me
    and (pause)
I was chased from Enoshima. I soon
Turned to blackmail and the badger
    game

(Gestures with pipe)

For my daily bread and pulled some
    petty
Extortion jobs using the techniques
    my
Grandpa taught me. My name?

(Taps brazier to remove tobacco)

It's Benten Kozō Kikunosuke!

(He makes a wide swinging gesture with the pipe and then slams it down at his side. At the same time, he draws his left arm into his sleeve. The last word, ''Kikunosuke,'' is delivered in a greatly

heightened manner, almost sung, with the syllable "no" being spoken in a higher pitch than the rest, the voice then dropping sharply for "suke." As soon as that last syllable is uttered he thrusts his left arm out of the breast of his kimono in a fist held near the right knee, forcing the garment to drop from his shoulder, revealing an arm and shoulder covered with tattoos of blooming cherry blossoms. The tattoos are on a skintight, shirtlike garment. Simultaneously, he grabs the big toe of his left foot and brings the foot up over the knee of his right leg. He finishes with a revolving motion of the head timed to the beating of the tsuke. He glares, crossing one eye. Tattoos covering his thighs are visible. The pose is called the miawarashi mie *or "revelation pose."*)

That's who!

(*As Nango now begins to speak Benten slowly relaxes, after holding his pose for about five seconds, and begins smoking again. He places the towel on his left shoulder. Seeing that his pipe is clogged he quietly picks up the rosette hairpin lying at his feet and uses its point to clean his pipe. He then wipes it with the paper used earlier for his forehead, fills it, and smokes.*)

NANGO:

*Me, I've been his partner and
    support in crime*

*From the shadows of Mt. Fuji to the
Town of Odawara. Born a
    fisherman's son,
I cast anchor aboard the leading
Deep sea fishing boats, taking up a
    life
Upon the waves where I netted a
    healthy
Profit in gambling with loaded dice,
Filled my pockets with the suckers'
    loot,
Grew gutsy living an inch away from
A watery hell, and blackmailed and
    robbed
The fisherfolk, until my crimes were
As heavy as a ship's speed is slow.
Today you'll find me in the East,
    tomorrow
In the West, never staying in one
    place long.*

(*Reaching a minor crescendo*)

I am Nango Rikimaru!

(*Pause*)

And don't forget it!

(*He glares fiercely as he speaks, moving his head and pipe rhythmically to accentuate the pose.*)

NIPPON: You're from that five-man gang of Nippon Daemon's we hear so much about, aren't you?

BENTEN: Right. I'm the scrap end of the five thieves.

(*This is spoken in a highly rhythmic manner, which accentuates each syllable of the names, as Benton points to his left hand with his pipe and, starting with the thumb of his left hand, closes his fingers one by one until all the fingers are closed.*)

First, there's Nippon Daemon, Nango Rikimaru, Tadanobu Rihei, Akaboshi Jūzō, Benten Kozō (*pause*), and I'm the last of the lot.

NANGO: To get right down to it, we won't be going anywhere with this. Here's the one hundred ryō we squeezed you for.

(*He turns and tosses the money to Kōbei, who is seated on the platform upstage of him.*)

BENTEN: Well, now that you've found us out you can call the police. I've even put on a nice new loincloth for the occasion.

NANGO: I'm also ready for anything, come what may! Hey, boy! Let's have some tea!

SHOP BOY: (*As before*) Y-e-e-e-s!

BENTEN: Sounds like a ghost in there, doesn't it?

NANGO: His answers do take forever, don't they?

BENTEN: Yeah.

SHOP BOY: Here's your tea.

(*Stands at Nango's right*)

NANGO: What? You dare serve tea while standing?

(*Takes a sip and spits it out*)

Ptu! Do you think I can drink burned tea?

(*He tosses the tea in the boy's face. The boy is startled, then raises the round tea tray in his right hand as if to strike Nango, pauses; Nango glares at him menacingly; the boy thinks better of it, and runs off to the tea shop, wailing. Nango tosses the teacup by the entrance-way and the boy picks it up on his way out.*)

SHOP BOY: Waaaa!

BENTEN: Well, the sooner all this is finished, the better. We'd appreciate it if you'd get moving, tie us up, and hand us over to the cops before it gets dark. We don't know if we'll ever return to this corrupt world as we are but we can guarantee (*to Nippon*) that, as a token of our gratitude, we'll have no problem in visiting your place, my kind friend, even if we've lost our heads.

NANGO: Right! There's no greater disgrace than to be afraid of death and cling to life like a fool.

BENTEN: Correct!

NIPPON: (*Considering what they've said*) Your skillful masquerade has been discovered so what do you do? Do you rise and leave, disconsolate? No. You have the nerve to say "turn us over to the cops!" If it wouldn't cause this family trouble you two would soon breathe your last . . .

(*He grabs his sword with his left hand.*)

BENTEN: (*Mocking*) How's this? How's this? Playing around with his sword? Did he say he would kill us? Go ahead, have fun! It's always been my ambition to see two heads chopped off at one stroke by an amateur using a rusty sword.

(*He points to and strikes his left arm as if chopping it.*)

NANGO: Right you are! Right you are! How glorious it will be to die on these tatami mats and be carried forth (*pointing outside*) from this shop like heroes!

BOTH: Remember, you get no money if you fail to draw blood! Go ahead, we're waiting!

(*They turn on their knees simultaneously and face right on a slight diagonal.*)

NIPPON: If that is what you want . . .

(*He takes his sword and begins to rise. Kōbei and Sonosuke instantly gesture to stop him. They bow low to address Nippon.*)

KŌBEI: Please wait a moment, sir. If you murder these two scoundrels we will be obliged to bring your name up in the affair and . . .

SONOSUKE: We realize how furious you must be and they certainly are a wicked pair . . .

KŌBEI: But we ask you to forgive them.

NIPPON: Yes, I have been angry but, from the beginning, had no taste for this affair.

(*Puts sword down*)

KŌBEI: Then you'll forgive them?

NIPPON: Yes, I will.

SONOSUKE: Oh, thank you very much.

BENTEN: Well, are you going to kill us quickly or not?

NANGO: If you're turning us in instead . . .

KŌBEI: Now listen!

(*Rises and crosses down to Benten's left where he sits*)

Keep a civil tongue in your heads! I'll be the one who says whether you are to be bound and handed over to the police. Since I'm in business and don't want a fuss I'll overlook everything and let you go just as you are.

BENTEN: No sir! We won't leave!

(*He speaks to Kobei over his shoulder.*)

KŌBEI: And why not?

BENTEN: (*Gesturing with his pipe*) I said I was the daughter of Hayase Mondo of the Nikaidō clan . . .

(*He shifts position so that he is sitting on his left hip with his right leg out to the right, knee raised, while his left leg is under him; he leans on his left hand.*)

and dressed like this to prove it. My ruse was discovered so I handed you back the one hundred ryō I took you for. Right? You haven't lost a penny, but me—I'm called a thief, beaten by a mob, and get a goddamn scar on my forehead.

(*Points to it with his pipe*)

What do you propose to do about that?

KŌBEI: Well, as for that, I suppose I must apologize and if it will help to settle the affair I'll give you a tidy sum that should soothe your feelings.

BENTEN: Let's talk the matter over. If we can come to an understanding, we'll be happy to leave.

KŌBEI: Wait a second, please.

(*Kōbei takes some money from his wallet and wraps it in a sheet of paper. While waiting, Benten ad-libs with Nango, asking him to look at his gash, telling him how much it hurts, and receiving his friend's commiseration; he also curses the clerk and his abacus.*)

It's not much but please take it and leave us be.

(*He puts the money down by Benten.*)

BENTEN: (*Picks up the money and puts his arm back in his under-kimono sleeve so that he will be more properly dressed for the moment. He chats breezily.*) Thank you, master, thank you. I understand very well the kind of trouble we've caused for you, you being such a respectable man and all.

(*As he talks he is looking at the money; he realizes it is, after all, only a small amount and makes an expression of surprise. His manner is now changed.*)

Eh? Hey, master, you said you'd give us a tidy sum but you couldn't have meant only twenty ryō, could you? How do you think we'd feel if people said that Benten Kozō and Nango Rikimaru had flopped at blackmailing a dry-goods shop and came away with only ten ryō apiece. Here's your money back!

(*Puts it down with a thud and slides it over toward Kōbei; he then turns away.*)

KŌBEI: (*Threatening*) If it's not enough, I'll think of something else...

BENTEN: Yeah! I'm not after pocket money, you know.

(*Kōbei attempts to get Benten's attention, saying, "Please, please."*)

NANGO: Now, now, Benten, we can probably get thirty or forty ryō out of him if we press him long enough but we'd have to hang around here till it was too late. Let's take this cash and go, okay?

(*He crawls over to Benten, on his knees.*)

BENTEN: Hey, Nango, you're not yourself tonight, are you? How can we leave with only ten ryō apiece?

NANGO: True enough, true enough.

(*At this point there is a great deal of ad-libbing between the pair, Benten refusing to accept the money and Nango urging him to take it. The exchange lasts a few seconds, gets faster, and reaches a climax when Nango says, loudly and slowly,*)

But remember (*pause*), the master here was just talking of certain measures he might have to take.

(*Nango is at Benten's right, elevated slightly above him on his knees. With slow and deliberate emphasis*)

The money will come in handy if the cops ever get their hands on us.

(*At the end of this speech he is rhythmically pointing his hand at the money near Benten. There is a long pause, then the pair nod knowingly at each other.*)

BENTEN: Well (*taking the money*), it's a shame I have to get scarred for nothing more than pocket money.

(*He points to his forehead, acting as if he had suffered great pain.*)

NANGO: I guess you're right, having to leave like this and all.

(*This following section requires a considerable amount of ad-libbing as Benten and Nango rise and begin to dress for the road. Nango busies himself at the rear with the bundle they are to carry. He is assisted by the stage assistant who has brought out a dummy set of swords wrapped in fabric to substitute for the hakama and swords removed earlier. Benten removes his outer two kimono and wears only his red undergarment which he adjusts by tucking it up at the rear. He looks at himself and says what a fool he looks like. Nango offers him his haori jacket which Benten puts on and poses with. Then Nango tells Benten he can't go out with a woman's wig on as he looks ridiculous. Benten puts his hands to his head in surprise as if to say, "Ooops! You're right" and, getting an idea, takes the polka-dot towel, unfolds it, puts it in his mouth while he tucks the loose piece of crepe hanging from the topknot into place, and places the towel on his head. He folds it backward near his jaws, twists the material into a knot under his chin, and picks up the rosette from the floor, tucking it into his sleeve. Then, as if he just remembered, he sees the piece of crepe on the floor, makes a remark about not forgetting it, picks it up, and puts it into his sleeve as well. He turns to Kōbei.*)

BENTEN: Don't worry, we'll be back. I mean, twenty ryō is a mere drop in the bucket these days. I'm sure your shop can provide a better price, master.

KŌBEI: Now, please be reasonable...

SONOSUKE: And leave us alone.

BENTEN: We're going but we'll be back from time to time.

YOKURŌ: Not on your life!

BENTEN: That's a laugh! You may have told me to stay away but I'll be back when my money runs out.

(*To Yokurō*)

You've got a mouth like a tea spout, you little runt!

(*He and Nango move to the entranceway of the shop. Nango steps into his sandals but Benten notices that his have red thongs.*)

Hey, boy! How the hell can I wear red sandals? Let me have those white ones.

(*He points to a pair lying nearby.*)

SHOP BOY: They're the head fireman's.

BENTEN: I don't give a damn if they're the head's or the tail's! Give 'em to me!

SHOP BOY: Yes, sir.

(*He brings over Seiji's sandals and Benten slips them on.*)

BENTEN: (*Turning slightly to Nippon*) One day, Mr. Samurai, I'll pay you back for this.

NIPPON: Anytime you have a complaint...

BENTEN: I won't forget!

YOKURŌ: (*Turning over to Benten*) Come back the day before yesterday!

(*He pushes Benten on the shoulder.*)

BENTEN: What the...

(*He turns and aims a sharp slap at Yokurō's downstage cheek; the tsuke accentuate the blow.*)

YOKURŌ: Aiii!

(*He falls to the floor in a sitting position, below the platform, his back to the audience.*)

BENTEN: How do you like that?

(*To those in the shop*)

Hope I haven't caused you too much trouble.

(*He thrusts his hands inside his kimono, keeping them at his chest, his sleeves dangling. Nango holds the bundle over one shoulder and puts his other hand inside his kimono, too. They casually proceed to the hanamichi, ad-libbing freely. The lines that follow are mainly from the acting script but they are merely a skeleton on which the actors embroider their improvisations. Nango and Benten stop at the shichi-san. The shamisen music called shinnai bushi is played offstage as accompaniment.*)

BENTEN: The clouds look pretty big. It'll probably rain again tonight.

NANGO: Hey, are you sure you haven't forgotten something?

BENTEN: (*Puzzled*) We've brought everything with us.

NANGO: Since we didn't divide it yet, let's do it now.

(*Realization dawns and Benten immediately slips his hands into his sleeves and searches there for the money. He takes out the packet, holding it forth, his hand protruding from the breast of his kimono.*)

BENTEN: Right. This is your share.

(*He flips some coins into Nango's hand, also thrust forth from his kimono at the breast. They quibble a bit over their spoils. Then, referring to the bundle carried by Nango*)

That load is a real pain, isn't it?

NANGO: Why don't we play "The Priest Holds the Bag"?

BENTEN: How do you play that?

NANGO: Whenever a blind masseur comes along the other person must carry the load.

BENTEN: Okay. it's fine with me.

(*Nango hands Benten the bundle. They begin to walk on very slowly. A masseur enters the hanamichi tapping his blind man's cane. He is bald and wears a simple gray kimono and wooden clogs. A blue hand towel is tucked into his obi on one side and a cylindrical whistle at the other.*)

MASSEUR: (*Singing it out*) Massage, acupuncture...

BENTEN: (*Happily*) A masseur. Here, you carry it.

(*Gives load to Nango*)

NANGO: That was fast, wasn't it?

(*The masseur stops, seems to have forgotten something, and turns back the way he came.*)

Hey, the masseur is leaving. Now it's your turn.

(*Hands load to Benten*)

BENTEN: Son-of-a-bitch masseur.

(*He puts load on his shoulder and begins to sing in shinnai bushi style as he strolls down the hanamichi, eyes downcast, almost closed. Meanwhile, the masseur, having felt for his whistle and towel and realizing he has had them with him all the time, turns to go on his original route. Nango sees him coming and holds his sleeves out, making a wall so that Benten does not see the masseur go by. Benten is singing.)*

Amari doyoku na, mada mada.

MASSEUR: (*Now almost by the stage itself*) Massage, massage, acupuncture . . .

BENTEN: (*Hearing him*) Ah! A masseur, huh?

(Tries to give bundle to Nango)

NANGO: (*Not taking it*) Yeah, but your singing canceled the deal.

BENTEN: Damn and double damn!

(The two casually stroll off the rest of the way while the masseur, blowing his whistle, exits at stage right.)

KŌBEI: (*Shamisen music accompanies his dialogue.*) If it hadn't been for you, sir, they would have gotten away with one hundred ryō.

SONOSUKE: Without your help we could never have avoided being robbed.

KŌBEI: We would like very much to give you something for your trouble; if you would be kind enough to step into the rear of the shop for a cup of sake . . .

NIPPON: Since you put it like that, it would be rude to refuse.

KŌBEI: (*Bowing gratefully, as do the others in the shop*) Sir.

NIPPON: Then, I shall (*taking up his sword*) be glad to accept.

(Music and singing are heard from the geza. Sonosuke crosses to the center doors, kneels, and opens them for Nippon to go through. The curtain is pulled across the stage on this tableau as the ki are struck together faster and faster.)

CURTAIN

THE MUSTERING SCENE AT THE INASE RIVER

(While the scenery is being changed for the present scene the lights in the theater are dimmed to half their intensity. Throughout, a drum can be heard beating in the geza giving a sense of great excitement to come. No formal intermission is taken and the interval lasts only about four to five minutes. Shortly before the curtain opens there is a sharp beat of the ki that soon begin to beat more and more rapidly as the curtain is pulled across the stage. Singing and shamisen music—the so called maigo narimono *[lost child music]—is heard. The sound of the big drum beating in the background represents the sound of waves. When the main curtain [jōshiki maku] opens, a pale-blue sky curtain [asagi maku] is revealed, hiding the sce-*

nery upstage from it. Cries of "Lost child! Lost child!" are heard as drums and bells are beaten. Two men enter from either end of the curtain and come to the center. They have scarves on their heads and carry bamboo matting around them to protect them from the rain. Two carry drums and sticks, the others carry bells. They are actually policemen [torite] in pursuit of the five thieves but have adopted this disguise to allay suspicions. An occasional gong can be heard in the background amidst the beats of the drum banging out the sound of waves.)

POLICEMEN: (*Entering and beating their instruments*) Lost child! Santarō, where are you?

(*They cross to center.*)

POLICEMAN #1: We've searched the area from the Hase Temple to the Inase River but found nothing so they may have headed for Matsura . . .

POLICEMAN #2: And we don't know how far they've gone so if we watch carefully for them from here to there . . .

POLICEMAN #3: It's for sure that they can only go one way and before they can escape . . .

POLICEMAN #4: Our vigilance will pay off . . .

ALL: Lost child! Lost child! Santarō, where are you?

(*They pass one another and exit at opposite ends of the stage. Sound of gongs and drums. At a sharp crack of the ki the big blue curtain drops suddenly and is carried offstage by several stage assistants. The scene so swiftly revealed is a striking one picturing an embankment at the Inase River in Kamakura on a drizzly day. A background of blue sky is framed at the top of the stage by two borders of hanging artificial cherry blossoms. Several cherry trees in bloom are depicted in cutout form at the rear of the embankment. The waters of the river are painted on the lower portion of the background panel and a distant landscape is seen beyond the waters. The embankment itself is a platform about three feet high running across the center of the stage, parallel to the footlights. It is painted green as if to represent a riverbank. Ramps lead off at its ends and, at left, a small four step staircase leads up to the upper surface. Cherry trees in bloom are painted on the side panels of the stage. Lively nagauta music called* kari to tsubame *["geese and swallows"] is heard and the thieves begin to make their entrances. Before each thief enters on the hanamichi, he thrusts his umbrella out through the curtained doorway leading to the hanamichi. The word* shiranami *[bandit] is written on each white paper umbrella in bold black characters. Benten enters first. About halfway down the hanamichi he poses, holding the umbrella over his head in his right hand, extending his left foot. He and all the other thieves wear gor-*

geous purple kimono, each with a specific design always worn by these characters in this scene. Benten's is of a huge lute [biwa] around which a snake is coiled. There are also chrysanthemum patterns scattered on the design. Tadanobu Rihei's is a cloud and dragon pattern. Akaboshi Jūzaburō's [Jūzō for short] is of a cockfight, Nango's is of a dog and lightning design, and Nippon's is of waves, an anchor, and a hawswer. Each also wears clogs and carries a pipe case and tobacco pouch hanging at the right hip from a silver band tucked into the obi. The sight of the thieves lined up on the hanamichi or stage is vastly impressive and has been likened to a fashion show. Benten wears a wig with the forelock portion grown in, as seen on many wakashu heroes. A red cloth scar is attached to his forehead. Tadanobu wears the sakaguma wig, which is similar to Benten's, Nango wears the waribuchi no fukuro tsuki wig, and Nippon's is the gojūnichi fukuro tsuki no ginko mage. As each enters and poses in a mie the tsuke are struck. Benten, after posing, moves down the hanamichi toward the stage, where he stands facing the auditorium wall on the spectators' left. During Benten's entrance the geza singer intones the following lines of verse.)

CHORUS:

The bandit gang assembles here.
The mere name of Goddess
    Benzaiten of Enoshima.

With lute in hand, Benzaiten revels
In a sailor's ditty of the ocean blue.

(This is accompanied by daibyōshi ["big rhythm"] music of the large drum [ōdaiko] and shamisen. Tadanobu Rihei now enters. He poses by snapping his head rhythmically to the beat of the tsuke and then moves on to stand about three feet from Benten in the same position. As he enters, taisoiri music of the large hand drum [ōtsuzumi] and small hand drum [kotsuzumi] accompanies the geza singer.)

CHORUS:

Tadanobu, whose name reminds us
Of a famous drum
The resting place for a dragon's
    wings.

(Akaboshi Jūzaburō enters, poses gracefully in an almost feminine manner, and moves down to a position on the hanamichi near Tadanobu Rihei. He is a wakashu role, the type of handsome young man often played by female impersonators. Sōban music of the sōban gong and ōdaiko drum play in the background for his entrance.)

CHORUS:

Like the single or double early cherry
    blossoms
In the twilight mist
Is Akaboshi, the evening star.

(*Nango enters, swings his umbrella in a bold movement until it rests on his right shoulder, raises the hem of his kimono on his left leg with his left hand, and stamps his left foot about two feet from his right, bending his right knee slightly. Nango is the only one of the thieves not wearing a white pocket towel on his left shoulder. His is tied loosely around his neck, supposedly because of his background as a fisherman. His topknot is purposely worn somewhat awry. He moves on to stand near Akaboshi. The music for his entrance is sōban, like that for Akaboshi, but the tone is much more vigorous.*)

CHORUS:

From the waves of
Crashing, pealing, thunder-clouds
Nango comes along the sandy path.

(*Last comes Nippon Daemon. He poses by snapping his head in time to the tsuke and moves on.* Taikoiri *music employing the taiko drum supports his entrance.*)

CHORUS:

Like that of a deep-sea boat
His hawser binds the thieves together.

(*When all five thieves are arranged in a line facing the same direction, their umbrellas held aloft in their right hands, they turn in unison to face the central part of the theater. The following is a famous example of "pass-along" speech*

[*watarizerifu*]. *The shamisen music heard in the background is called* komuso.)

BENTEN:

After crossing the mountains from
Yukinoshita
This is the first place to which we
have fled...

TADANOBU:

On this brief spring eve when the
seventh hour tolls
And our fate seems clear, we'll to the
Mutsura River...

AKABOSHI:

Escaping by the boat to freedom
Before the sun comes up...

NANGO:

Leaving our homes behind
And sailing from Miura round
Misaki
Into the open sea...

NIPPON:

Where, on the waves,
Unlike the land, men's eyes need not
concern us...

BENTEN:

But, before we reach the Mutsura
We must steer a narrow course
through Enshu's
Fierce and open sea...

TADANOBU:

And battle mountain winds,
But whether we encounter favorable
Tail winds or the gales of those
*   behind us...*

AKABOSHI:

We will row with long swords if our
*   oars should fail*
And row until our sword shafts snap
*   in twain...*

NANGO:

Then lay about us with a show of
*   strength*
But should we be overcome we'll
*   fight until*
The bitter end...

NIPPON:

Then cut loose our anchor...

ALL:

And let them try to take us!

(*As the kari to tsubame music is heard again the thieves walk to the main stage and take up positions there with Nango on stage right, then Akaboshi, then Tadanobu, and then Benten. Nippon now moves to the first position, at stage left, so he has the longest distance to traverse, having been last on the hanamichi. They all face the rear of the stage, backs to the audience. Ten policemen rush on to the upstage platform from stage left and line up across it, facing the thieves,* below them. They each wear a black kimono of the type called yoten. It is tucked up at the armpits by a white sash. Each wears a white headband around his forehead, black leggings, black tabi, and carries a jitte, a steel weapon with a prong on it used to thrust off sword blows. They stand with the jitte held before their foreheads in their right hands while their left hands are held slightly before their waists, palms open and facing downward, elbows bent a bit and about six inches from the body.)

POLICEMEN: Don't move!

NIPPON: Well? What is it you want?

POLICEMAN #1:   What do we want? Just this! Nippon Daemon, leader of this notorious band of thieves...

POLICEMAN #2:   And the rest of you, as well —do not resist! Place your hands...

ALL: Behind your backs!

NIPPON: Well! Have we five thieves come this far...

THIEVES: Only to be ambushed?

POLICEMAN #5:   We made as if we were searching for a lost child while we carefully spread our net...

ALL: And waited patiently.

NIPPON: Now that we're discovered we will not run away like cowards. First we'll tell you, one by one, who we are, and then we'll give ourselves up...

BENTEN: To receive...

THIEVES: Our just deserts.

POLICEMAN #1: Let the first one...

ALL: Step forth!

(*The thieves all turn around slowly to face the audience and take four steps in unison downstage. The policemen put their hands down at their sides.* Gion hayashi *music of taiko drum and shamisen beings.*)

NIPPON: Although it's absurd to be asked to tell my name, I will tell you this. I was born at Hamamatsu in Enshu. I left home at fourteen and took up a life of piracy upon the seas. Although I robbed and pilfered I never acted cruelly. From the Kake River to Kanaya they speak of me as the compassionate and chivalrous bandit; notice boards demanding my arrest are set up here and there; my life is in constant danger but man's span is a mere fifty or sixty years and I am already over forty. I am the leader of that band of thieves hidden in this embankment—Nippon Daemon!

(*The name is expressed with great dramatic, almost operatic, power. This is true for each character's name announcement. At the moment of the speech's climax, Nippon switches the umbrella to his left hand, holds it straight up, draws his right hand into its sleeve, and moves his head in time to the double beat of the tsuke. As Benten begins to speak he*

slowly *relaxes from this mie pose and places the umbrella against his left shoulder.*)

BENTEN: Next is one who was raised as a page at the Iwamoto Temple at Enoshima. Since I dressed like a girl in a kimono with hanging sleeves I combed my hair in the female style called Shimada. Drenched by the waves of Yuga Beach, I passed myself off as a girl and acted as the bait in blackmail schemes but despite great caution, the bubble burst, and my name was dragged through the mud as I was thrown into one dungeon after the other. As the years flew by I passed through the gates of many shrines and became known to the parishioners of Kamakura's Hachiman Shrine as a homeless rogue. Brought up on Enoshima, they call me Benten Kozō Kikunosuke!

(*His left hand grabs the umbrella and places it against his left shoulder. He draws his right hand into his kimono, thrusts it out at the breast in a fist. At the same time he stamps his left foot out to the left about a foot and a half, bends his right leg slightly, and revolves his head to the beating of the tsuke. Then, as Tadanobu speaks he slowly straightens up and takes the same posture as Nippon Daemon. Each thief does the same following his mie.*)

TADANOBU: Then comes me, a son of Edo. I was light-fingered even as a brat. I ran away from home to make a pilgrimage but decided to turn criminal and wandered throughout

Japan, winding up at Mount Yoshino. I met with great success in the Ōmine Mountains and then in Nara, passed myself off as a chess master, found my way into temples and wealthy homes, and made off with glittering mountains of loot, my crimes piled up as high as a pagoda. I made my escape and hid out from the law. I am he who takes his name from Yoshitsune's famous vassal. I am Tadanobu Rihei!

(*He takes the umbrella in his left hand, places it on his left shoulder, puts his right hand inside his sleeve, and moves his right foot forward slightly, moving his head in time to the striking of the tsuke.*)

AKABOSHI: I come next in line. As a young boy I earned my pay as a samurai's page. Later, I learned the art of robbery for the sake of my former master, kept my dull and rusty sword sharp by polishing it on unsuspecting victims at Koshigoe and Togamigahara, and followed my youthfully ardent love for thievery, slashing, and grabbing at such places as Yatsuchigō and Hanamizu Bridge in willow-green Kamakura, until my fame rivaled that of the great Yoshitsune. Though in disguise my form is well known to those of Tsukikagegayatsu and Mikoshigatake. The stars and moon in the evening sky will soon fade as will my very life. My name is Akaboshi Jūzaburō.

(*This speech is delivered in the peculiar near-falsetto of the wakashu role-type. At its conclusion Akaboshi poses by placing the umbrella in his left hand and*

drawing his right hand back, palm downward, against the hanging sleeve of his left arm. At the same time he takes a gentle step forward, almost pigeon-toed, and revolves his head softly to the beat of the tsuke.)

NANGO: Finally, there's me. I, who was raised by the Koyurugi shore, where I learned to bend before the strong sea breeze like the pines. Following the code of the underworld, I took to the waters as a pirate, robbing passengers on the Shira River night boats and threatening them with my sword, which flashed upon the waves like a bolt of lightning. Talk of my crimes, which have grown as heavy on my back as the famous Tiger Stone, has spread with the swiftness of tigers to every nook and cranny. I will end up with my head nailed to a tree but I am remorseless and will not pray for salvation. No, not I, Nango Rikimaru!

(*This is the most theatrical of the mie. As he shouts his name, Nango, holding the umbrella in his right hand, describes a wide sweeping arc with it from left to right, bringing it to rest on his right shoulder. As he does so, he pulls the hem of the kimono up over his left knee with his left hand and stamps sharply with his left foot, bending his right leg at the knee. The head movement is timed to the beating of the tsuke.*)

NIPPON: (*Closes his umbrella as he talks and holds it upside down at his right side, his hand inside the folded part*) We five men resemble the Karigane gang of old...

BENTEN: (*Same action with umbrella*) And though it may surprise you, the five thieves lined up here...

TADANOBU: (*Closes his umbrella and holds it by the top, right side up*) Will cause their names to everafter boom like thunder...

AKABOSHI: (*Umbrella business as per Nippon*) For among 1,000 few thieves reach our pinnacle...

NANGO: (*Same umbrella business as Tadanobu*) Or can boast of guts and spirit such as ours so...

NIPPON: If it will bring you honor...

THIEVES: Just try and take us!

POLICEMAN #1:   (*Loudly*) Now!

(*Rousing drum music plays as a brief fight scene* [tate] *ensues. Two policemen come down the steps and walk to Nippon Daemon whom they escort up the platform to the center. As this is a very theatrical scene, there is no actual struggle. Meanwhile, the other eight policemen jump down to the stage floor and divide into pairs, two men going to each of the four thieves and standing on either side of them. They do some stylized thrusts with their jitte. One of the men fighting Nango does a flip and remains in position on the floor after landing. The thieves parry with their umbrellas. The action is rather leisurely and is accompanied by the beating of the tsuke. Then the company slowly assumes a final tableau, and each thief poses in a posture of victory, performing a mie over his assailants. The curtain is pulled closed on the tableau as the ki are struck.*)

CURTAIN

Figure 1. Yokurō chats with Benten and Nango about the theater (*Nango*, Nakamura Kichiemon; *Benten*, Ichikawa Somegorō; *Yokurō*, Ichikawa Nakanosuke).

Figure 2. Benten looks through the textile goods as Yokurō adds figures on his abacus (*Nango*, Nakamura Kichiemon; *Benten*, Ichikawa Somegorō; *Yokurō*, Ichikawa Nakanosuke).

Figure 3.   Benten slips a piece of silk into his kimono (*Nango,* Nakamura Kichiemon; *Benten,* Ichikawa Somegorō; *Yokurō,* Ichikawa Nakanosuke).

Figure 4.   The clerks rush over to thrash Benten as Seiji holds Nango back (*Nango,* Nakamura Kichiemon; *Benten,* Ichikawa Somegorō; *Yokurō* [with abacus], Ichikawa Nakanosuke).

Figure 5. Nango shows his receipt to Yokurō (*Nango,* Nakamura Kichiemon; *Yokurō,* Ichikawa Nakanosuke).

Figure 6. Nango: ''I seem to have no alternative than to sever the head of each and every one of you'' (*Benten,* Ichikawa Somegorō; *Nango,* Nakamura Kichiemon; *Kōbei,* Nakamura Kichijūrō).

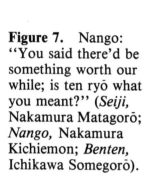

Figure 7. Nango: "You said there'd be something worth our while; is ten ryō what you meant?" (*Seiji,* Nakamura Matagorō; *Nango,* Nakamura Kichiemon; *Benten,* Ichikawa Somegorō).

Figure 8. The clerks hustle Seiji off as he throws his towel at Nango (*Seiji,* Nakamura Matagorō; *Benten,* Ichikawa Somegorō).

Figure 9. Nango (ready to draw his sword): "I cannot leave without drawing blood" (*Benten,* Ichikawa Somegorō; *Nango,* Nakamura Kichiemon; *Kōbei,* Nakamura Kichijūrō).

Figure 10. Nango: "since you are resigned to your fate I'll accept these one hundred ryō" (*Benten,* Ichikawa Somegorō; *Nango,* Nakamura Kichiemon; *Kōbei,* Nakamura Kichijūrō).

Figure 11. Nango: "He's a pretty impressive samurai" (*Nango,* Nakamura Kichiemon; *Benten,* Ichikawa Somegorō; *Nippon Daemon,* Matsumoto Kōshirō; *Kōbei,* Nakamura Kichijūrō).

Figure 12. Benten (Derisively): "I beg your pardons" (*Benten,* Ichikawa Somegorō; *Nippon,* Matsumoto Kōshirō).

Figure 13. Benten stretches as he opens his kimono (*Kōbei,* Nakamura Kichijūrō; *Benten,* Ichikawa Somegorō; *Nippon,* Matsumoto Kōshirō).

Figure 14. Benten: "If you still don't know, then lend me your ears" (*Nango,* Nakamura Kichiemon; *Sonosuke,* Matsumoto Kingo; *Kōbei,* Nakamura Kichijūrō; *Benten,* Ichikawa Somegorō; *Nippon,* Matsumoto Kōshirō).

Figure 15. The "revelation mie" (*Benten,* Onoe Kikugorō VII).

Figure 16. Benten: "Hey, Nango, you're not yourself tonight, are you?" (*Sonosuke,* Matsumoto Kingo; *Nango,* Nakamura Kichiemon; *Benten,* Ichikawa Somegorō).

Figure 17. Nango: "But remember, the master here was just talking of certain measures he might have to take" (*Sonosuke,* Matsumoto Kingo; *Nango,* Nakamura Kichiemon; *Benten,* Ichikawa Somegorō).

Figure 18. Benten puts on Nango's haori and poses (*Sonosuke,* Matsumoto Kingo; *Nango,* Nakamura Kichiemon; *Benten,* Ichikawa Somegorō; *Nippon,* Matsumoto Kōshirō).

Figure 19. Yokurō: "Come back the day before yesterday!" (*Nango,* Nakamura Kichiemon; *Benten,* Ichikawa Somegorō; *Yokurō,* Ichikawa Nakanosuke; *Sonosuke,* Matsumoto Kingo; *Kōbei,* Nakamura Kichijūrō).

Figure 20. Benten and Nango play "The Priest Holds the Bag" (*Benten,* Ichikawa Somegorō; *Nango,* Nakamura Kichiemon).

Figure 21. Four men enter below the *asagi-maku* beating drums and carrying bamboo matting.

Figure 22. One by one, the thieves poke their umbrellas through the *agemaku* before entering the hanamichi.

Figure 23. The thieves line up on the hanamichi in the Mustering scene (*Nippon,* Matsumoto Kōshirō; *Nango,* Nakamura Kichiemon; *Akaboshi,* Nakamura Jakuemon; *Tadanobu,* Ichikawa Komazō; *Benten,* Ichikawa Somegorō).

Figure 24. The thieves line up across the stage (*Nango,* Nakamura Kichiemon; *Akaboshi,* Nakamura Jakuemon; *Tadanobu,* Ichikawa Komazō; *Benten,* Ichikawa Somegorō).

Figure 25. Ichikawa Ennosuke as Nango Rikimaru performs a powerful mie.

Figure 26. The policemen attack the thieves.

Figure 27.   The final tableau.

2

Sugawara's Secrets of Calligraphy

(*Sugawara Denju Tenarai Kagami*)
A Kabuki Adaptation of a Puppet Play by
Miyoshi Shōraku, Namiki Senryū, and Takeda Izumo
Pulling the Carriage Apart (*Kuruma Biki*)
The Village School (*Terakoya*)

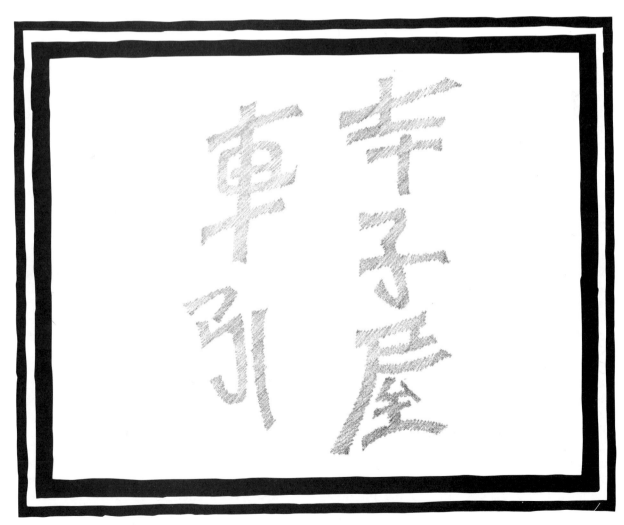

BACKGROUND TO THE PLAY

Like other works in this book, *Pulling the Carriage Apart* (*Kuruma Biki*) and *The Village School* (*Terakoya*) are scenes derived from a longer play but often presented as independent pieces. They are part of the famous masterpiece, *Sugawara's Secrets of Calligraphy* (*Sugawara Denju Tenarai Kagami*), one of the triad of great puppet plays written by Takeda Izumo II (1691-1756), Namiki Senryū (later Sōsuke, 1659-1757), and Miyoshi Shōraku (1706-1772) during the height of puppet theater popularity in the mid-eighteenth century. As with the other two outstanding works created by this group, *The Loyal Forty-seven Samurai* (*Kanadehon Chūshingura*) and *Yoshitsune and the Thousand Cherry Trees* (*Yoshitsune Sembon Zakura*), this play was almost immediately adapted by the Kabuki following its successful presentation at the Takemoto Theatre (Takemoto-za) in 1746. The first Kabuki version was in October 1746 at Kyoto's Asao Gengorō Theatre (Asao Gengorō-za). August 1747 saw a production at Osaka's Naka Theatre (Naka no Shibai) while Edo produced the work in May of that year, at both the Ichimura Theatre (Ichimura-za) and the Nakamura Theatre (Nakamura-za).

The legend of Lord Sugawara already had been told in dramatic form in Chikamatsu Monzaemon's *The Chronicle of Lord Sugawara* (*Tenjinki*), a play that has many things in common with *Sugawara's Secrets of Calligraphy*. A main point distinguishing the new treatment was the focus on the samurai triplets, Umeomaru, Sakuramaru, and Matsuomaru. (Their names refer to the plum, pine, and cherry trees, each of which is thought to have salient features summed up in the respective characters of the three brothers.) The recent birth in Osaka of triplets was a sensational news item of the day on which the clever playwriting team was quick to capitalize.

Group dramatization was usually accomplished by each writer's being assigned a specific act to write. In the present case, Shōraku wrote the second act, Senryu the third, and Izumo the fourth. Lesser playwrights employed at the theater handled the play's other acts. A novel element was added when the three main dramatists decided that each would write his major scene on the theme of the separation of a parent and child. *The Village School* was the most famous result of this approach.

Pulling the Carriage Apart was originally a brief and unimportant scene placed as a curtain-raiser to the main scene of Act III. When taken over by Kabuki it was performed in the dynamic bravado style called *aragoto* ("wild style") and, in its perfected form, was so outstanding a vehicle that the puppet theater dropped its own method of performing the scene in favor of the Kabuki approach. The piece has since come to be considered a quintessential example of the aragoto style, a style which has long been the domain of Tokyo actors, ever since it was created by the first Danjūrō (1660-1704) and developed by his descendants. Aragoto is known as the "family art" (*ie no gei*) of the Danjūrō line and actors in this family have made a number of distinctive contributions to the play's performance. Two of the chief roles, Umeō and Matsuō (shortened forms by which Umeomaru and Matsuomaru are often called), are classic examples of the aragoto superman type though their brother, Sakuramaru, is always played in the *wagoto* ("gentle style") tradition, a far more delicate and romantic style. When the play is produced in the Kyoto-Osaka area the aragoto qualities are slightly reduced as that region favors the wagoto style.

Pulling the Carriage Apart has barely any plot, merely being a confrontation between Sakuramaru and Umeō with their supposed traitor-brother, Matsuō, and his lord, Fujiwara no Shihei. Yet, the thirty minutes or so that the play takes up in performance provide audiences with one of the most brilliant displays of Kabuki spectacle and excitement. The piece is a perfect example of the printed page's limitations in conveying the magic with which theatrical performance can infuse a script. When, in 1973, spectators at the Kennedy Center's Eisenhower Theatre in Washington, D.C., were treated to a performance of this work by the young actors in training at Japan's National Theatre, they understood at once why writers such as Hamamura Yonezō have called this "the most Kabuki-esque of all Kabuki plays."

Although Namiki Senryū is known to have written the third act's major scene, *The Seventieth Birthday Celebration,* it is not clear who wrote the original *Pulling the Carriage Apart.* It is likely that the actors themselves developed the dialogue and action, with minimal formal participation by a playwright.

The Village School is one of the ten most often performed Kabuki plays. It has long been known in the West, having been the inspiration for John Masefield's drama, *The Pine.* A version titled *Bushido* was popular in the United States early in the twentieth century; its most important production was at the hands of the Washington Square Players, shortly before they became better known as the Theatre Guild. Following World War II it was one of the plays proscribed by the Occupation authorities as being too overtly feudalistic in theme. Earle Ernst, who later wrote a definitive book on Kabuki, was an Occupation official, in charge of censoring postwar theater; Ernst actually forbade performances of this play, though he was eventually to change his mind. He ultimately included a free translation of the puppet play text in his *Three Japanese Plays from the Traditional Theatre.*

Scholars today claim that, rather than exalting feudal virtues, the play actually criticizes them, but in a necessarily indirect way. Kawatake Toshio, for instance, asserts that the Japanese masses were not enthralled by plays that glorified a system that could force a man to have to substitute his own son for another's. Such critics feel this subversive criticism is implicit in Genzō's famous line, "It is painful indeed to serve one's master."

Whereas *Pulling the Carriage Apart* is performed in aragoto style, a subcategory of the jidaimono or history play genre, *The Village School* is an example of the sewamono or domestic play genre, albeit with a number of elements suggestive of the history classification. As a full-length work, *Sugawara's Secrets of Calligraphy* is classed as a history play of the kind known as *ōdaimono* or *ōchomono,* that is, plays dealing with Imperial society during the Nara and Heian periods of Japan's middle ages.

Since the war, very few full-length productions of *Sugawara's Secrets of Calligraphy* have been offered, although several of the more famous scenes are sometimes staged on the same program. *Pulling the Carriage Apart* and *The Village School* are seldom played together as part of a program unless other pieces from the complete play are produced as well. For instance, in November 1975, Tokyo's Kabuki Theatre produced a matinee program consisting of these scenes plus the one called *Dōmyō Temple* (*Dōmyōji*), from an earlier part of the play. Though part of the same work, the performance style of the different scenes differs sharply. Thus, the make-up, costume, and wig worn by Matsuō in *Pulling the Carriage Apart,* as well as the acting technique used for the role, is noticeably different from that of *The Village School.* The respective excellence of these scenes, despite their violently contrasting natures, clearly demonstrates the range of Kabuki's stylistic eclecticism.

PLOT AND KATA

Sugawara's Secrets of Calligraphy skillfully places the story of the rivalry between Lord Sugawara no Michizane and Fujiwara no Shihei against the background of the samurai triplets and the loyal but suffering Takebe Genzō. One reason the work has held a position of esteem for so long is that Sugawara was posthumously deified, is known in Japan under several venerable titles, and is the patron saint of calligraphy.

Briefly, the play concerns the successful machinations of the evil Fujiwara family minister, Shihei, to discredit the renowned Lord Sugawara so as to increase his own power. When Sugawara is forced into exile, Genzō, Sugawara's faithful disciple, takes his master's young son, Kan Shūsai, and flees with him to safety, away from those seeking to destroy Sugawara's family. He sets up a calligraphy school in the country where he passes the boy off as his own. The play's other main subplot concerns the fortunes of the samurai triplets Matsuō, Umeō, and Sakuramaru. Matsuō has alienated his brothers by taking service with Lord Shihei, the mortal enemy of the house of Sugawara, to which the triplets' family owes allegiance. Sakuramaru gets into trouble by presuming to arrange a tryst between his master, Prince Tokiyo, and Tokiyo's mistress, Kariya, Sugawara's daughter. Discovered in their rendezvous by Shihei's men, Tokiyo and Kariya are forced to escape. The tryst is used by Shihei as an excuse for bringing about Sugawara's disgrace and exile. These events form the background to the action of *Pulling the Carriage Apart.*

Scenery for "Pulling the Carriage Apart." Pulling the Carriage Apart takes place at the Yoshida Shrine in Kyoto. The set described in the text is that of the Tokyo production style, by far the most prevalent. However, the Osaka-Kyoto style is still used. In this latter a light blue curtain (the asagimaku) hides most of the set after the striped curtain opens. The blue curtain may have a landscape with trees painted on it. When Umeō and Sakuramaru exit the curtain is dropped, revealing the set described in the translation. Another variation is to have a mud wall depicted across the set. This is removed when the brothers enter. A rationale for the double set is that its use avoids the artificiality of having the brothers exit and then reappear in the same setting. There is some cramping of the acting space when the blue curtain is used, though. When the young actors-in-training at the National Theatre of Japan played in Washington, D.C., in 1973, they used the latter style.

After an introductory passage recited by the *gidayū* chanter (a convention borrowed from the puppet theater), Umeō enters on the hanamichi and his brother, Sakuramaru, comes on from stage right.

Hanamichi and Costume Kata. Frequently, two hanamichi will be used for this entrance. Umeō will then make his entrance on the regular (*hon*) hanamichi while his brother will arrive on the temporary hanamichi set up on the stage left side of the auditorium. Since Kabuki's leading family of actors, the Ichikawas, often play Umeō it is customary for this entrance procedure to be used. However, since Sakuramaru was once a great success for actors in the Kikugorō and Sōjūrō lines, when actors from these traditions play the role, they may be allowed use of the main hanamichi for their entrance.

The brothers are dressed in thickly padded costumes with long, thick, rope-like obis (the *maruguke*). Umeō's obi is much thicker than Sakuramaru's. It is over three inches thick and about twelve feet long. To tie this obi, four men must cooperate in a complex procedure during which the obi is wrapped three times around the actor and formed into a bow at the rear. Since it must be tied as tightly as possible, at least one or two feet are usually pressed against the actor's back in the process. On opening day, the obi is a bit too thick and short but after being pulled strongly day after day it stretches considerably.

Each brother wears a red removable collar though some experts claim that these should be black. Most scholars would agree, however, that red is more appropriate as it accentuates the youth of the characters.

Umeō and Sakuramaru speak to each other of the chagrin they feel because of their recent misfortunes. Sakuramaru would prefer to commit suicide for his part in the Lord Tokiyo/Lady Kariya scandal but realizes that he must first attend his father's imminent seventieth birthday celebration. The brothers weep by lightly moving their heads rhythmically.

A Weeping Kata. There is an old tradition that Umeō cries by moving his head in the pattern of the Japanese symbol for the sound of "ri" (り) whereas Sakuramaru's head movement resembles that for "no" (の). Since the brothers are wearing large straw hats the head movements must be done carefully so as not to make the hats shake clumsily.

A herald appears and interrupts the mood of sadness by announcing the coming of Lord Shihei to the shrine. He treats the brothers with contempt, then leaves. Umeō and Sakuramaru, seething with rage, exit on the hanamichi with Umeō doing so in the difficult *tobi roppō* style.

The Tobi Roppō Exit. Kikugorō VI described the tobi roppō or "flying in six directions" as follows:

> First, Umeō arrives at the hanamichi where he begins his exit by thrusting forth his right foot, raising his left foot as if pulling it up, then moving ahead in a double hop step; he puts forth his left foot, "pulls" up his right, and repeats the double-hop. While thus alternating legs in double-hop steps, he moves in a way expressive of power and roundness, the body seemingly hurtling forward freely.... The hanamichi in the larger theaters is good for about six and one-half or seven bounds before reaching the agemaku curtain, but since one gains momentum and cannot possibly stop oneself, an apprentice stands waiting within the agemaku room to seize the actor and halt his progress, if there is no young "catcher" waiting, the actor will crash right through to the front entrance of the theater.[1]

Whereas most performers do their tobi roppō from the beginning of the hanamichi, Danjūrō IX did his from the stage itself as he spoke his parting line.

Such a kata is considered more difficult. Danjūrō kept both hands glued to the hilt of his sword as he exited, this being another variation of the usual method.

As for Sakuramaru's exit, Kikugorō VI wrote that he "grabs the hilt of a sword with his right hand, then places his left on the other hilt, and, in double steps, lowering his shoulders, moves off in a slightly coquettish way, evoking a feeling of softness and sex appeal." He points out that this was the kata of Kikugorō V whereas he, "taking my stoutness into account, make the exit in single step movements, moving my shoulders in a way intended to suggest sexiness."[2]

Shihei's carriage can now be heard and, after a moment, it enters at left with a retinue of white-robed retainers. Once it is in position, Umeō and Sakuramaru come bolting back in on the hanamichi, calling to the procession to stop. Umeō is now wearing three extra-long swords rather than the two he wore at the play's opening.

Kata of the Three Swords. The use of the three swords is really supposed to be restricted to actors of the Ichikawa line though others make use of it too. One reason the usage is associated with the Ichikawas is said to be because the samurai of Kōshū, whence an Ichikawa ancestor hailed, wore three instead of the customary two swords. Whether this is true or not, it cannot be denied that the effect of the three huge swords adds a perfect

1. *Gei* (*Art*) (Tokyo, 1948), pp. 205-206.

2. Ibid.

touch to the exaggerated style in which Umeō is acted. When Matsuō enters shortly afterward, the actor playing him may also elect to wear three long swords.

A young retainer, Sugiomaru, steps forth to answer the challenge.

Sugiomaru. The character of Sugiomaru does not appear in the original version of the play. He was added by the actor, Kō-shirō V (1764-1838), who wished to make his own entrance as Matsuō even more impressive by the inclusion of this role.

The brothers exchange some fiery remarks and posturings with Sugiomaru and then four lesser retainers come forth to do battle with Sakuramaru and Umeō. They are easily bested by the powerful brothers. Matsuō now enters from the left, carrying a long, folded umbrella and harangues his brothers. Like Umeō he is an aragoto character.

Matsuō's Side-Facing Mie. Matsuō's first mie pose is done in profile. Kōshirō V, who loved to pose in profile to show off his magnificently high-bridged nose, created this side-facing mie (*yoko mie*).

Matsuō removes the upper portion of his outer kimono, preparatory to engaging his brothers in combat. He reveals a white under-kimono in doing so.

Matsuō's Under-Kimono. Matsuō originally wore a red under-kimono like his brothers but Kōshirō V created the kata of wearing a white one to make Matsuō

more prominent. Today, the white under-kimono is almost always worn. However, when the National Theatre produced the play in 1966, Onoe Kuroemon, son of Kikugorō VI, returned to the red under-kimono which he says his father wore for a 1935 performance of the role.

There is some powerful posing and movement as the confrontation between Matsuō and his brothers reaches its climax. At one point they strike a dynamic tableau at center holding the long umbrella off the floor in a horizontal line as they snap their heads in time to the background percussion music. In those rare cases where Matsuō wears a red under-kimono the tableau is performed on the hanamichi, near the shichi-san. At its conclusion Umeō forces Matsuō back to the stage in the manner of an *oshimodoshi* (a Kabuki superman-type whose generic name means "queller of demons").

Presently, the carriage is dismantled by Sakuramaru and Umeō. This reveals its occupant, the ferocious-looking Lord Shihei. Shihei is an excellent example of the Kabuki role-type called *kugeaku,* villainous noblemen attached to the Imperial Court. Sakuramaru and Umeō attempt to overcome Shihei but his awesome magical power overwhelms them. The brothers argue once more but Shihei forbids Matsuō from battling with Umeō and Sakuramaru because he does not wish to commit sacrilege on holy ground. The scene ends as the company assumes a final tableau of impressive grandeur.

Following *Pulling the Carriage Apart* is an act titled *The Seventieth Birthday Celebration* (*Ga no Iwai*). In it the triplets and their wives arrive at the home of Shirodayū, father to the three men, to celebrate his birthday. Matsuō and Umeō quarrel bitterly. Shirodayū shames Matsuō for having betrayed his trust to Sugawara by taking service with Shihei. The act ends with the suicide of Sakuramaru, who kills himself to atone for his involvement in the Tokiyo-Kariya affair.

This act is followed by *The Village School*. Takebe Genzō had been the most able disciple of the great calligrapher, Sugawara. He had, however, incurred his master's displeasure by falling in love with the lady-in-waiting, Tonami. This unfortunate incident led to the establishment by Genzō and Tonami of a small temple school in the country where they have to earn a living by teaching calligraphy to the children of local farmers. When Genzō and Tonami learned of the exile to which Sugawara was condemned by Shihei, they smuggled Sugawara's son, Kan Shūsai, out of their lord's palace and installed him as a pupil in their school, giving out that he was their own son.

When *The Village School* opens the children in the school are seen lined up across the stage doing their schoolwork. Among them is the noble-looking Kan Shūsai.

Stage Positions of the Schoolchildren. As described in the translation, the children are lined up across the upstage platform. Such an arrangement is typical of productions in the Kyoto-Osaka area but is rare in Tokyo. Tokyo productions usually have all the boys seated on the stage floor, just downstage of the platform, with Kan Shūsai seated on the platform alone at right center. His elevated position clearly marks him off from the others in the room. Sometimes he is reading, as in the present version, and sometimes he is practicing calligraphy like everyone else. The number of children is usually nine, though this number is open to debate, as will be seen below.

The Village School may be divided, for the sake of analysis, into eight sections. This first part is called *terairi* (admission to the village school). It is an excellently written scene, filled with superb moments of emotional expression for its chief character, Chiyo, yet it is often cut from modern productions. Fortunately, it was staged in the present production and is described here in detail. Its humorous portions are in the typical vein of Kabuki farce and serve to set off the later scenes of tragedy by the vividness with which they contrast with them in tone. When the scene is cut the business with Yodarekuri is greatly abbreviated and Genzō enters only a few moments after the curtain's opening.

Though the children are supposed to be practicing their calligraphy, the fifteen-year-old rascal, Yodarekuri, would rather draw funny pictures. He is berated by Kan Shūsai for his attitude and, when he talks back to the young lord, the other boys gang up on him for his rudeness.

Yodarekuri is something of a simpleton; he is usually played by an actor of children's roles (*koyaku*) but, on occasion, more mature actors of the clown-type (*sanmaime*) enact the role.

Tonami, hearing the fuss in the schoolroom, enters from upstage center and punishes Yodarekuri by making him stand on his desk. As soon as she leaves, Chiyo enters on the hanamichi with her young son, Kotarō, and her manservant, Sansuke.

> *Chiyo's Entrance.* Onoe Baikō VI wrote that Chiyo's entry here is a very difficult one for the actor. Chiyo must be very sad yet must not cry or overtly reveal her grief (she is bringing her son to meet his death). Nevertheless, tradition holds that a smile to cover her sadness is also taboo. The actor's attitude, wrote Baikō, must be somewhere in the margin between crying and not smiling.[3]

Sansuke goes to the door of the school to learn if it is the place his mistress is seeking. He and Yodarekuri have a comic argument revolving around a pun on the words *takeppera* (bamboo spatula) and Takebe (Genzō's family name). Sansuke asks if this is the home of Takeppera Genzō but Yodarekuri replies that he must have the wrong house as no one here sells takeppera. My translation makes use of a far racier pun suggested by an actor in the Brooklyn College production of the play. Though the translation is by no means literal it provides a good laugh and is perfectly in keeping with the comic spirit of such Kabuki scenes.

Tonami reenters and invites the small group into the schoolroom. Chiyo explains that she wishes to enroll her son in the school. She asks to see Tonami's son and Tonami points to him.

Reference to Kan Shūsai. The original version of the play had Tonami calling Kan Shūsai over to meet Chiyo but this was cut long ago, to speed up the action. Also, whereas the original had Tonami state that the boy was "over here," modern productions must substitute "over there" because of the increased size of today's stages.

Chiyo is the wife of Matsuō. Kan Shūsai's presence in the school has been discovered and Shihei has ordered his head cut off. Chiyo and Matsuō, realizing that this is the perfect time to show their true allegiance to Lord Sugawara, have decided to place Kotarō in the school in the hope that Genzō will kill him instead and use his head as a substitute to deceive the official who will come to verify that the head is indeed Kan Shūsai's. Genzō is now in the village, being given the order to hand over Kan Shūsai's head. Tonami knows nothing of this yet. Now, when Chiyo asks to see Tonami's son, it is with the express purpose of assuring herself that her son will make a suitable substitute.

> *Chiyo's Comparison.* According to tradition, Chiyo must not be overly obvious in her comparison of the two boys' faces. Her line, "My, what a lovely child," must be spoken quite casually. Baikō VI noted that Chiyo can see perfectly well which boy is Kan Shūsai as the rest are all obviously the children of peasants. She simply wishes final confirmation, wrote Baikō, that her son will be worthy as a substitute. A few moments later she asks Tonami whether Genzō is not at home.

3. *Joen Shiryoshu* (*Collection of Research Materials*) (July 1968), p. 16.

The answer to this, too, is known to her as she is aware that Genzō has been called to the village headman's home where her husband, Matsuō, also has gone.[4]

During the following action, Yodarekuri's bawling distracts Chiyo, who then begs Tonami to forgive him.

Chiyo's Compassion. Baikō VI felt that Chiyo expends her compassion on Yodarekuri because of her inability to do likewise for Kotarō. She also imagines that her deed of mercy will help her son on his journey to the afterworld.[5]

Chiyo prepares to leave but Kotarō tries to stop her, pleading for her to take him with her. She disengages herself and leaves but, overcome with a desire to see her boy one more time, returns on the pretext of having forgotten her fan. When Tonami points out that Chiyo has it in her hand, the women laugh lightly and the inwardly grieving Chiyo makes her exit. Tonami and Kotarō go within.

A farcical scene ensues between Sansuke and Yodarekuri in which the pathos of the scene of Chiyo and Kotarō's parting is mimicked. Such scenes of "parroting" (*ōmu*) are a convention of certain Kabuki plays. A moment after Sansuke departs, Genzō, wrapped in a cloud of gloom, makes his appearance on the hanamichi. The section now beginning is called *Genzō modori* (Genzō returns).

4. Ibid.
5. Ibid.

Genzō's Entrance and Costume. Genzō's manner of entering should immediately communicate his concern over the dire command he has received: to hand over the head of Kan Shūsai. There are some who say that the success or failure of the entire performance hinges on the effectiveness of this entry. Most actors perform it in the manner described in the translation, said to have been created by Danjūrō IX, but there are also several variations seen occasionally. For example, there is the Kikugorō kata of entering the hanamichi lost in thought, arms folded, and, at the shichi-san, stumbling slightly, and looking back to see if he has been followed or not. Then, his mind made up to perform the substitution of another boy's head for Kan Shūsai's, he folds his arms once more and moves to the gateway. The Sōjūrō kata has Genzō entering at his wit's end and going straight to the gateway without pausing. Yet another kata has the village headman accompany Genzō as far as the shichi-san.

There used to be small theaters (*koshibai*) performing Kabuki in contrast to the large theaters (*ōshibai*) such as those still producing today. Though these koshibai lacked the prestige of the "majors" they often performed interesting variations on the traditional kata. One such was the kata of having Genzō be so distracted by his thoughts that he walked right past his house on reaching the stage.

Genzō's costume differs today from that worn in the past. The main difference is that he now appears without the formal divided trousers (*hakama*) formerly worn. It would be more realistic for him to wear the hakama as he is coming from a formal call paid to the village headman. The puppet version of this play retains the use of the hakama.

Genzō enters the schoolroom and looks at the faces of the boys there. Hoping to find one suitable for use as a substitute for Kan Shūsai he is depressed at the plainness he sees in their faces and bearing. His manner toward the children is harsh and when Tonami enters she chides him for the nasty tone in his voice.

Greeting of the Children. In the present production, the boys remain on the platform at their desks during this business but other versions have them rush to greet Genzō at the door where they kneel as he looks down into their upturned faces.

Although Tonami usually enters at this point with Kotarō the original version of the play never had the boy exit at all. He remained on stage near Kan Shūsai following Chiyo's departure. Because of the feeling that Genzō would notice him immediately if he saw Kotarō next to the young lord, most modern productions have the boy exit earlier with Tonami. The major full-length production given as the inaugural presentation of the National Theatre (1966), however, arranged the text so that both Kotarō and Kan Shūsai went off with Tonami in the earlier scene.

Tonami presents Kotarō to Genzō. When the schoolmaster sees the new boy he is over-joyed since he realizes how excellent a substitution he will make. The children are dismissed. As they leave, they pile their desks upstage right. When the desks are piled up, Kotarō's desk and book box (brought on earlier by Sansuke) remain as is, below them. This is important, as it later prompts Matsuō to question Tonami about the number of desks on the platform.

Kiku-Kichi Kata. One of the most famous Matsuō-Genzō acting teams in Kabuki history was Onoe Kikugorō VI as Matsuō and Nakamura Kichiemon I as Genzō. They also were lauded when they played the opposite roles but the Kikugorō-Matsuō/Kichiemon-Genzō combination is said to have been supreme. Faubion Bowers, who often saw this team play together recalls that "Kiku was larger-faced and suited the more Kabuki-esque role of Matsuō. Kichi, being smaller, suited the less grand, lower, more humble role of Genzō. But, by contrast, and this gave the combination its extraordinary flavor, Kiku was the more realistic (in a nonrealistic role) and Kichi was more Kabuki in the realistic role of Genzō. A further contrast that meshed in performance marvelously was that Kiku brought a dance element into everything he touched (being a dancer, all was grace) and Kichi, being a nondancer, matched the earthiness of Genzō better."[6] This team's productions will be referred to hereafter as "Kiku-Kichi."

6. In a letter to the author.

Kiku-Kichi's kata at the point we have reached differed from that described for the present production. Genzō picked up his sword in his left hand, rose, saw the children off, turned front, made a prayer gesture with his right hand, went to the door, opened it, looked outside, closed the door, walked to upstage center, and then came down left center wrapped in thought. He sat down in a semierect posture. Tonami then took Kan Shūsai off into the shoji room at left, placing his desk there, too, before returning to the stage proper. Thus, Kan Shūsai did not go off up center as described in the present version. This, of course, led to variations in later business that will be described in due course.

Tonami and Genzō are now alone. Genzō reveals that he has been ordered to hand over Kan Shūsai's head but that he plans to substitute the new boy instead. He declares that, if necessary, he will kill the mother when she returns. During this powerful emotional scene Genzō speaks the famous line, "It is painful indeed to serve one's master."

A Controversial Line. Critics often have stated that this line (*semajiki mono wa omiyazukai*) sums up the theme of the play. Because of its antimilitaristic implications the line was changed by Danjūrō IX and the change was performed from the Meiji period through the end of World War II. Danjūrō's revision made the line read, "Now we can truly serve our lord!" Obviously, the second version was more in keeping with the chauvinistic mood of late-nineteenth-century Japan, a mood that eventually led the Japanese to global conflict. Nevertheless, Kikugorō VI and Kichiemon I reverted to the original line in their early performances together in the late 1910s. This pair, however, seems to have gone back to Danjūrō's revision in the militaristic 1930s, possibly because of official pressure. Following the war, they brought the original back into use.

Tonami and Genzō resolve to do what must be done. Voices are heard from nearby and the couple goes within. As Matsuō (in a palanquin), Gemba, and a retinue of policemen and farmers enter, Kan Shūsai is hidden in the shoji room at left.

A Variant "Hiding" Kata. In contrast with the business described in the text of the translation, Genzō, in the Kiku-Kichi version, after rising, held Tonami to him, looked meaningfully at her, and pointed to the doorway. Understanding, she went to it, looked about, locked the door, placed her back to it, and stared at Genzō. This was all done quickly. Meanwhile, Genzō went up to the platform, placed his sword in front of the closet, entered the shoji room, came out with Kan Shūsai, hid him in a closet built into the upstage wall, ad-libbed, "Be patient for a while," closed the closet door, and bowed to the now hidden child. This business of hiding the child in the closet is more common than that of the production method described in the text. A gidayū line, omitted here, follows the off-stage cries of the farmers which begins this section. It reads: "Tonami hides Kan Shūsai/in a nearby closet." The line having been cut in the present version, the business of hiding the child took place a bit later in the play and was slightly different from that indicated for the Kiku-Kichi production.[7]

The fearsome Shundō Gemba, vassal of Lord Shihei, has come to oversee the act of head inspection. The head inspector is none other than Matsuō, the father of Kotarō. Only he is said to know the face of Kan Shūsai well enough to verify the head's authenticity. Matsuō, of course, is aware that the head he is about to see most likely will be that of his own son but he dare not let on to anyone that this is the case. Matsuō steps out of his palanquin and joins Gemba at the doorway to the schoolhouse. A group of farmers, the parents and grandparents of the children, have entered. They are lined up nearby, ready to take their children home with them. The scene now commencing is called *terako aratame* (the inspection of the schoolchildren).

Matsuō warns the farmers not to try to sneak Kan Shūsai off as one of their own. During his harangue he breaks into a highly theatricalized fit of coughing.

The Coughing Kata. There are four main approaches to the coughing business. One is the way indicated in the transla-

tion; a second is at the line, "get him out of here"; a third is on a line in Matsuō's next speech—"examined their faces"; and a fourth would be to omit all coughs completely. The second approach is aimed at hinting to Genzō, within, that he should sneak Kan Shūsai off as one of the farmer's sons. When Kikugorō V performed this business he altered it slightly and said the line by turning a bit toward the door to the school and reacting appropriately. Many have followed this kata, including Uzaemon XV, but some critics feel it is a gross error. Genzō is convinced that Matsuō is an enemy, they claim, so no matter what Matsuō says, even as a hint, he will definitely not believe it. Gemba's presence also militates against Matsuō doing this kind of hinting. Moreover, Matsuō would have to increase his volume to make Genzō hear him but Matsuō must speak in a low voice until the moment of Kotarō's death. If he did not, the boy might hear him and come running out to see his father.

If the actor chooses to cough on "examined their faces," Matsuō seemingly choking on his spittle while raising his voice, the same objection as was made to the second method can be raised. Takechi Tetsuji, a critic-director who often attempts to "psychologize" Kabuki in his interpretations, feels that Matsuō's line, "I will most gratefully take my leave as requested," is a better one for him to cough on as it puts him under a debt of obligation to Shihei who granted his leave. Matsuō's conscience

7. A very detailed account of the Kiku-Kichi production is in *Jōen Shiryōshū* (July 1968), pp. 23-38.

rankles at the thought of being obligated to Shihei and he coughs on his next line when the gall rises in his throat upon his having had to praise his evil master. Takechi says, "The way indicated by the original text is by far the best even when looked at from the psychological angle."[8]

Matsuō now demands that the parents call their children out one at a time so that he can examine their faces. At this point, Genzō and Tonami appear inside the room and hide Kan Shūsai in the shoji room.

Hiding Kan Shūsai. As already noted, some productions, notably that of Kiku-Kichi, have the schoolmaster and his wife hide the boy in a closet in the upstage left wall during a previous section. The most recent exit of the couple would have been into the shoji room and not up center as in the production described in the text. Thus, Genzō and his wife enter from up center here while other productions would have them come in from the shoji room. The other business, however, is basically the same. One major difference is that in the present version, Genzō notices Kotarō's sandals at the door and rushes over to hide them. This is not always done in other productions.

When the sandals are allowed to stay by the door Matsuō may, upon entering the room, enact a kata of noticing them.

Takechi writes that Kikugorō VI did nothing to show that his Matsuō noticed the sandals. Bowers, however, notes that he recalls Kikugorō giving the sandals a cursory glance as he entered.[9] To notice them more obviously would require that he ask whose they were; this would make his later question about the number of desks meaningless. Why bother with the business of the desks, intended as it is to verify Kotarō's presence, if Matsuō already knows he is there from having seen the sandals? The counting of the desks would then become a mere taunting of Tonami in order to gain Gemba's confidence and Matsuō's later line about having counted the desks in order to see if Kotarō had arrived would be an untruth. A subtle glance such as Bowers remembers, however, would merely be one more assurance to Matsuō that his son was present and, for a man in Matsuō's position, all risks should be avoided.

As each child is called out, he stops at Gemba's knee. Gemba lifts each of their faces with his fan and seeks Matsuō's reaction. Each then goes off with his parent.

Inspecting the Children. Kichiemon I wrote that the most important point in Matsuō's role, according to his father, Nakamura Karoku III (1849-1919), was the inspection of the children's faces. As Matsuō looks at each face he wonders to himself what he will do if his own son

8. *Kari no Tayori* (*Missives*) (Tokyo, 1969), pp. 68-70. See also Tomita Tetsunosuke, "Sugawara Denju Tenarai Kagami Saiken" ("A Close Look at '*Sugawara's Secrets of Calligraphy*'"), *Kabuki,* 10 (1971), 118.

9. In a letter to the author.

comes flying out into his arms. When, finally, Kotarō fails to appear, he thinks to himself, "Ah, thank goodness!"[10] The difficulty in acting this is its subtlety. It must be done so even the audience is unaware of it. Here is a perfect example of the inner depth of much Kabuki acting which the uninitiated often takes to be a thing of merely outward splendor.

Takechi notes that some actors scarcely look at the children's faces while others stare intently at them and then shake their heads, "No." The most interesting method, he says, was when Kikugorō VI, shortly before the first boy came out, turned his head to gaze at the doorway. The feeling conveyed was his wonder as to who would be the next boy to emerge. Kotarō? Someone else? Matsuō's nervousness was vividly depicted.[11]

When all the children have gone, Gemba and Matsuō enter the schoolroom for the climactic scene, that called *kubijikken* (the head inspection). Gemba and Matsuō sit at stage left on high stools (*aibiki*).

The Sitting Kata. Danjūrō VII (1791-1859) created a kata of having Matsuō sit on a red cushion with an armrest rather than on an aibiki stool. This is rarely seen today, though, since the process of getting up and down from a position on the cushion is simply too bothersome for most actors. Kataoka Nizaemon XI (1857-1934) was one of the few to follow this kata. He used the cushion throughout, including the head inspection scene, leaning on the armrest as though he were ill. However, even Nizaemon eventually gave up use of the cushion in favor of the stool.

Matsuō and Gemba order Genzō to go within and sever the head of Kan Shūsai. Matsuō warns Genzō not to attempt using a substitute. He says, "you won't fool me by using a substitute head...."

Matsuō's "Hint" to Genzō. Ichikawa Chūsha VII (1860-1936) and Kōshirō VII were actors who played this line as if Matsuō were hinting to Genzō that he *should* substitute Kotarō for Kan Shūsai. They stared hard at the schoolmaster and spoke the words slowly, as though Genzō's mind could be pierced.[12]

Takechi writes that he is dissatisfied with most actors' delivery of these lines.

> There is no doubt that Matsuō's intention here is to tell Genzō that he must by no means attempt to escape but he also means to fortify thoroughly Genzō's resolve to kill Kotarō instead of Kan Shūsai. Thus, "using a substitute head" is spoken with no special need to give Genzō any hints. This is because, first, Matsuō realizes that Genzō

---

10. See Kawatake Shigetoshi, *Nakamura Kichiemon* (Tokyo, 1955), pp. 366-370.
11. *Kari no Tayori*, p. 71.

12. See Kima Hisao, *Kabuki* (Tokyo, 1958), pp. 144-150, for an account of Chūsha's highly praised performance as Matsuō.

considers him an absolute enemy. Matsuō, even if he faces Genzō on speaking "using a substitute head," should understand more than anyone else that Genzō is exercising vigilance and caution and would never entertain the idea that Matsuō might be hinting something to him as a favor. Number two, Matsuō recognizes the necessity of deceiving Gemba by inspiring his confidence in Matsuō's behavior. So, even earlier he faces Gemba and warns him against letting any children depart too hastily. Later, he does such things as grilling Tonami about the number of desks [for the same reason]. . . . Thus, since Matsuō has to be on guard to the nth degree and must go so far as to put on a show for Gemba's benefit, there is no chance that he would actually be giving secret hints to Genzō.[13]

Following Matsuō's order, Genzō rises and, with a great show of resolution, takes the head box within.

Genzō's Exit. When this exit was made by Danjūrō IX he slipped his outer kimono off one shoulder, revealing the special cords (*tasuki*) used to tie back the under-kimono for deeds of action. Most actors first disclose these cords when they attack Chiyo, later in the play. Chūsha VII felt that to do so here was to detract

from Matsuō, who should be the central focus in this section.

Matsuō looks around the room after Genzō has gone and notices that there seems to be one desk too many.

On the Number of Desks. Matsuō's line, "We counted only eight brats but there is one extra desk here," has called forth much controversy. The problem is that, according to the text, Matsuō has inspected eight children yet he clearly sees nine desks, one being apart from the rest in most productions. This would apparently verify to him that there was one extra child in the school, possibly his Kotarō. Yet he cannot be sure that the extra desk does not belong to Kan Shūsai. To complicate matters, Tonami, as noted, removed Kan Shūsai's desk earlier in the play. If she had not there would now be ten desks on stage. Tonami removed the desk before becoming aware of Genzō's situation. The present arrangement of the desks, which seems to be the most common, leaves open for Matsuō the question: whose desk is it? Tonami's removal of Kan Shūsai's desk seems to have been designed to circumvent the problem of having ten desks on stage, despite the apparent illogicality of the action in terms of motivation.

There have been actors, however, who felt that Tonami should not remove Kan Shūsai's desk. Kōshirō VII was one of these. He believed that it should be piled up at the rear with the other desks as should the desk of Kotarō. His ap-

13. *Kari no Tayori*, pp. 73-74.

proach was to use seven children for the inspection rather than eight. Matsuō would then notice that only seven children had left despite there being nine desks on stage. He would do some mental arithmetic, saying, "We counted only...," then realize that only seven children had left, and, to forestall Gemba, add "eight" immediately, with emphasis. Other actors, such as Kikugorō V and Baikō VI, his son, felt that Kan Shūsai's desk should be taken off but that Kotarō's should remain; its position, however, would not be apart from the others but rather would be amidst them in the upstage right corner.

Kawarazaki Chōjūrō, an actor, has said, "When Matsuō sees the number of desks and that one is placed separately, he is sure that his son has come to the school. Further, his line, 'there are nine desks here,' is intended to deceive Gemba and he uses the contradictory number as the source of his plan, revealing the fact in order to guarantee Gemba's trust."[14]

Takechi Tetsuji feels that Matsuō's later remark to the effect that he counted the desks in order to verify his son's presence contains a contradiction. If he had merely wanted to verify the fact, there would have been no need to say anything about it. He could simply have thought to himself, "Ah, Kotarō's desk is here." Takechi agrees that the whole purpose of bringing up the subject here is to throw Gemba off guard.[15]

Tonami comes up with an excuse to Matsuō's barbed query and presents the desk to Matsuō for his inspection.

The Name Tag Kata. Kyoto-Osaka actors often perform the kata of having Tonami notice that there is a name tag with Kotarō's name on the desk. Tonami will secretly remove it and only then present the desk to Matsuō. At any rate, Matsuō does not pursue the topic any further.

Several moments later the sound of a head being severed is heard from within. Matsuō loses his self-control and bumps into Tonami. He screams "Brazen woman!" (*bureimonome*) at her and strikes a powerful mie, which has come to be a major highlight of the play.

The Bureimonome Kata. According to Tōbe Ginsaku, the well-known critic, the basis of this moment is Matsuō's almost unconscious act of rising with his attention fixed on what is happening offstage (the death of his son), his crossing toward center, and his collision there with Tonami, who must time her move precisely, in accordance with the rhythm of the chanter and shamisen player. Tonami, the supporting role, must enhance the performance of the actor playing Matsuō, so the moment is a good test of the supporting actor's skill. Too conspicuous a performance will disturb the necessary balance.[16]

14. Ibid., p. 76.
15. Ibid.

16. *Kabuki no Engi* (*Kabuki Acting*) (Tokyo, 1955), p. 183.

Takechi points out that

Kikugorō VI, on hearing the sound of decapitation, faced front with a slight facial reaction and, Tonami, startled, faced upstage and began to rise. Kikugorō turned his face in that direction and, [when bumped into] shouted his line and began to cough; he coughed for a moment (his body being positioned to face left slightly)...as he brought his hand to his mouth and then to his head, with his thumb pressed against the temple, the other four fingers widely splayed, as if hiding his features from Gemba; he then blinked several times.[17]

On certain days, rather than saying the conventional line, Kikugorō shouted *"Susariirō!"* ("Get back!") instead. He would also, on occasion, change the kata and, with his right hand holding the sword, switch it to his left, and perform the actions described by Takechi with the opposite hands. Although Kikugorō was one of the most intelligent and rational of modern Kabuki actors, one who always endeavored to bring fresh insights to the interpretation of classical roles, it is likely that he made such changes as indicated in the last sentence not so much from a psychological point of view as from the need to add variety to his acting. It is not unlikely that even Kabuki actors seek to vary their performances in roles with which they have long been associated; such variations may derive from no more potent an inspiration than the desire to relieve the monotony of playing the same role in precisely the same way time after time.

Other approaches to the bureimonome kata include those of Danjūrō IX, Kikugorō V, Chūsha VII, Nizaemon XI, and Danzō VII. Danjūrō banged his sword on the ground with his right hand and then pressed his left to his head in the rather realistic style for which he was famous. Kikugorō would strike the floor directly before him with the sword in his right hand in performing the mie. Chūsha also thrust the sword on the ground with his right hand; he then opened his left hand wide and, with a broad gesture, placed it over his right on the sword's pommel. Nizaemon would slam the sword on the ground with his right hand, shout out the line, thrust his left hand into his sleeve, pose, take the sword in his left hand, and place his right elbow on the pommel of the sword. He would then hold his right hand's fingers splayed open near his head in the "headache repressing" kata, as it is known. At other times, he would face upstage, rap the sword on the floor with his right hand, thrust his left into his sleeve, and turn back to glare over his shoulder, his body continuing to face the upstage wall. Danzō (1882-1966), however, neither spoke the line nor did a mie, feeling that Tonami should be the scene's focus, not Matsuō.[18]

---

17. *Kari no Tayori*, pp. 78-79.

18. Tomita, "Sugawara Denju Tenarai Kagami Saiken," p. 122.

Descriptions of past actors' kata would seem to show that actors who performed the pose as does Kōshirō VIII, described in the text, included Kichiemon I (Kōshirō's father-in-law and teacher) and Uzaemon XV.

As Hamamura Yonezō states, the word translated here as "brazen woman" is not in the puppet theater text of the play; it is used only in Kabuki. Its first use occurred in the Meiji era, since which time it has become a second major climax of the play, in addition to the head inspection mie. For Kikugorō VI, in fact, the bureimonome mie was even more significant than that of the head inspection.[19]

After his dramatic pose, Matsuō settles down again and Genzō enters carrying the head box.

Genzō's Reentry. Many players of Genzō enter through the upstage center curtains in such a way as to cause one-half of the curtain to remain on their shoulder for a moment. Danjūrō IX made this entrance by appearing without his tabi socks or haori jacket (other actors usually remove their haori earlier). To emphasize the pathos of the entry he put white powder on his lips to make it seem as if Genzō had blanched at the deed he has just performed. He later licked his lips to remove the powder.

Genzō sets the box down and takes a position at stage right center where he can strike out at Matsuō if the deception does not succeed. The policemen take up positions to prevent Genzō from taking any untoward actions as Matsuō begins to perform his inspection duties.

Staging of the Head Inspection Scene. The number of policemen is generally ten but a photograph exists to demonstrate that, in at least certain performances, more have been used. This photo, found in the opening section of Kima Hisao's book, *Kabuki,* shows Chūsha VII performing his famous head inspection kata. Five constables are lined up below the shoji room at left, and five are arranged in a group near the doorway, right. There is a gap of about eight feet between the two groups. On the platform upstage another eight men are standing with a three- or four-foot space between those on the left and those on the right. The stance taken by these policemen is also considerably more dynamic than that normally seen.

Matsuō moves to the box and kneels a foot or two upstage of it. The lid of the box has a mark on it so that when the actor lifts it the head will surely be facing in his direction. The tension builds as he prepares himself mentally for his task.

Kichiemon I was notoriously fastidious about the head used in the scene. Even though the audience sees only the

---

19. *Kabuki*, p. 54. Leonard Pronko, in a pioneering article on the subject of the variations in Kabuki kata, deals extensively with the bureimonome kata and other major stage business in *The Village School*. See "Freedom and Tradition in the Kabuki Actor's Art," *Educational Theatre Journal*, XXI (May 1969), 139-146.

back of the head, its facial expression is of great importance to the actor, who must convey the anguish of a man gazing on the head of his own son. Kichiemon would demand to see the head as opening day approached. The property people would have to repaint the head for each new production since Kichiemon would carefully inspect its color and expression to guarantee that it was just right. An expression of innocence is usually depicted on the face; the gentle eyes are shut, the lips faintly painted red to suggest that Kotarō died with a peaceful heart. If, however, Kichiemon felt that the eyebrows or mouth evoked a feeling of misery, he rejected it. He would order it repainted again and again until he was satisfied.[20]

Kōshirō's head inspection kata, described in the text, is basically that of Kichiemon I. The style is relatively uncomplicated with a greater emphasis on the moment leading up to the inspection than on the inspection itself. Kichiemon said that "when Matsuō opens the lid and quickly glances at the head he sees instantly that it is his son. He must not take a sharp breath or do any such indicating of his emotions at this moment as Gemba is so close. He must stifle his feelings as much as possible."[21]

Early in his career Kichiemon was noted for his kata of placing a wad of paper in his mouth while performing the inspection. This was a formal gesture, intended to show respect for the object being examined. At his April 1932 performance he decided to give up the paper and do the scene in a manner similar to that of other actors, such as Uzaemon and Kikugorō. Miyake Shūtarō, a respected critic, has written that the kata of having the paper in his mouth made Matsuō seem very much the expert at affairs dealing with the sword.[22]

One of the most conspicuous head inspection kata is that done by actors in the Danjūrō line, such as the late Danjūrō XI and his son, the present Ebizō X. Matsuō, fearing that Gemba will say he recognizes the head, loosens his sheath and then opens the box. Impatiently, Gemba lifts the head on its stand himself and, with his back to the audience, leans right in Matsuō's direction, thrusting the head at him for his verdict. Suddenly, Matsuō draws his sword and, holding it out pointed at Genzō, performs a mie with the fingers of his left hand opened wide, hiding his face from Gemba. His intention is to slay Gemba if he should prove dangerous. Matsuō has his hand on the head box at his left. Since Gemba says nothing Matsuō relaxes and completes his inspection. After approving the head as genuine, he holds the sword up vertically in his left hand and makes a congratulatory gesture toward Genzō with his right.

20. Fujinami Yohei, *Shibai no Kodōgu: Sōi to Denshō* (*Theatrical Properties: Their Creation and Traditions*) (Tokyo, 1974).

21. Shigetoshi, *Nakamura Kichiemon,* p. 367.

22. *Kabuki Kenkyū* (*Kabuki Studies*) (Tokyo, 1942), p. 221.

Nizaemon XI, as mentioned earlier, used a cushion and armrest during this scene. He sat holding his sheathed sword in his left hand, its point on the ground. Gemba was at his left. He removed the lid, looked first at Gemba, then at the head, conveyed an expression of grief but then switched to one of caution, stared at the head, and, though weeping inwardly, gradually leaned over and said, in an unconscious manner, "Well done, Genzō. This is surely the head of Kan Shūsai." He then placed his sword on the ground. Following this he covered the head with the lid, making a sharp sound as the lid went into place, said, "You have done an excellent job," and then painfully rested his right hand on the box, put his right elbow on the box, opened his fingers wide, and made a gesture as if pressing his fingers to his forehead, without actually touching it. Many critics feel that the most effective kata was that of Chūsha VII, who used to place the lid at his left side, put his right hand on it across his body, and open his left hand wide at the side of his face, as if supporting it.

Ichikawa Danzō VIII's special kata was to open the lid, notice Gemba peeking at the head, replace the lid quickly with a snap, turn his body to the same angle in which Gemba was standing, facing down right, lift the lid again, and look at the head. This has been criticized since it makes Matsuō's vigilance appear too obvious and reduces the character's stature. The actor playing Matsuō, says Tōbe Ginsaku the critic, must demonstrate his ability to act from within as well as his technical skill. For actors better on the technical side this is Matsuō's most difficult scene, but for actors who specialize in inner technique the later scene where Matsuō reveals his true nature is his most exacting.[23]

Most actors presume that Gemba has no knowledge of Kotarō's appearance and the same would have to hold true of the ten or so policemen who accompany him. There is, however, one chance in a million that one among them just might recognize the head, so the police are almost always positioned in the fashion of an open book with their focus concentrated on Genzō, not the head. As is often the case with Kabuki's famous kata, a number of anecdotes have come down to the present age concerning the kubijikken kata. One such anecdote sounds as if it were originated among adherents of the Stanislavski system of acting. It illustrates clearly the psychological underside of even the most overtly conventional Kabuki acting. According to this story, Danjūrō VII selected his disciple, Ebijurō, to play Genzō to his Matsuō. The grateful actor performed diligently but one day he set the head box down before his master (then known as Ebizō), having forgotten to put the head inside. Ebizō opened it and saw that no head was there. The audience had also noticed so he was forced to ad-lib, "Genzō, I will give you another chance to bring out the head." Ebijurō quickly

23. *Kabuki no Engi,* pp. 184-185.

grabbed the box and went within. To fill the pause, Ebizō improvised with Gemba. "Gemba, isn't it only natural that a man who would go so far as to cut off his own master's head would forget the head itself?"

Later, he questioned the disciple in this way: "Anyone can make a mistake but, tell me, when you went within, what did you actually do?"

Ebijūrō replied, "Well, actually, I wiped off my sweat and took a breather."

Ebizō's expression changed and he said, "This is the theater but if it were real life, you would ostensibly be cutting off the head of your master while really doing it to a substitute, another man's son. Therefore, it is of the gravest importance that you deceive the envoys who have come to inspect the head. It is not a time when you would wipe your sweat or drink a cup of tea. When you do so you go from being Genzō, the schoolmaster, to Ebijūrō, the actor, and end up by forgetting the head."

Although most of the above discussion of the kubijikken has been concerned with Matsuō, Gemba's role during the sequence also has been commented on, notably by Kikugorō V, who warned actors playing the role not to keep looking back and forth from the head to Matsuō, as some were prone to do, as it distracts attention from Matsuō. Since Gemba obviously does not know the head, there is no special reason for him to look at it. "The head has been brought out," wrote Kikugorō,

and even though Gemba does not know it, he might glance at it just as illiterate people will stop to watch a billboard being painted. In this way, when Matsuō lifts off the lid Gemba might wonder just what sort of face the boy has and glance at it; then, wondering what Matsuō will say, he would stare at him. This, I believe, is the gist of Gemba's role at this point.[24]

Matsuō finally declares the head to be that of Kan Shūsai and takes his leave.

Matsuō's Exit. An exit kata for Matsuō somewhat different than that described in the text was that of Kikugorō VI who, on occasion, would leave the room by closing the door with his left hand, go out, open the door a bit with his right foot while looking down and supporting his weight on his left foot, strike his left hand with the hilt of his sword, look into the house one last time, pause, tilt his head back, weep, take the sword in his left hand, turn, and enter the palanquin. This kata clearly reveals Matsuō's emotional turmoil far more vividly than that used for the usual exit. Despite its psychological validity in revealing Matsuō's anguish, the kata has a built-in weakness: an open display of Matsuō's emotions at this point of the drama will detract from

24. Much of the foregoing information describing the kubijikken kata is drawn from Tomita, "Sugawara Denju Tenarai Kagami Saiken," pp. 123 ff.

the surprise effect produced when Matsuō reappears later in the play and reveals his true character. To those unfamiliar with the play, Matsuō must appear a villain until he has a chance to redeem himself in the play's closing sections.

Gemba departs after some cruel remarks to Genzō. The head box is carried off by the chief policeman.

Who Should Carry the Head Box? According to most critics, this type of exit with the head box entrusted to the leader of the policemen is decidedly inferior to the one where Gemba exits carrying it himself. They argue that Gemba ultimately must hand the head over to Lord Shihei and that, entrusted with so important a mission, he would never take a chance by allowing someone else to carry it off.

The brief sequence now enacted is called *goshiki no iki* ("breathless with joy"). Tonami and Genzō are so overjoyed they cannot speak. Kan Shūsai is brought out of the shoji room. They bow to him and take him off again.

Obeisance to Kan Shūsai. In the Kiku-Kichi version Tonami took the boy out of the closet instead of the shoji room. Genzō went to him from the doorway and dropped before him on his knees in respect. He took his short sword from his waist with his left hand, placed it near the long sword already on the floor, staggered to the platform, approached Kan Shūsai on the boy's right, embraced his shoulders in joy, then helped him off into the shoji room. Tonami closed the closet and went stage right. Genzō emerged from the shoji room, closed the door with his right hand, placed his left on the pillar of the room to support himself, leaned back against the pillar, sank down in exhaustion, crawled on his knees towards Tonami, tried to stand but could not, resolved to do so, rose, and approached his wife. As with most of the Kiku-Kichi kata, this business reveals a far greater complexity of detail to heighten the psychological overtones of the action than does the production described in the text.

The excited beating of wooden clappers signals the hurried hanamichi entrance of Chiyo. Her entrance begins the section called *Chiyo nidome no de* (Chiyo's second entrance).

Doubling as Chiyo and Gemba. There used to be a tradition wherein the actor playing Gemba would make a quick change and reappear here as Chiyo. He would make his exit as Gemba sooner than indicated in the text, giving his final speech to the leader of the police. In order to gain even more time he would, after knocking at the door as Chiyo, turn his back to face upstage and apply tooth-blackener to his teeth (part of his makeup as a married woman).

Tonami leaves and Genzō goes to the door, prepared to kill Chiyo at an opportune moment. After some uncomfortable conversation, Genzō lashes out but Chiyo wards him off successfully, blocking his best blow with Kotarō's book box lid.

Chiyo's "Shield." The use by Ganjirō, the actor playing Chiyo, of only the lid is rather unusual. Most actors of Chiyo prefer to use the whole box as a shield. Then, when the lid falls off the contents are dramatically revealed. Since Ganjirō chooses not to use the box itself, he must run over to it to retrieve the materials present within it.

Chiyo removes a prayer banner for her son's funeral from the box, revealing that she knew all along her son had come to the school to die. Genzō is further confused when Matsuō appears. Not knowing that Matsuō is Chiyo's husband he tries to strike at him but Matsuō holds him off and removes his swords, showing that his purposes are peaceful. This new section is called *Matsuō honshin* (Matsuō's true character).

Matsuō proceeds to explain all that has transpired. He is grateful that his son's sacrifice has given him the chance to redeem himself in the eyes of men. He reveals that he counted the desks earlier as a means of assuring himself of his son's presence.

Matsuō's Reference. It is not clear why Matsuō mentions the desk-counting to Genzō since the latter was not on stage when that business occurred. Matsuō's remarks would make sense if Tonami were now present but she does not reappear for several minutes. Similarly, when Tonami enters she is clearly aware of what has been revealed during her absence in another room of the house. Obviously, the audience is expected to overlook these dramaturgic inconsistencies—or else to assume that offstage characters can, through the paper-thin walls, hear what is being said on stage. In *Benten Kozō* Kōbei enters fully cognizant of the events that have occurred prior to his own appearance.

When he learns that Kotarō died with a smile on his face, Matsuō's pride knows no bounds.

On Kotarō's Last Moments. A number of critics and actors have debated the truth of Genzō's encouraging remarks concerning Kotarō's death. There are those who feel Genzō is lying about Kotarō's noble behavior in order to soften the moment for Matsuō though others claim that he truthfully depicts the young boy's courage at meeting death. This latter argument holds that the truth will not soften the parents' grief but will actually intensify it.

Matsuō tries to laugh but sobs intervene. This scene of laughing-crying is an extremely difficult one and often elicits applause when well done. It is a good example of the influence of modern psychology on Kabuki acting. Not surprisingly, the kata was created by Kikugorō VI. The awesome difficulty of the kata actually has kept some actors from performing it.

Matsuō states that Kotarō's death reminds him of his late brother, Sakuramaru, and, unable to dam up the feelings inside himself, bursts into torrents of tears.

The Motive for Matsuō's Weeping. Most actors today interpret this moment as Matsuō's weeping, not over Sakuramaru, but over his dead child. He merely uses Sakuramaru as a cover to allow him to give vent to his pent-up emotions. The effect is a truly powerful one, especially as magnified by the larger-than-life manner in which Matsuō is acted.

Kan Shūsai, hearing his distraught saviors, emerges and expresses his regret at having caused so much pain. He is now dressed in a very formal costume befitting his rank.

Kan Shūsai's Costume. There is a rare kata where the boy appears with his schoolboy costume, as earlier, but with a trailing robe put on over it. It was seen in a production of Ganjirō I. Asked the reason for the innovation, Ganjirō replied, "Who could have helped him change?" If one were to produce the play with total attention to logic, however, one would have to agree with the nineteenth-century journalist-playwright, Fukuchi Ōchi, and bring the boy on in the clothes of the dead Kotarō, thus thoroughly effecting the substitution.

Matsuō steps outside for a moment and signals for a palanquin to be brought on. From it appears Lady Sono no Mae, Kan Shūsai's mother, whom Matsuō has successfully hidden from Sugawara's enemies. The mother and child are united once more.

The play's final section, the *iroha okuri* (A-B-C funeral ceremony) begins at this point.

Staging the Play's Ending. Two main ways exist of staging the final part. In one only the gidayū is heard as a funeral ceremony is acted out in pantomime by the actors. This is the Kyoto-Osaka style. In the other method, a number of lines are broken up among the actors and spoken in "pass-along" dialogue form. The translation indicates those lines that may be spoken by the actors. There are also some differences in the acting between the two funeral sequence styles. Both end in a final tableau like that described in the text.

The final tableau is in the manner of a "pulling mie" (*hippari no mie*) with each character concentrating on a different focal point. Though Matsuō's position is generally the same in most productions, Genzō's often varies. Aside from the differing seated or kneeling positions assumed, there are those actors, like the late Kanya XIV (1907-1975), who stood at this moment, facing front with both hands on the hilt of his sheathed sword, and leaned his weight in the direction of Lady Sono no Mae and her son. Probably the most unusual final tableau is that used by the present Ebizō and Onoe Tatsunosuke (1946-) for their 1968 alternating-role production at the National Theatre. According to the photographs, they adopted the traditional tableau (supposedly shaped like a mountain with Lady Sono as the peak and called the *Fujisan kata* after Mt. Fuji) when Tatsunosuke played Matsuō; on Ebizō's Matsuō days he concluded the play by standing at left center, his hands before his waist, on a slight diagonal to the front of the stage. Chiyo (Ichikawa Monnosuke VII [1928-]) stood at his right shoulder, facing front. Lady Sono and Kan Shūsai knelt at up center instead of standing and Genzō and Tonami knelt at stage right in a mirror image of their conventional positions.

The closing scenes of *Sugawara's Secrets of Calligraphy,* not translated here, present the death of Sugawara, who dies after learning of the rescue of his wife and child, followed by the return of Sugawara's ghost to haunt the evil Shihei. Umeō aids Sugawara's daughter and Kan Shūsai in slaying Shihei, and Sugawara is ultimately exonerated and his reputation and honors restored.

THE PLAYWRIGHTS

Takeda Izumo II was the son of Takeda Izumo I, the famous manager of the Takemoto Theare. Izumo II became one of the main playwrights of the mid-eighteenth-century puppet theater and collaborated on many plays, including the three masterpieces mentioned earlier. Among his other famous works are *Chronicle of the Rise and Fall of the Heike (Hiragana Seisuiki)* and *Diary of Two Butterflies in the Licensed Quarters (Futatsu Chōchō Kuruwa Nikki).* However, it is not certain to what degree he actually participated in the writing of these plays. There are some who believe he may merely have used his name as chief playwright to help promote the works without actually having had an active part in their creation. This theory stems from his activity as manager of the Takemoto Theatre, a position he inherited from his father.

Namiki Senryū was an Osakan who first wrote plays for the Toyotake Theatre (Toyotake-za) and later switched to its rival, the Takemoto. Most of his plays were collaborative works. He returned to the Toyotake Theatre where he wrote the outstanding play, *Chronicles of the Battle of Ichinotani (Ichinotani Futaba Gunki);* he died shortly thereafter. Among his major works are *Mirror of the Summer Festival in Osaka (Natsu Matsuri Naniwa Kagami)* and *Diary of Two Butterflies in the Licensed Quarters.* He is known to have been the main influence in the writing of these plays. Many of his disciples became leading Kabuki and puppet theater dramatists.

In addition to his work on the three masterpieces previously mentioned, Miyoshi Shōraku, third member of the triumvirate, collaborated on such great puppet plays (later adapted by Kabuki) as *The Tragedy on Mount Imose (Imoseyama Onna Teikin)* and *Strife at Uji (Ōmi Genji Senjin Yakata).*

The translations are based on the text in the *Kokuritsu Gekijō Jōen Taihonshū* (Collection of National Theatre Production Scripts), Vol. I, Tokyo, 1968, and that in *Meisaku Kabuki Zenshū,* Vol. II. The chief actors in the production of *Pulling the Carriage Apart* on which the stage directions are based were Nakamura Tomijūrō V (1929-) as Umeomaru, Nakamura Kichiemon II as Matsuomaru, Sawamura Kiyoshirō I (1943-) as Sakuramaru, and Ichikawa Yaozō IX (1906-) as Shihei (Kabuki Theatre, Tokyo, May, 1975).

The stage directions for *The Village School* are mainly those of the production starring Matsumoto Kōshirō VIII as Matsuomaru, Nakamura Shikan VII (1928-) as Tonami, Nakamura Ganjirō II (1902-) as Chiyo, Kataoka Nizaemon XIII (1903-) as Genzō, and Ichikawa Yaozō IX as Gemba (Kabuki Theatre, Tokyo, January, 1975).

A good recording of *Pulling the Carriage Apart* is available. It is KK2 on King Records (Japan). *The Village School* may be heard on the excellent Japan Columbia album, CLS-5141-2.

PULLING THE CARRIAGE APART

(For about ten minutes before the curtain opens the muffled sound of wooden clappers can be heard at intervals from behind the striped Kabuki curtain. After a double clack the geza music called haya kagura *["fast sacred music"] starts up. This is a very lively accompaniment using flute, ōdaiko and taiko drums. As the music plays the ki get faster and faster in time to the opening of the curtain. When the curtain is completely opened, the music stops and the chanting of the gidayū begins. The gidayū combination is seated, unseen, in an alcove over the curtained entranceway at left. Their presence is concealed by a gold rattan blind. The setting revealed by the opening of the curtain represents the area outside the Yoshida Shrine in Kyoto. It is a vivid setting dominated by bright red coloring. At left, on an angle to the front of the stage is a large red torii gate, usually seen at Shinto shrines. Along the back of the stage is a low red fence [tamagaki, a kind of shrine fence] behind which runs a corridor. Spaced at equal intervals above this fence are three trees, two cherries and a plum. Further upstage and running along the rear of the stage is a backing representing the outer walls of a shrine building. A hanging border [tsuri eda] of red and white plum blossoms decorates the upper edge of the proscenium arch.)*

GIDAYŪ:

*The chicks have left their nest
And the fish have left the sea.*

*This allegory of unnatural events
Aptly fits Lord Sugawara's vassals
Umeomaru and Sakuramaru
Who are now without a master.*

(Miya kagura *[shrine music] of shamisen, ōdaiko and taiko drums, and flute begins in the geza as Umeō enters with heavy strides on the hanamichi and walks to the stage. Sakuramaru enters from left at the same time. Umeō stops at right center and Sakuramaru at left center. Each wears a thick padded* dotera *kimono of large purple and white squares [the do-shigoshi pattern]. Around their waists they wear a padded black obi tied in the rear in butterfly fashion. On their feet are* fukuzōri *sandals which have three-layered soles on the forepart and a four-layered heel section. Each has two swords in his obi at the left. Their faces are completely hidden by basketlike straw hats [amigasa] tied beneath their chins by white cords. On their knees are the small pads called* sanriate. *Their kimono are hitched up slightly at the waist so that their feet are exposed to the shins. We can see that Umeō's feet are white with the bold red lines of a kumadori makeup pattern outlining their musculature. The actor wears tights of silk with this pattern painted on them. A similar design is seen on Umeō's hands, also part of a skintight costume accessory. Sakuramaru's hands are white as are his feet. He, however, wears red leggings that reach to his ankles. Each wears a red silk collar attached to his under-kimono. These are removable and are not worn when they*

make their second entrance later in the
scene. Though they are dressed in almost
identical costumes, Umeō presents an
image bordering on rotundity, almost as
if he were a sumo wrestler. Sakuramaru
is much more elegantly slim in appearance. This is in keeping with their role-
types. Sakuramaru is played in the
slightly effeminate manner of the wakashu whereas Umeō is one of the prime
examples of Kabuki's manly aragoto
style. The difference in their makeup and
wigs will be described below. When they
reach their positions the music stops.
Each tilts his hat slightly with his right
hand as they look at each other.)

SAKURAMARU: (*In a delicate voice*) Is that
you, Umeomaru?

UMEOMARU: (*Powerfully*) Is that you,
Sakuramaru?

SAKURAMARU: There's something I must
tell you.

UMEOMARU: There's something I must ask
you.

(*After a slight pause, the brothers move
to opposite positions, counter-crossing.
After exchanging places they pause as
two stage assistants enter and place stools
designed to look like tree stumps behind
them. Umeō's is slightly higher than
Sakuramaru's. They sit on these with
their legs wide apart, hands on laps.
Umeō's hands are clenched in fists.*)

GIDAYŪ: (*As they move to their new
positions*)

The brothers lift
their hats
In the shadow of the trees.

(*Kagura music begins. It continues during Umeō's speech and then during Sakuramaru's.*)

UMEOMARU: First, what I want to ask you is
this: I know you left your wife, Yae, behind
that fateful day at the Kamo River and set off
in search of young Lord Tokiyo and Princess
Kariya. Were you able to locate them?

SAKURAMARU: (*Looking down and speaking
in a voice deep with feeling*) Yes, I did,
indeed, overtake them on the road. When I
told them that Lord Sugawara had been exiled
they said they wished to see him. I therefore
accompanied them to the coast at Yasui but
they were prevented from visiting with the
lord. They were forbidden from returning to
Kyoto and were forced to part from each
other. The princess went to the home of her
aunt in Haji Village and Lord Tokiyo entered
service at the tonsured Emperor's palace.
Though the matter appears to be a thing of
the past, it is not yet over for me since I,
despite my humble station, brought about
Lord Sugawara's unjust downfall by acting
as a go-between for the noble lovers. When I
think that none of this would have happened
without my interference my heart feels as if it
would burst. I even wonder whether I should
not commit ritual suicide today or kill myself
tomorrow but when I reach for my sword I
remember that my beloved father, living in
Sada Village, will soon celebrate his seventieth
birthday, an auspicious event. His greatest

happiness will come from seeing his three sons and their wives together again.

(*He holds forth one finger of each hand and slowly brings them together.*)

If I were to be absent I would be adding the crime of filial ingratitude to that of disloyalty. It is only for this seventieth birthday celebration that I have shamefully prolonged my life to now, as you can guess.

(*Pause*)

Umeomaru...

GIDAYŪ:

He clenches his fists and grits his
   teeth
Overwhelmed by remorse for his
   shameful deed.
Aware of the reason for his brother's
   actions
Umeō is silent for a time.

(*As the gidayū sings Sakuramaru raises his left arm slightly and gently slaps it with his right hand in an act of self-castigation. He then repeats this gesture with the opposite hand and arm. He lifts his hands slowly to his face in a gesture of weeping. As Umeō begins to speak he replaces his hands on his lap. His gaze is toward the floor. Kagura music continues.*)

UMEOMARU: (*As if taking a deep breath*)
Yes! You are right! You are right! Since our lord has been exiled there's no reason for me to stay in the capital but, ever since the downfall of his house, the whereabouts of his wife, Lady Sono no Mae, who could not remain in Kyoto, have been unknown. Should we search for her or should we visit our lord's place of exile?

(*Gestures briefly with right hand*)

Caught between these choices we must yet bear in mind that our aged father's birthday celebration is this month. Each of us is filled with the same boundless agony of delay.

(*He holds the vowels in his last words in a powerful vocal display of emotion.*)

SAKURAMARU: Umeomaru.

(*Shifts position slightly in direction of Umeō*)

UMEOMARU: Sakuramaru.

(*Same business*)

SAKURAMARU: Such must always be...

BOTH: (*Holding the vowels emotionally*) The way of the world.

(*Each lifts his hat a bit with his upstage hand. They bend slightly in alternate directions as they silently gaze at each other, then shift back to original positions facing front. Each raises his hands to his face, weeping.*)

GIDAYŪ: (*During the above business*)

*The brothers look intently at each
    other
And just as tears begin to form
The banging of a metal staff
Announces the coming of a herald.*

HERALD: (*Offstage*) Hi, ho! Clear the way!
Clear the way!

(*The voice is quite loud and powerful,
rising to a crescendo on each sentence in
a rhythmical fashion. The drum and flute
music of kagura starts up in the geza as,
from left, the herald appears in exaggerated aragoto costume and makeup, carrying a tall metal pole with rings dangling
from its top. This is held in his right
hand. His costume is a* han suo *of green
and rust with the hakama trousers tucked
up exposing his legs to the thighs. Sanriate pads are worn on his knees. His
tabi-clad feet are encased in thick fukuzōri sandals. His makeup is the somewhat comical kumadori pattern called
kani [crab] guma. As he enters, banging
his staff at regular intervals, the brothers
rise, look at each other for a moment,
and cross upstage right where they stand
with their backs to the audience. Sakuramaru is closer to stage right. The stage
assistants remove the stumps.*)

HERALD: (*Entering*) Hi-i-i, h-o-o-o! Clear
the way! Clear the way!

(*Umeō gestures to Sakuramaru with his
open right hand. They turn and walk
downstage two steps in unison.*)

UMEOMARU: (*Facing the herald, who is at
right center*) Aiya! You there! Just who is it
that's coming through here?

HERALD: (*Astonished at their affrontery*)
Yaa! You scurvy dog! How dare you ask me
who is coming? It is his most gracious
excellency, the exalted and most excellent
Minister of the Left, Lord Fujiwara no
Shihei, who has come to worship at
Yoshidaya Shrine. Now, get out of the way
(*pounds staff sharply*) before you taste the
thrust of my steel staff!

(*He practically screams the last sentence,
then crosses to the edge of the hanamichi, right. The music stops.*)

GIDAYŪ:
And as he goes, he shouts . . .

HERALD: Hi, ho! Clear the way, clear the
way!

(*He revolves his head and glares down
the hanamichi in a mie as the tsuke beat.
Kagura music plays during his exit down
the hanamichi. As he goes the brothers
raise their right hands to their hat brims
and look off after him. They then cross
slowly to center and face front. A stage
assistant enters and crouches behind
each. Seeing that the herald is out of
sight they nod to each other. Each places
his right hand on the brim of his hat,
crouches a bit, lifts his left leg high, knee
bent, and brings his foot down in front.
[Sometimes this begins with the right
leg.] When the foot is on the ground it is*

loosened from the sandal thong and the sandal is abruptly slid backward to the crouching stage assistant. Moving with rhythmic precision the same action is repeated with the other foot. They then crouch slightly, legs apart, and, in time to the shamisen, untie the cords under their chins. They take three steps forward in unison then slowly begin to raise their hats from their faces, using both hands. Umeō lifts his right foot high and thrusts it out sharply before him on the ground, slowly moves his hat till he is holding it at the rear of his head, framing his face, and puts his weight on his left leg, which is bent at the knee. He completes the mie as the tsuke strike. His right foot's big toe is pointed upward. At the same time, Sakuramaru moves his left foot forward gracefully, his weight on his right foot, holding his hat with both hands at his right side. He too completes his mie to the beating of the tsuke. His mie is much gentler in aspect than Umeō's. The resulting tableau with Umeō at left center and Sakuramaru at right center, each in their respective poses, is called an emen mie or "picture mie." The movements of Umeō especially are suggestive of the puppet theater that, of course, first produced the piece. Umeō and Sakuramaru's makeup is now visible to the audience. Umeō wears the highly stylized series of red lines painted on a white base called nipponsujiguma. It is also called Shikansuji after an actor who was instrumental in its creation. His wig is a wild-looking affair with anywhere from five to seven spokes of lacquered hair protruding from either side. Its forelock is a sort of high pom-pom. The wig is called kuruma bin ["carriage sidelocks"], presumably because of its spokelike projections. Sakuramaru wears a highly theatrical wig, too, though not as grotesque a one as Umeō. It is the maechasen, worn with a divided, lacquered forelock. His makeup is the mukimi [a kind of shell fish] guma, consisting of a red line drawn beneath each eye and rising at the outside corners of the eyes to the temples. Another red line connects the inner end of the eyebrows with the inside corner of the eye. This is a quite attractive makeup in keeping with Sakuramaru's gentle nature.)

UMEOMARU: (*Looking at Sakuramaru and speaking in time to the gidayū shamisen*) Did you hear that, Sakuramaru? It's Minister Shihei, he who is responsible for the grief of Lord Tokiyo and Lord Sugawara.

(*Almost shouting*)

We've got plenty to say to him, don't we-e-e?!

(*He straightens up, holding his hat with both hands at his left side. He leans his head sharply to the right, like a puppet, to look at Sakuramaru.*)

SAKURAMARU: Indeed, indeed! Our timing couldn't have been better!

(*He too straightens up.*)

UMEOMARU: (*Seething with rage*)
Sakuramaru, come on, come on, c-o-o-me
on!

(*As he says these words, lively kagura
music begins. He throws his hat upstage
with his right hand. Sakuramaru throws
his down, too. Umeō moves directly below his brother to the hanamichi and,
gripping his sword hilt, flies off down
the hanamichi in tobi roppō* ["*flying in
six directions*"] *fashion without stopping. This entails a manner of moving
with both hands waving broadly as the
actor leaps from foot to foot while ca-
reening down the runway.* [*See the introduction to this play for details on its execution.*] *Sakuramaru comes to the hanamichi a moment later, and, gripping the
hilt of his sword with both hands, runs
quickly off in his graceful, almost coy
manner. The kagura music ceases.*)

SHIHEI'S LACKEYS: (*Offstage left*) Hi, ho!

GIDAYŪ:

Before long, the grating rumble of
 an ox-cart
Bearing Minister Shihei, decked in
 finery,
Can be heard as it rolls along the
 narrow road.

(*As this passage is chanted a group of
twelve men dressed in white tunics and
black caps bring a creaking ox-carriage
on from left. Hitched to the front of the
fancy black lacquered cart is a large
black ox—actually a costume with two*

*men inside it. When the carriage reaches
center it stops, its side facing the audience. The ox kneels. The lackeys, retainers of Fujiwara Shihei, stabilize the
carriage by placing black sawhorses
under it at front and rear. The men then
line up at the rear, six on either side of
the carriage, to its left and right. Ongaku
music of odaiko and* suzu *bells begins to
play in the geza in a spirited fashion as
Umeō and Sakuramaru enter quickly on
the hanamichi.* [*The word ongaku here
refers to a specific type of Kabuki music
though the word also may be used to refer to "music" in general.*] *They come to
the stage and stand downstage right,
their backs to the audience. Sakuramaru
is closer to stage right. Umeō now has
three huge swords stuck into his obi. The
brothers have removed their red silk
under-kimono collars. They stand with
their hands on their swords. The music
stops.*)

GIDAYŪ: (*As the brothers enters*)

The brothers spring out from the
 shadows.

UMEOMARU: Stop that...

BOTH: Carriage!

(*The brothers turn front and perform a
powerful mie as they thrust their right
feet out, and spread their hands wide to
either side, the left hand slightly higher,
in a gesture of halting the carriage. They
face front as they do so. Tsuke beats
accent the pose.*)

GIDAYŪ:

> They yell "stop the carriage" and
>   block its way.
> Sugiomaru, vassal of Lord Shihei,
> Steps forth with arrogant demeanor.

(*During this action the rear of the carriage, unseen by the audience, is dismantled by stage assistants, and a black curtain is set up before a false door in the set's rear wall. The brothers straighten up and Umeō stands with his hands thrust out of his kimono at the breast while Sakuramaru has his hands on his sword hilt. Sugiomaru, a retainer of Shihei's, enters through the torii gate at left. He is a young man, in the wakashu category. He wears a red kimono with three white horizontal stripes on it. Over this is a white tunic such as the other vassals wear. His wig is the* chigomage, *which has a forelock symbolizing his youth. Straw sandals are on his feet. He is made up in a mukimi guma pattern similar to Sakuramaru's. A black cap hangs by a white cord on his back.*)

SUGIOMARU: (*At left, looking at the brothers impudently*) Yaa! Look who's here! If it isn't Matsuō's brothers, Umeomaru and Sakuramaru. From what I hear you've lost your master, lost your stipends, and have run amuck! However, whether or not you knew you were stopping the carriage of the great Lord Shihei, I, Sugiomaru, will show you no mercy!

(*Sugiomaru performs the same business with his sandals as was done earlier by Umeō and Sakuramaru. He then pulls back each of his kimono sleeves in turn, turns to face upstage, leans his weight sharply on his left leg, his right being thrust out to the side, brings his right fist in the air to the left, and juts his chin out in the direction of the brothers, completing the mie as the tsuke are struck. He then straightens up.*)

GIDAYŪ:

> The white robed retainer of Shihei
> Rolls back his sleeves
> And prepares to seize the brothers.
> But Umeō merely laughs in his face.

UMEOMARU: (*Laughing in a very highly stylized manner*) Ha, ha, ha, ha, ha!

(*As noted above, Umeō's hands are thrust forth at the breast. He now makes a rhythmic gesture of spitting into his left hand, then his right, then clapping the hands together twice. He follows this with a powerful move as he shoves the kimono off his shoulders [*hadanugi*], revealing a bright red under-kimono with a design of scattered plum blossoms and cloud patterns embroidered on it. As he whirls his arms overhead like a windmill, he steps forward on his left foot, then his right, and then his left again. He lifts his legs quite high as he does so. He grips the sheath of his longest sword in his left hand and pulls it out of the obi most of its length, twisting it so that it curves* *away from the body. It is held erect, almost perpendicular to the floor. He whirls around to the left and when facing front again thrusts his right foot out straight before him, his right fist held beneath his chin, elbow out to the side, and completes the mie as the tsuke beat. This is a variation of the so-called Gen-roku mie [named for a period in Japanese history, 1688-1703]. The sleeves of his outer kimono, hanging at his sides, are held up by a stage assistant crouching behind the actor. They seem like wings and help make the pose look more impressive by increasing the actor's size. He finishes the dialogue in this position. The shamisen music, which played throughout the posing, continues during his line and the business of Sakuramaru which follows.)*

I'm not crazy and I know perfectly well that this is Shihei's carriage!

(As he finishes his line, Umeō turns to face upstage, then does a mie by sharply cocking his head to the left, staring in Sugiomaru's direction. He continues to hold his sword erect, only its tip remaining in the obi. Sakuramaru now poses as he removes his kimono from the shoulders. This allows the audience to see the bright red under-kimono he is wearing. It has a scattered cherry blossom design embroidered on it, as well as a stylized gold cloud pattern. Sakuramaru takes three large steps forward, first on his left, then his right, then his left foot. He

thrusts his left foot out and raises his hands over his head, performing a mie without accompanying sound from the tsuke. At the end of this pose Umeō turns to face front and stands with his hands crossed before him, wrist over wrist, elbows extended to the sides, arms raised, fingers pointed upward, thumbs toward the body.)

SAKURAMARU: Because of Shihei's evil lies, Lord Tokiyo and Lord Sugawara have been banished from the capital. The strength of our hatred for him will still be as fresh as today if we should meet here one hundred years from now.

(He leans his weight onto his left leg, crossing his hands before him in a manner similar to Umeo's.)

If I, Sakuramaru ...

(With his crossed hands before him, his palms facing outward, his right hand holding back the sleeve of his left arm from his wrist, he does a shuffling step [aizariashi] in a semicrouching position called hako [box], moving forward several inches, then straightens up)

UMEOMARU: And I, Umeomaru, don't take an ox-herder's bamboo stick and beat Lord Shihei's pride-filled fat behind, two, three

(he sharply thrusts his right hand over his left, near the chest, palms outward, then crouches slightly, leaps up and lands with

a bang in a semicrouch; he places his right hand before his mouth and explodes in a typical aragoto vocal sound effect, something like the rapid fire from a machine gun; it bears some resemblance to the sound of clearing the throat but is delivered in a very theatrical manner)

Ka, ka, ka, ka, ka, ka, ka, ka!—five or six hundred strokes, we will never live down the shame!!

(He has risen to full height during this. He grabs his longest sword with his left hand, slowly inches forward in a shuffle step, straightens up at the end, feet together at the heels, flips his sword around so it stands erect and curving away from his body, thrusts his right foot out, leans his weight on his left leg, and brings his right fist out to the right in a Genroku mie.)

SAKURAMARU: Get your nasty toady's face . . .

UMEOMARU: Out of here . . .

SAKURAMARU: Or we'll . . .

BOTH: Destroy it for you!

(They each thrust forth their right foot, place their weight on the left, and perform a mie with their arms outstretched, as earlier.)

GIDAYŪ:

They swing their arms wide
And take a threatening stance.

SUGIOMARU: Yaaa! You filthy lawless bastards! Take them!

(Sugiomaru turns his back to the audience, raises his right arm as a signal, then steps right a few paces.)

LACKEYS: Haa!

(Haya kagura music begins. Umeō and Sakuramaru pose with their hands raised aloft. Four lackeys leave the rear lineup and stand in a row behind the brothers. Each brother makes a stylized gesture of striking a blow, one hand at a time. As they do so, the nearest attackers do a forward flip, landing on their backs. Sakuramaru and Umeō perform a mie as the tsuke beat. Umeō has his left leg bent, the weight on it, his hands crossed before his chest, palms facing outward. Sakuramaru stands with both hands aloft, his weight on the right leg, his left thrust out a bit before him.)

GIDAYŪ:

Matsuō glares with hatred.

(They straighten up, Umeō still with his hands crossed. Sakuramaru places his hands on his hilts.)

MATSUOMARU: *(Offstage left)* Wait! Wait a moment!

(Geza music of taiko and tsuzumi drums begins as Matsuō enters from the torii at stage left. He walks on pompously, hold-

ing a long, white, folded ceremonial umbrella in both hands, resting it against his right shoulder. He stands in profile facing right as he speaks. He wears a white tunic over the same purple and white checkerboard-patterned kimono as his brothers. On his head is a black hat tied with a long white cord knotted beneath his chin. His legs are pure white, his feet in the fukuzōri *or thick-soled sandals seen earlier on his brothers' feet. His* kumadori *makeup is red on white, the so-called* ipponguma *variety. His wig is made with stiff, flat sidelocks and a high, divided forelock. It is the* itabin no maegami. *He wears two long swords with green tassels like those on Umeō's swords. Facing right, he performs a mie by moving his head rhythmically to the beating of the tsuke.)*

Yaaa! You wild and reckless fools! Don't show them any mercy just because they're my brothers! I'm not at all like them! Watch me, your brother, Matsuō, show you what it is to be loyal to one's lord!

(He turns front, flips the sleeves of his tunic back, hands the umbrella to Sugiomaru who comes down to take it and stands with it at left. Matsuō does the same business with his sandals as was done earlier by Sakuramaru, Umeō, and Sugiomaru, removes his tunic, thrusts his hands out at the breast of his kimono, unties the white cords of his hat, flips the cords over his shoulders, while a stage assistant proceeds to remove his hat, shoves the kimono free from his shoul-ders, and reveals an under-kimono of white with green pine trees and gold cloud patterns embroidered on it. He grabs the sword in his left hand, twists it so that it is perpendicular to the ground and curving away from his body, brings his right fist in rhythmic jerks before his upper chest, juts his right leg out powerfully, the weight on his left, and completes a Genroku mie, as the tsuke beat. During this process the gidayū shamisen plays a rhythmic accompaniment. Also, the group of lackeys shout the meaningless phrase, Aaarya, koorya! *throughout. This shouting of encouragement is called* keshōgoe [makeup voice].)*

LACKEYS: Aaarya, koorya! Aaarya, koorya!

MATSUOMARU: *(Holding his pose)* Let's see you try to stop this carriage if Matsuō pulls it. That would be a feat to brag of! Sa, sa, sa!

(He laughs derisively.)

Ha, ha, ha, ha, ha, ha!

(Matsuō leaps up in the air and lands hard in a semicrouch, feet wide apart, and inches forward in a shuffle step until he is standing erect.)

GIDAYŪ:

*Taking the oxen by the snout
He pulls it with him.*

(He now does the same coughlike sound-effect done earlier by Umeō and he brings his right hand to his mouth. He

thrusts his right foot way out, grips his sword with his left hand, pulling it nearly the entire way out of his obi, spins to his left until facing his brothers on a profile to the audience, rises on his toes, and slowly raises his right hand overhead, fingers splayed, in the famous "stone-throwing" pose [ishi nage no mie]. He holds the sword hilt thrust forward in his left hand and shouts at the top of his voice.)

MATSUOMARU: Try and stop it. Eeeee!

SAKURAMARU: Sakuramaru...

UMEOMARU: And Umeō are here so if...

SAKURAMARU: You dare to move it...

UMEOMARU: By an inch...

SAKURAMARU: Or even half an inch...

UMEOMARU: We promise...

BOTH: You'll be sorry! Eeeee!

(Matsuō takes the umbrella from Sugio-maru. He moves to center as Umeō, with right hand raised, crosses left above him. Sakuramaru, at right, takes the upper end of the umbrella in his left hand while Umeō takes the handle in his right hand. The triplets strike a pose with Umeō standing erect at the left, his left hand thrust straight out to the left, palm open, fingers pointing upward. Sakuramaru does precisely the opposite while Matsuō poses with his right foot out to the right, weight on the left, hands crossed before him, palms open. The umbrella appears

to rest across his shoulders. The mie they now perform by moving their heads to the beating of the tsuke is a "picture" mie [emen no mie]. At this point there is a passage of geza drum music called itsu no gashira ["the five heads"] and, in time to the taiko drumbeats, the triplets snap their heads in unison to the left, right, and left almost as if they were wooden puppets. They end in a mie facing front. This is the hippari no mie. *During the itsu no gashira section Umeō and Sakuramaru pull the umbrella to either side as they snap their heads. Sarashi music, in which the taiko drum figures, begins as Umeō and Sakuramaru turn their backs to the audience. The brothers pick up two black lacquered carriage shafts and, in unison, mime the action of breaking the carriage apart as if with ramrods. They hold the shafts in both hands and, backs to the audience with Umeō slightly more upstage and to the left than his brother, thrust three times at the carriage with the shafts. The movements are emphasized by the tsuke. During this, a number of stage assistants dismantle the carriage, placing two of its side walls against the wheel that faces the audience. The walls are placed so they each balance on a lower corner, forming a sort of double flag pattern. Dorodoro drum music [played on the ōdaiko], used for scenes of magic or mystery, begins as Shihei makes his appearance through a trick door in the upstage wall and mounts a ladder set up for him behind the carriage. He appears on top of the carriage now as though he had been in it all along.*

When he comes into view Umeō and Sakuramaru cross downstage right, facing front, and hold the shafts somewhat to the right, left legs bent, while glaring upstage center at Shihei. The three of them perform a mie as the tsuke are struck. Shihei is an awesome figure. He is made up in kugeaku kumadori *makeup of blue lines on a white ground, his face resembling the fearful* hannya *mask of the Nō theater. On his head is a gold nobleman's hat* [kammuri] *and his lacquered hair falls in a shower over his chest on each side. His silver robe has a design of clouds embroidered on it. He holds a silver scepter in his right hand. The lower half of his costume consists of dull red hakama of the long, trailing variety* [nagabakama]. *A high aibiki stool is placed behind him for him to sit on.*)

GIDAYŪ: (*As Shihei enters*)

*The powerful Minister of the Left,
Fujiwara no Shihei,
Now reveals himself.*

SHIHEI: (*Standing on the carriage; his voice is frightening.*) Yaa! If you miserable vermin, who are fit only for being fed to my ox, attempt to stop this carriage, I'll throw you in the wheel ruts and ride right over your filthy carcasses.

UMEOMARU: (*Powerfully*) The Minister who says this...

UMEOMARU AND SAKURAMARU: Will be run over instead!

(*They straighten up, thrust their right feet out, whirl around to face the carriage, and thrust at it with their shafts as the tsuke beat and dorodoro drum music plays in the geza. They turn front and thrust the shafts, then turn their backs and thrust, but Shihei merely inclines his head and, glaring fiercely at them, raises his scepter aloft, whirls his long sleeve over his left arm, and projects such a great magical force that Umeō and Sakuramaru are forced back several steps. They each stamp strongly with their feet, renew their grip, and brandish the staffs as if about to attack the carriage, but Shihei once more flips his sleeve and glares at them, thrusting his flame red tongue out in doing so. Overcome by his devastating power, they raise the shafts and fling them down with a thundering crash. They do a mie as Umeō moves his left leg out straight and puts his weight heavily on his right leg, bending it deeply at the knee, his hands crossed before him, left above, right below, as before. Sakuramaru does a similar pose but his right leg is not so deeply bent. They move their shoulders up and down rhythmically as if experiencing extreme chagrin. As they are shrinking back the first time they exclaim*)

What is this?

GIDAYŪ:

*In spite of themselves the brothers
Find themselves staggering
    backward,
Overcome by Shihei's magic power.*

They can do nothing but curse their state.

MATSUOMARU: (*He rises from the camp stool he has been sitting on.*) Now!

(*With great mockery*)

Have you seen the power of my lord? If you still wish a confrontation, I, Matsuō, will slice you both in two!

(*He opens his right hand and brings it before his chest as he leans over slightly toward the right on his last words. He then straightens up, gripping his sword hilt. Ongaku music begins. Umeō now stands erect at right, his hands still crossed before him. Sakuramaru is at right with his hands on his hilts.*)

SHIHEI: (*Sitting on his stool*) No! Wait a moment, Matsuō!

(*Matsuō removes his hand from the hilt and bows his head respectfully.*)

I am entrusted with the task of overseeing the government. If blood is spilled before me while I am wearing the sacred gold crown and white tunic my pilgrimage to this shrine will be defiled. Although I hate to aid these scoundrels I will do so out of deference to your spirit of loyalty.

(*To Umeō and Sakuramaru*)

You crawling vermin! You have been saved by Divine Providence!

(*Shihei rises, holding both arms out to the side, his mouth wide open, his red tongue sticking out, and does a mie. He sits. Umeō and Sakuramaru stand quietly at the right.*)

GIDAYŪ: (*During this*)

He glares about and rises.

MATSUOMARU: You are indeed fortunate to have a brother like me. You should bow three times in thanks for my having saved you.

SAKURAMARU: (*As if wounded*) Yaa! Though we have a complaint with you, too, it must wait until the completion of our honored father's seventieth birthday celebrations. Right, Umeō?

UMEOMARU: (*Powerfully*) Very true! Very true! Moreover, (*referring to Matsuō, whose name means "pine tree"*) we will break the pine branches, cut the roots out, and dry up our enemy's leaves.

MATSUOMARU: (*Equally violent*) And the same goes for me, Matsuomaru. When our father's celebrations are concluded the plum and cherry blossoms will all be scattered. Get out before you regret it!

(*Each brother turns to look at Matsuō when their "names" are mentioned, Sakuramaru for "cherry" and Umeō for "plum."*)

UMEOMARU: (*Trembling with rage*) Hell! Why should you...

UMEOMARU AND SAKURAMARU: Give us orders when to leave?!

MATSUOMARU: (*Angrily*) Why you . . .

(*Matsuō rises from his stool and grips his sword. Sakuramaru and Umeō pull their swords way out of their obis, twisting them so they curve away from their bodies. Gripping their hilts, they do a shuffle step, crouching slightly, toward Matsuō. Sakuramaru has his right hand aloft as Matsuō makes a similar crouching, shuffle-step movement from left to right. Umeō and Matsuō are almost nose to nose at center. They toss their heads rhythmically as the tsuke beat.*)

SHIHEI: Let's get this carriage moving quickly!

(*Sarashi drum music begins. The brothers rise from their crouch and extend both hands to either side in a broad gesture of blocking the way. Umeō crosses left, above Matsuō, while the latter moves to center. All turn to face upstage. Matsuō holds his hands wide at his side in a gesture of respect for Shihei. He looks left, then right, at his brothers. They all turn front and take the final tableau pose, each performing a mie, the total effect being in the fashion of a "pulling" mie.*)

LACKEYS: (*During the above*) Aaarya, koorya! Aaaarya, koorya!

(*Matsuō looks at Sakuramaru, stage right, then Umeō, at left, then front. With his sword held up perpendicularly, its tip in the obi, he thrusts his right foot forward, brings his right hand out wide in a fist and pulls it up before his chest, and leans his weight on his left leg, completing a Genroku mie. Umeō holds his right hand in a fist overhead, his weight leaning on his left leg, his left hand holding his sword pulled high out of his obi and pointed toward stage right, his right foot straight and pointed upstage left, his head tilted to look at Matsuō as he completes the mie. His whole body is turned only one-fourth to the audience. At right, Sakuramaru stands facing front in three-quarter position, his open right hand in the air to his side, his left hand on the hilt of his sword, left foot thrust forward gracefully. He looks at Matsuō. Sugiomaru, at left, leans his weight on his right foot, points his straightened left foot toward the left, leans the long umbrella against the left side of his neck, its shaft running to the floor in a line parallel with the line of his left leg, holds his right hand out in a gesture of respect for Shihei, and lowers his head slightly. Shihei stands on the carriage, his right hand aloft holding its scepter, his left arm straight out to the side, its sleeve flipped around it, his red tongue thrust forth, his eyes glaring. The final crack of the ki is heard during this business followed by the resounding sarashi music coming from the geza. The complex musical finale reaches a crescendo accompanied by the beating of the ki and the curtain closes on this scene of static power.*)

CURTAIN

THE VILLAGE SCHOOL

(*Several minutes before the curtain opens the sound of the ki can be heard being clapped together sharply at intervals of approximately thirty seconds. Finally, there is a double beat and "country music" [zaigō uta] begins to be sung and played in the geza music room. The clappers begin beating faster and faster and the curtain opens rapidly from right to left. The scene disclosed is of Takebe Genzō's village school in the village of Seryū. The stage shows a typical Kabuki interior/exterior setting. A platform about eighteen inches high runs across the rear of the interior section. It is reached from the stage floor proper by a single step placed at its center. Strips of thin straw matting run lengthwise across the downstage area of the room. On the wall to the right of the upstage doorway leading into the living quarters of the schoolmaster and his wife a small shinto altar [kamidana] is hung. In some productions this altar is hung above the doorway. Within it is a scroll containing Lord Sugawara's secrets of calligraphy, entrusted to Genzō, who has hidden it here. Noren curtains with a bracken design on them hang in the doorway. The stage-left end of the platform is in the form of a small room shut off from the audience's view by shoji screens [the structure is called shōji yatai]. Sliding panels are painted on the area facing the audience to the left of the upstage doorway. At the right side of the platform and perpendicular to it is a wooden gateway with a sliding door. This latticework gateway is portable and can be moved intact. Upstage right is a landscape of the surrounding countryside; some thickets of grass are placed before this. A tree "cut-out" stands here, too. Since the play is a Kabuki adaptation from the puppet theater there is a platform on stage left for the chanter and shamisen player combination [chobo]. At the moment it is unoccupied. Seen on stage are a class of country children practicing their calligraphy. They are seated across the front of the upstage platform, one next to the other, at low desks at which they must kneel to write. Four children are arranged in a row from left to right; after a space of two feet or so five more children are seated. At the inside end of the group on stage left sits Yodarekuri [literally, "dribblepuss"], a fifteen year-old mischief-maker, older by several years than any other in the group. At the extreme left, next to the shōji yatai, is Kan Shūsai. He is set off from the others in that he is behind a reading stand, not a writing desk, and is reading from a book. Also, his noble appearance is clearly distinguishable from the rusticity of the others by its white face, long hair, and noble mien. Each boy, except for Kan Shūsai, has a large writing tablet opened before him, its used portions hanging over the front of the desk. These papers are seemingly messed up with unsightly black scrawls. The boys are busily making ink with their inkstones, dipping their writing brushes into the ink, and practicing their calligraphy. Some, especially*

Yodarekuri, have ink stains on face and fingers. When the curtain opens, the geza music fades and the voice of a gidayū chanter can be heard reciting from a position at left. He is seated with the shamisen player in a booth about eight feet over the stage floor; just beneath him is the platform area where he later appears. At present, a bamboo blind hides him from the audience's sight. His words are chanted to the shamisen's accompaniment.)

GIDAYŪ:

> *Of all the world's treasures*
> *More than silver or gold is*
> *The power to read and write.*
> *Kan Shūsai sits among the students*
> *Who have come to learn calligraphy.*
> *Takebe Genzō and his wife*
> *Have taken him under their wing.*
> *The oldest boy is Yodarekuri*
> *The son of Gosaku, a farmer.*

(During much of the play, when no chanting is heard, shamisen music played in the geza accompanies and accentuates the stage action. At other times the shamisen played by the musician accompanying the gidayū performs the same function. Geza shamisen music is now heard during the following business.)

YODAREKURI: Hey fellas! Take a look at this! Why waste time practicing while the master is gone! Look, I've drawn a picture of a priest's bald head! Hey fellas! Take a look! Take a look!

(He holds up his picture so all can see.)

How do you like it, huh! How do you like it, huh!

GIDAYŪ:

> *The fifteen-year-old Yodarekuri*
> *Shows his picture to the boys*
> *But the young lord*
> *Does not misbehave.*

KAN SHŪSAI: *(Speaking each word in a carefully measured falsetto)* If you learn one character a day you can learn three hundred sixty in a year. You should not be drawing such things but should be practicing your calligraphy.

GIDAYŪ:

> *The eight-year-old*
> *Scolds his senior.*

YODAREKURI: Hey, you've got a nerve, you've got a nerve!

CHILD #1: Don't talk back to your superiors!

OTHERS: Let's teach him a lesson! Yaaaa!

(The boys all rise, except for Kan Shūsai, and, ad-libbing, chase Yodarekuri downstage center, flailing him with their fists. Tonami, Genzō's wife, enters up center and the boys run back to their desks. As she talks she goes to Yodarekuri's desk and places it left center, below the platform. She sends a boy off to get something. The writing utensils formerly on the desk are placed on the floor in the desk's former position. Yodarekuri is forced to stand on the desk as Tonami

hands him a teacup filled with water and an incense stick, the objects for which the boy had been sent. Yodarekuri's punishment consists of being made to stand on the desk holding these objects in his hands. He begins to bawl loudly. Tonami is dressed in the classic costume of a well-bred country lady, the plum-colored kokumochi *kimono, worn with a black obi and a carefully folded tenugui towel tucked into the obi at the right. This tenugui is a distinctive part of her costume's appearance and is frequently removed and used for a myriad of gestures.*)

TONAMI: (*As she enters*) What is going on here? Are you quarreling again? I suppose I must punish you, mustn't I? Here, hold this stick of incense and this teacup.

(*Business described above*)

CHILDREN: (*Mocking*) Yaa, yaa!

(*As Tonami makes Yodarekuri stand on the desk, dialogue such as the following is improvised.*)

YODAREKURI: Oh no! Please forgive me!

TONAMI: Now you stand there, Yodarekuri.

YODAREKURI: I mean it, I apologize . . .

TONAMI: Now you must stand here and not move. And you must hold this cup and stick of incense. I will not forgive you so easily today. Well, well, everybody, put your noses to the grindstone now and study, do you hear me, study.

GIDAYŪ:

A man comes along
Carrying a desk and school supplies
Slung across his shoulder.
With him is a lady
And her bright young seven-year old.

(*Zaigō uta is played in the geza. Chiyo, Kotarō, and Sansuke enter on the hanamichi and stop at the shichi-san. Chiyo is a noble looking lady of about thirty, dressed in a black montsuki kimono with the white silk collar of her undergarment showing at the neck. Her gold silk obi is tied in front. Her son, Kotarō, is wearing hakama divided trousers and formal montsuki kimono over which he wears a silk haori jacket. He carries one sword. Sansuke is the family servant and is dressed rather rustically, with his kimono hitched up at the thighs. Chiyo is obviously troubled by something. As the group arrives at the shichi-san, Chiyo speaks.*)

CHIYO: Sansuke, go see if this is the place.

SANSUKE: Yes'm.

(*He moves on past his mistress and goes to the doorway of the house. Chiyo and Kotarō come up behind him and stand several feet to the right. Sansuke's manner is rather loutish and should be played for laughs.*)

Excuse me in there but I'd like some information please. This wouldn't be the home of Takeapeea Genzō, would it?

YODAREKURI: (*Getting off his desk and going to the door*) Takeapeea? You take a peea here and you'll be in hot water.

SANSUKE: Ah, you say this is the place, huh?

YODAREKURI: No, I said it isn't!

SANSUKE: It is, huh?

YODAREKURI: No, it's not!

SANSUKE: Yes, it is!

YODAREKURI: Not, not, not, not, not!

SANSUKE: (*Simultaneously*) Is, is, is, is, is!

YODAREKURI: What are you talking about?

(*This sequence, which is ad-libbed in a manner similar to that indicated, goes on for a moment or two until Tonami enters from upstage center. She claps her hands and Yodarekuri jumps back up on the desk at left, innocently.*)

TONAMI: What is going on?

(*She crosses to the doorway, opens the door, steps back onto the matting, and bows low.*)

CHIYO: (*Moving to door*) I beg your pardon but I would like to ask you something. Is this the home of Takebe Genzō?

TONAMI: Yes, this the home of Takebe Genzō. But I don't believe I am acquainted with you, madame. Please do enter my humble home.

CHIYO: Thank you so much. I will be honored to do so.

(*The trio enters. They remove their sandals at the edge of the matting near the doorway. As Chiyo takes her seat, right, she speaks.*)

I am very happy to make your acquaintance. I live modestly in the next village. When we sent to inquire whether you would accept our naughty boy in your school and you agreed to do so, we were so delighted with your kind reply I decided to come here with him right away.

(*Sansuke, on entering, has taken a seat up right, near the platform, where he is now busying himself unloading and arranging the school materials he has brought for Kotarō. He wipes all the pieces with a cloth as he sets them up neatly, putting the desk with the book box on it on the platform above him.*)

TONAMI: Ah? Is that so? Then, is this the child who wants to enter our school?

(*This section is played at a leisurely pace with geza shamisen music performed in the background. Chiyo has taken a small paper fan out of her obi and uses it to gesture with as she speaks.*)

CHIYO: Yes, it is.

TONAMI: A fine looking lad, isn't he? And what, may I ask, is the little man's name?

CHIYO: We call him Kotarō.

TONAMI: My, what an excellent name he has.

CHIYO: I have heard that you too have a son. Which one is he, may I ask?

TOMANI: That is he over there, my husband Genzō's heir.

(*Chiyo looks at Kan Shūsai.*)

CHIYO: My, what a lovely child.

(*Pause*)

Oh, Sansuke, please put the things you've brought over here.

SANSUKE: Eeee.

(*Sansuke takes a red-lacquered box, covered with a lid, and places it before Tonami. He does this in formal fashion, bowing on his knees, back to audience, on a slight diagonal, then returns to his former position, up right. The box contains rice cakes. Soon after he returns, Sansuke falls asleep with his pole resting against his left shoulder.*)

CHIYO: This really isn't anything much, but we want our boy to make a good impression so there are some sweets here for the other children. Please do me the honor of accepting it.

TONAMI: Well, well. You really have arranged everything so carefully. I'll distribute these to the children later.

(*Yodarekuri begins to bawl loudly.*)

CHIYO: Ah! That gave me a start! What did the boy do to be punished?

TONAMI: He simply can't stop playing the clown so I've made him stand there like that.

CHIYO: I see, I see. It's really none of my business but since this is my boy's first day at your school please do forgive him.

TONAMI: Oh, oh. Please don't pay any mind to him.

YODAREKURI: Wa-a-a-a!

CHIYO: I do find it most vexing, you know.

(*He rises and crosses to Yodarekuri; Tonami counter-crosses to Kotarō.*)

Just for today, if I apologize for you won't you be a good boy and learn your lessons?

(*He nods.*)

Now, come on down. That's right. . . . Please behave yourself from now on.

(*To Tonami*)

Please do forgive him, won't you?

TONAMI: All right, I will.

(*To Yodarekuri*)

Don't you think you should say thank you to the nice lady?

YODAREKURI: Ah, yes, yes.

(*Very flippantly*)

Many thanks, m'am.

(*He picks up his desk and runs back with it to his former position, where he sits. Chiyo crosses back to Kotarō at right and Tonami counter-crosses to center. They sit. As they pass each other Yodare-kuri rises and runs to the red box, grabs a rice cake, and rushes back to his desk where he proceeds to eat.*)

TONAMI: (*Noticing Yodarekuri's theft*) You can see why I have to punish him.

(*The ladies laugh lightly, covering their mouths with their sleeves. Chiyo removes a small gift of money wrapped in paper from her kimono and places it on her fan.*)

CHIYO: Please honor me by accepting this insignificant gift.

(*She places the fan before Tonami. Tonami takes the gift from the fan, puts it away in her kimono, then pushes the fan back to Chiyo.*)

TONAMI: How very kind of you. Thank you so much. Unfortunately, my husband, Genzō, was asked to attend a reception in the village today and has not yet returned.

CHIYO: So the master is not at home?

TONAMI: He has been taking a long time. If you'd like I'll just go out and fetch him.

CHIYO: No, no. That's really not necessary. Fortunately, I only have to go as far as the next village so I will be returning in just a little while.

TONAMI: Certainly. My husband will surely be here before long.

CHIYO: (*To Kotarō*) Listen to me, Kotarō. I'm just going to the village so I want you to study and wait here for me like a good boy.

(*Turning to him slightly and putting her hand on his shoulder*)

Don't misbehave, all right? All right? Now, I'll be off.

(*She rises and crosses right a few steps. Pause. Kotarō clings to her sleeve as she passes. He is on his knees at her left side, looking up at her imploringly. She can barely look at him for emotion. They hold this pose.*)

KOTARŌ: Mama! I want to go with you!

CHIYO: Are you still being unreasonable, even though I gave you instructions on how to behave before we came here? Aren't you ashamed, a big boy like you running after his mother?

(*She lightly removes his hand from her sleeve.*)

Even though he's big he's still quite helpless.

TONAMI: It's only natural, after all.

(*She sits with her fingertips touching the ground before her in a semibow. Then she rises and crosses to Kotarō at right as Chiyo moves to the doorway to put on her sandals.*)

You and I are going to have a nice time here, aren't we?

(*To Chiyo*)

We'll be waiting for your return.

CHIYO: (*Going out*) Yes, yes. Well, I'll be leaving now.

(*She takes a few steps but, unable to tear herself away, returns quickly to the doorway. Tonami sees her, moves to the boy's right, and kneels respectfully. Kotarō rises at her side. Tonami bows.*)

GIDAYŪ:

*Pulled back by motherly love
Chiyo returns to the school.*

TONAMI: Did you forget something, madam?

CHIYO: Didn't I leave my fan behind?

(*The following sequence is based on what was originally an ad-lib scene although it is pretty much fixed today. Chiyo goes back into the school for a moment, standing near the doorway. Kotarō moves to her and they look at each other with longing. Tonami, meanwhile, rises and, walking in a wide circular pattern, looks around the room for the fan. As she returns to Chiyo, the latter steps outside the doorway, somewhat embarrassed.*)

TONAMI: Please wait a moment.

(*Looking around*)

I don't see a fan anywhere.

(*She sees that the fan is in Chiyo's hand.*)

Ah! Isn't that the fan in your hand?

CHIYO: (*Seeing it*) Oh!

(*Laughs lightly, hand to mouth*)

My goodness, isn't that just like me?

(*They laugh.*)

Goodbye again.

(*She moves to the hanamichi, stops at the shichi-san, pauses, and turns, looking back with sadness and longing.*)

GIDAYŪ:

*As she leaves her son behind
She can't help looking back, looking
   back . . .*

(*Chiyo, after a few seconds, takes out her fan, flips it open sharply, and covers her face on the left side with it, holding it in her right hand. Her left hand holds the bag of her right sleeve. Keeping this pose, she moves on down the hanamichi.*)

TONAMI: Well, you'll be meeting the master a bit later, but for now why don't you come inside with me? Come, let's go on in.

(*They are near the doorway, Kotarō standing and looking off, Tonami at his side on her knees. She speaks her lines and then rises, slides the door shut, takes Kotarō with her to center where she stoops to pick up the box of cakes, and exits up center. The scene that follows is a farcical parody [ōmu] of the previous actions. The scene begins with mimed action as Yodarekuri, who has cut out a long paper curlicue, quietly steals down to Sansuke and pastes it on his head. Sansuke has been sleeping upright for several minutes, his carrying pole resting against his shoulder. His behavior now is rather illogical when considered rationally, but the audience accepts the parody on its own terms and does not worry about the logic of cause and effect. After pasting on the curlicue with his saliva, Yodarekuri paints big circles around Sansuke's eyes and also applies a mustache and beard. He uses his calligraphy brush and ink for this purpose. The first few lines are ad-libbed to the following effect.*)

YODAREKURI: Hey, his mistress has left. What prank can I pull now? I know, I'll write all over his face.

(*Above business*)

Hey, not bad, not bad.

(*Shouts in Sansuke's ear*)

Hey, you! Wake up, wake up!

SANSUKE: (*Startled*) Wha..., wha..., wha...?

YODAREKURI: Your mistress has left already.

SANSUKE: Where, where, where?

(*He jumps up with a start.*)

Tell me, tell me, which way'd she go?

YODAREKURI: (*Confusing him and pointing in every direction*) Here, no there, no here, no there!

SANSUKE: Here? There? Here? There?

(*The pair walk around in circles, Yodarekuri moving from center stage in a counterclockwise direction while Sansuke moves in a clockwise direction. They come back to their starting position at center.*)

YODAREKURI: (*As they go around*) No, there, there. Here, there. There, here, here, there, here.

(*Pause, at center*)

I haven't the slightest idea.

SANSUKE: She could have at least told me she was going.

YODAREKURI: (*Imitating Kotarō*) Mama, I wanna go wif you!

(*They have crossed to stage right, near the doorway. Yodarekuri takes Sansuke's hand in a mock version of Kotarō's behavior with Chiyo.*)

SANSUKE: (*Imitating Chiyo*) Now, what is all this about? See (*as if speaking to Tonami*), even though he's big, he's still a baby.

YODAREKURI: (*Twirling himself around in a circle on his knees; when he faces front again he is imitating Tonami.*) It's only natural, after all.

SANSUKE: (*As Chiyo*) Of course. I'll be leaving now.

(*He walks out and comes back to the door. He is carrying his sandals in his kimono. His pole is thrust through his obi.*)

GIDAYŪ:

As she leaves her son behind
She can't help looking back, looking
  back . . .

YODAREKURI: Did you forget something?

SANSUKE: Yes, didn't I leave my carrying pole behind?

YODAREKURI: Your pole? Your pole? Your pole?

(*He raises his hem in a manner similar to Tonami's and walks around as if looking for the pole. He returns to Sansuke.*)

Why, isn't that it at your side?

SANSUKE: (*Seeing it in his obi*) Oh? Isn't that just like me?

(*They each laugh in imitation of the ladies but in a farcically exaggerated manner.*)

I'll be leaving now.

(*Sansuke walks to the shichi-san on the hanamichi, stops, looks back, then turns, and, taking out his sandals, holds them to his face in much the same manner as Chiyo with her fan. He exits down the hanamichi. Yodarekuri, who has been watching from the doorway, runs after him, saying, "Bye, bye!" and comes to the juncture of the hanamichi with the stage, waving to Sansuke's retreating figure.*)

YODAREKURI: Hey, Sansuke! Wait until they see your face when you get home! What a dumbbell! Ha! What a jerk!

(*Suddenly starts as if he sees something in the distance*)

Uh oh! The master is coming, the master is coming! He's on the way . . .

(*Shouting to the other students, he runs back into the classroom and takes his place behind his desk. The students immediately busy themselves with their brushes and ink and recite in unison the ABC of the Japanese syllabary.*)

CHILDREN: I ro ha ni ho e to . . .

(*Now, for the first time in the play, the gidayū chanter and shamisen combination come into view, as a revolve built into the floor of the stage left platform is turned from offstage with the pair seated on it. They wear the formal garb of the samurai class, called* kamishimo, *which consists of a black kimono over which a gray vest with stiff, winglike shoulder pieces is worn, with matching hakama divided trousers. The chanter intones his line slowly for several long moments before the lights on the hanamichi come up preparatory to Genzō's entrance.)*

GIDAYŪ:

Genzō, the master, returns to the school.
His face is ashen gray.

(Genzō comes slowly down the hanamichi. His hands are folded across his chest; his attitude is one of distraction. He stops at the shichi-san, pauses, then drops his arms, and moves on resolutely. He opens the door, steps into the room, turns quickly, and, standing with his back to the door, looks at the boys on the platform. He speaks his lines in a deliberate manner, with great feeling. All the boys look up at him, except Kan Shūsai.)

CHILDREN: *(As he closes the door)* Welcome back, master!

GIDAYŪ:

He looks over the poor faces
Of the children in the room.

GENZŌ: *(After a pause)* Aaah! Not one of them looks as if he were the son of a prosperous noble. Every face is that of a peasant.

(Turns front a bit)

I can't use them. There's no way out. Get to work! Get to work!

(Genzō removes his sandals at the edge of the matting, removes his long sword from the obi, carries it slowly to left center, and sits there, placing his sword at his left side. His gaze is on the floor. Tonami and Kotarō enter up center. Tonami sits at center, the boy at her right. She gestures to Kotarō to wait a moment. Genzō sits with his hands in either sleeve. His mood is very downcast and he seems preoccupied. He does not notice Kotarō.)

GIDAYŪ: *(As Tonami enters)*

His thoughts are deeply clouded
As his wife comes in to have a word.

TONAMI: *(Calmly)* I've never seen you so pale or your behavior so sodden. You must not speak so rudely to the children. Especially since a new child has entered the school today.

(Turns to Kotarō)

You don't want him to think you're ill tempered, do you? Now, cheer up and welcome him to the school.

GIDAYŪ:

She leads Kotarō to the master
Who sits there lost in thought.
The lovely child prepares to bow
To his new schoolteacher.

(As the gidayū chants Tonami moves to the boy, he rises, she adjusts his kimono,

and then brings him over to Genzō. She then crosses right center and sits. Kotarō bows low when speaking, fingers on the ground before him, head looking up to Genzō on an angle.)

KOTARŌ: Dear master, I humbly beg your favor from now on.

(Genzō looks at him distractedly as though the lad were a pest, stares at him vacantly, and then starts as if he had just realized something important.)

GIDAYŪ:

*The master vacantly looks up
And is stunned for a moment
By what he sees.
His stern face instantly relaxes.*

(After staring long and hard at the boy, Genzō, as if struck by the boy's appearance, moves his right hand into his left sleeve rapidly, in time to a sharp note from the shamisen. Then, as he speaks, he removes it.)

GENZŌ: Well, well. This boy is surely the son of some high-born noble. Marvelous! You're a splendid boy, aren't you?

(Holds Kotarō's face up with his right hand)

GIDAYŪ:

*Seeing his changed attitude
His wife echoes his words.*

TONAMI: Not only is he a splendid boy but he will surely be an excellent student in our school. This is superb. He is surely first-class.

(The pace of the dialogue quickens for the following segment.)

GENZŌ: What's his name?

TONAMI: He is called Kotarō.

GENZŌ: And who brought him here?

TONAMI: His mother.

GENZŌ: Where did she go?

TONAMI: Since you were out when they came she said she was going to make a brief visit to the next village . . .

GENZŌ: The next village, hm? That's fine, fine. Excellent.

(To Kotarō)

Since this is your first day of school why don't you go inside and play a bit with your new friends?

TONAMI: Children! Recess time! Take Kotarō inside with you.

CHILDREN: Hooray! Let's go in and play!

(Kotarō bows to Genzō. The boys all rise and take their desks to the upstage right corner of the platform and pile them there in two neat stacks of four each against the rear wall. They then exit up center. Tonami crosses to center meanwhile, with Kotarō. Leaving him there

momentarily she goes up left to Kan Shū-sai's desk, lifts it, and places it in the shōji yatai, offstage. She emerges and goes to the waiting Kotarō and Kan Shū-sai, who have not left yet, then watches as they leave up center with the waiting Yodarekuri. Tonami crosses down center to Genzō's right.)

GIDAYŪ:

Genzō looks about him sharply.

TONAMI: I couldn't figure out your behavior when you returned nor could I fathom it when you saw the new boy. I am afraid of what you may be thinking. Please tell me what you have in mind.

(She implores while placing her left hand on the floor, her right held before her breast.)

GIDAYŪ:

This is what Genzō replies.

GENZŌ: *(Speaking rapidly in a rhythmic delivery accompanied by the shamisen)* There is no need to worry.

(Drops sharply to his heels, places his sword down at his side, and puts both hands on his knees)

I didn't really go to a reception today. I was summoned to the village headman's home. It seems that Shundō Gemba, a vassal of the evil lord, Shihei, will soon be coming here. He is accompanied by that villain, Matsuomaru, who has betrayed his trust to the noble Lord Sugawara, our dear master. Matsuō is wasted from illness, they say, but he has been appointed official inspector and will be coming here soon. The fact that we have been harboring Kan Shūsai, Sugawara's only son, and passing him off as our own has been found out and we must cut the boy's head off immediately. If we don't they'll simply break in and seize him for themselves.

(Tonami seems shocked. Genzō motions to her with his right hand to keep calm.)

We have no way out. Since his head must be examined and certified as genuine I kept thinking all the way home as to whom of all the children in the school

(looks off left and up center)

we might substitute for Kan Shūsai.

(Looks off in distance and thinks)

I went over and over each one in my mind.

(Looking off up center)

Did this one

(inclines head)

look as though he were born into a noble family? Did that one look too like a peasant? I saw that we were at the end of our rope

(looking down)

and returned

(*his voice is filled with tears*)

as if coming home to a filthy slaughterhouse. But

(*faces Tonami and gestures off up center with right hand*)

heaven has seen fit

(*confidentially, almost whispering*)

to smile on us, for when I saw the new boy I realized that all was not yet lost. This Kotarō is truly a child of noble birth. We can use his head

(*looks down*)

to deceive the officials and then we can all flee from here to Kawachi.

(*Places hands on tatami mats*)

In a few moments

(*looks sharply at Tonami*)

we will know our fate.

GIDAYŪ:

His wife replies...

TONAMI: Wait a moment. It is well known that of the famous triplets, Sakuramaru, Umeomaru, and Matsuomaru, this Matsuō is by far the cruelest. And he knows the face of Kan Shūsai only too well.

(*She has both hands before her on the tatami.*)

GENZŌ: (*Almost angrily*) We

(*The tip of his right hand lightly touches the tatami.*)

have no choice in the matter.

(*Short pause*)

Besides, a dead face differs from a living one so there is a real chance he won't notice the substitution.

(*His hands are on his lap.*)

After all, this Kotarō closely resembles our young lord. But if our ruse is perceived I have resolved to cut Matsuō in two, kill the others, and flee.

(*He speaks now with great determination.*)

When all hope runs out we will die together with Kan Shūsai and travel with him to the world beyond.

(*He picks up sword with left hand, right hand gestures to stomach, face looks downward.*)

The main problem now is what to say to Kotarō's mother when she returns for him.

How can we get ourselves out of that dilemma?

(*Pause*)

TONAMI: (*Looks at doorway as if pondering what to do, then puts her hand on her knee decisively*) I don't think that that is really so serious a problem. I will speak to her as woman to woman and try to lead her off the track somehow.

GENZŌ: (*Strongly*) No, that won't work. She'll understand the truth.

(*With great feeling*)

We may have to kill the mother, too.

TONAMI: (*Shocked*) Oh!

(*She falls to her right side, her left hand on the ground.*)

GENZŌ: (*Holding the vowels for emphasis*) No one

(*faces away from her*)

must come before

(*places sword sharply on floor*)

our young lord.

(*Makes gesture of drawing both hands sharply from his lower to his upper lap*)

GIDAYŪ:

Tonami now steels herself.

TONAMI: (*Her voice moves into an almost soprano register as she holds the vowels in the following words, speaking with great emotion.*) You are right. We will fail if we are weakhearted.

(*Pause. On the word "demons" her voice rises to soprano register on the first vowel.*)

We must be demons.

(*She places each hand on the rear of her obi and slowly rises on her knees to a semierect position.*)

GIDAYŪ:

They look deeply
Into each other's face.

(*First they look at each other and then avert their gaze.*)

GENZŌ: Though we call them pupils

(*looks downward as if lamenting*)

they are truly like our own children.

(*Tonami uses her tenugui towel to dab her tears. She gestures with it in her right hand.*)

TONAMI: Whose karma is it, the child's or the mother's that brought them to our school today, of all days?

(*Places both hands on tatami, facing right*)

GENZŌ: And we must be the agents of their punishment.

TONAMI: (*With supreme emotional expression as she almost sings the line*) But we too

(*tenugui in her right hand is held to the breast, left hand on the tatami*)

shall be overtaken

(*pause*)

in our turn.

(*Sinks to floor in tears. Dabs tears with tenugui.*)

GIDAYŪ:

As the wife laments
The husband fights back his tears.

(*Genzō rises holding his sword in his left hand, his eyes shut tight. Tonami rises to one knee and puts one end of her hand towel in her teeth, pulling on it with her right hand. This is a typical Kabuki gesture for a female character in the throes of a deep emotion. Genzō puts one hand in his sleeve, holding his sword at his side. Moving his sword behind his back he turns to her and she to him; they look at each other with great intensity of emotion and he then drops to her side, in time to a sharp note from the shamisen. She*

puts her left hand on his lap, holding her tenugui in her right hand. He places an arm on her shoulder as she weeps.*)

GENZŌ: As the world well knows

(*pause, then, with terrific intensity, holding the vowels*)

it is painful indeed to serve one's master.

GIDAYŪ:

Their tears fall freely.

(*Genzō rises on his right knee. Tonami pulls herself up slightly; they look at each other, then avert their eyes. Genzō grabs the hilt of his sword in his right hand and places the tip of the sheath on the tatami. The voices of a group of farmers are now heard from the room at the rear of the hanamichi.*)

FARMERS: Please, please.

(*Genzō rises holding the sword in his left hand. Surprised, Tonami rises on her knees. They look at each other meaningfully. He whispers to her, then leads her off up center, slow step by slow step, each step becoming more rapid. As they go they look back fearfully in the direction of the hanamichi. Genzō takes a scroll from the small altar near the top of the up center doorway on his way out. This scroll contains the valuable secrets of calligraphy with which Genzō has been entrusted by the exiled Sugawara. The large drum [ōdaiko] in the geza begins to beat loudly, creating an atmosphere of tension.)*

GIDAYŪ:

There now appear Shundō Gemba
And the head inspector,
    Matsuomaru.
The latter, racked with illness,
Comes carried in a palanquin
Up to the school gate.
This fearsome pair are followed
By a crowd of village farmers.

(Gemba moves down the hanamichi with great authority. He is dressed in the ryū-jin maki *costume, the most distinctive element of which is the huge left sleeve shaped in the form of a square and kept stiff by splints placed inside its edges. Gemba is an aragoto-type character and is therefore acted in the bravura style. His speech and actions are quite exaggerated in order to produce an impression of power. His red kumadori makeup and unusual wig with a corkscrewlike topknot add to his impressive stature greatly. Behind come ten men, policemen dressed in black kimono* [kuroyoten] *with black leggings. Their kimono are hitched up to free their legs for walking and their sleeves are held back for action by white ribbons tied under and around their shoulders. White headbands encircle their brows and each one bears a jitte in his right hand. These are conventional Kabuki policemen* [torite] *and appear in a similar guise in a number of plays, as in the Inase River scene of* Benten Kozō.

The first of these policemen in the procession bears a box of paulonia wood. It looks something like a cylindrical hatbox and is light tan in color. Following the ten policemen is a palanquin [kago] *borne by two men with their kimono hitched up to expose their legs. Behind them comes a group of eight farmers, dressed in simple kimono. They are very subservient to the authorities. Gemba comes to the door of the school house. The constables take up a position up right before the scenic background. They crouch in two lines, facing forward. The palanquin is placed behind a stage thicket up right, only a part of it being visible. This is because it does not really bear the actor playing Matsuō. When Matsuō makes his entrance two stage assistants hold up a black cloth to the rear of the palanquin and the actor in the role of Matsuō uses this to screen himself so that he may appear as if emerging from the palanquin. Actually, he comes on from stage right. The farmers have taken up positions along the hanamichi bowing in the direction of Gemba. They are lined up on their hands and knees from the shichi-san down most of the hanamichi's length.)*

FARMER #1:   *(Clears throat)* I wish to inform your worships that we all have children in the school. They are all students of calligraphy.

FARMER #2:   If you slay the wrong child the damage can never be undone.

FARMER #3:   Please make your inspection as carefully as you can.

FARMER #4: And then please kindly allow them to go home with us.

FARMERS: Yes, yes, we humbly beg of you.

GIDAYŪ:

*Matsuomaru speaks to the nasty
  Gemba
From within the palanquin.*

MATSUOMARU: (*Apparently within the palanquin*) One moment! Wait one moment.

GIDAYŪ:

*Matsuō emerges from within
And stands with his sword as staff.*

(*Matsuō enters from right and crosses to Gemba's right. Two black-garbed stage assistants come out with narrow, high, black-lacquered aibiki stools for Matsuō and Gemba. These are placed behind the actors, who sit on them. The stage assistants crouch inconspicuously behind the actors. There is a pause as the process goes on. Matsuō is dressed in a splendid embroidered haori jacket worn over his kimono. He wears a very bushy wig, the gojūnichi, which is supposed to suggest that he has been too ill to shave his pate for many days. A purple band can be seen running through the wig around the head, a symbol of the character's illness. A piece of decorative paper called chika-ragami or "strong paper" adorns the rear of the wig. His manner and appearance is altogether impressive and awe-inspiring. As he is supposedly weak from illness, his manner is quite slow and de-*liberate *though filled with repressed strength. His voice is low and powerful. He uses his sheathed sword as a staff, holding it in his right hand with the sword knot at the hilt, his thumb resting on the top of the hilt. His left hand is on the small sword at his waist. Matsuō's makeup is a deathly white, his eyes and mouth being outlined in black. Together with his bluish beard he is immediately recognizable as a classic stage villain* [katakiyaku]. *When he is at Gemba's side he stands with his back to the audience for a moment, then turns to face front. He acknowledges Gemba with a nod and sits on the stool.*)

MATSUOMARU: If you'll allow me to say so these men can be treacherous. I have come here, though ill, to act as official head inspector since no one else is as familiar with the face of Kan Shūsai as am I. Since I am ill I will most gratefully take my leave as requested when my job here is completed though I will not retire until I have most scrupulously

(*He begins to cough but in a completely stylized way. He holds his left hand a bit before his mouth and barks out about nine coughs, one by one, pauses, then coughs six or seven times more, faster and faster, until he has no more breath. Pause. Then an exaggerated and forceful clearing of his throat occurs, his hand still held before his mouth. Another pause, about four seconds, as he comes to himself.*)

performed my duties. Sugawara has supporters in this village. They have infiltrated the ranks of the farmers and each is prepared to pass Kan Shūsai off as his son and get him out of here. You farmers can see that I know all your tricks!

(*He lifts his sword, brings it down with a bang, then flips his hanging left sleeve back over his wrist.*)

FARMERS: (*Dispirited*) Yes, sir!

MATSUOMARU: Now cut out the racket and call your brats out one at a time. They can go home after I've examined their faces.

(*He delivers this last line by holding the vowels and speaking with great emphasis.*)

GIDAYŪ:

Inside the house husband and wife
Steeled to their resolve,

(*Genzō and Tonami enter up center with Kan Shūsai. The boy wears Genzō's haori over his head and shoulders. Tonami hides the child in the shōji yatai at left while Genzō pauses at center. Genzō notices Kotarō's sandals at the doorway and rushes over to grab them. He crosses back to center where he poses as the tsuke are beat. This pose is performed with Tonami, who has come out of the shōji yatai and seems to be trying to cross to the doorway. He holds his sheathed sword across her body, preventing her*

from going any further. With the sword held thus in his left hand he moves left with Tonami, forcing her back, step by step, walking sideways; they enter the shōji yatai.)

Feel the pounding of their hearts
Reverberating like the sound
Of anvils being struck.
Outside a gray-haired farmer
Stands at the entrance
To call his son to him.

(*Toward the end of the gidayū passage the farmers move in a line to the stage proper where they take up positions on their knees before the stage right scenic wall fronting the geza. Farmer #1 rises and crosses to the school, passing by Matsuō and Gemba, to whom he bows his head. As soon as he calls his son he goes to the hanamichi to wait for him.*)

FARMER #1:   Chomayo! Chomayo!

GIDAYŪ:

As soon as he is called
The boy comes out,
His naughty face
All smeared with ink.
His face to that of Kan Shūsai
Is much like coal to snow.
"This isn't he," says the haughty
*   inspector*
And the boy is free to go.

(*As the gidayū sings the first line of the passage, a boy comes running out from up center, shouting, "Coming!" and goes directly to the inspector's area, right of the doorway. He stops at Gemba's right foot where he is forced to kneel. Gemba places his huge left sleeve at the back of the boy's head and puts his chūkei style fan under his chin, showing the boy's face to Matsuō. Matsuō lightly shakes his head "No" and closes his eyes. Gemba makes a slight movement with his left foot. The boy stands up and goes to his father on the hanamichi. The father takes the boy's hand and they exit.)*

FARMER #2:   (*Rises and goes to doorway*)
Where are you, Iwamatsu?

GIDAYŪ:

> *The voice that calls*
> *Is that of Iwamatsu's grandpa.*
> *The innocent child comes flying out.*

(Iwamatsu enters up center quickly, stops at Gemba's knee; same business of inspection.)

> *His young face*
> *Is like an eggplant.*
> *It isn't necessary to inspect him*
>   *closely*
> *And he is sent on his way with a*
>   *glare.*

(The boy rises and rushes to his grandfather on the hanamichi. The old man embraces him.)

FARMER #2:   Oh! What a fright I had. My darling grandson has barely escaped with his life.

(Looks the child over)

GIDAYŪ:

> *The old man hugs the boy*
> *And leaves with him.*

(The grandfather lifts the child in his arms and exits with him.)

> *The next one called is our*
> *Fifteen-year-old friend, Yodarekuri.*

(Yodarekuri's father goes to the doorway and calls within.)

FARMER #3:   Son! Oh, sonny-boy!

GIDAYŪ:

> *The old man beckons to the boy.*

(Yodarekuri appears up center carrying a broom to the end of which are attached strips of cloth. He makes believe he is a Kabuki actor and produces sounds supposed to be in imitation of the tsuke used in performing a mie. He wears writing paper hung over his chest like armor, a light blue tenugui around his forehead as a helmet, and brandishes the broom as a halberd. There is a duster stuck through his obi as a sword.)

YODAREKURI: Jyan, jyan, jyan, jyan, jyan!

(Handles the broom with both hands and does an awkward mie)

Pop? Wait there. I'm coming. Be right with you. I just had to do some sweeping.

(He removes the writing paper, tenugui, and duster, and puts them, together with the broom, behind the up center door, out of sight. He runs to the doorway, where he is stopped by Gemba's foot, and falls to his knees surprised. Gemba laughs lightly when he sees the boy's features. Gemba begins to look to Matsuō to see his reaction but, suddenly realizing that this scamp cannot be Kan Shūsai, strikes the boy on the head with his fan. This causes Yodarekuri to bawl loudly as he runs to his father on the hanamichi. When he gets to the old man he immediately plops himself on the floor, legs crossed.)

Waaaa! Waaaa!

FARMER #3: Oh, my boy. What happened, what happened?

YODAREKURI: *(Wailing)* That red-faced monster hit me all over my head!

FARMER #3: He did? He did? Well, he's a big shot so you'll just have to control yourself, that's all. There's nothing I can do about it. Nothing I can do. Tell you what. When we get home I'll buy you something nice. How about it? Now, let's go, let's go.

YODAREKURI: Hey, pop! Hey, hey, hey! How about carrying me home from here?

FARMER #3: What? Carry you home? What are you talking about? Your nose is running.

(Wipes Yodarekuri's nose with a piece of tissue paper)

Have a heart, will you?

(The boy appears adamant.)

Well, here goes.

(The old man bends down to allow Yodarekuri to climb onto his back. The boy leaps over his back, leap-frog style, instead, and the old man gets on his son's back. Yodarekuri then carries him off down the hanamichi.)

GIDAYŪ:

*The old man's face looks like a
    horse's
And the grasshopper has a sweeter
    voice.
Stop crying! Stop crying! he begs.
But the poor man gives in
To the boy's request
Only to be carried off instead
Like a piece of salmon
Stolen by a cat.*

FARMER #4: *(Rises and goes humbly past the inspectors to the doorway)* My son is very fine-looking so please don't make an error when you examine him.

GIDAYŪ:

So saying he summons his boy.

FARMER #4: Son, son!

GIDAYŪ:

*And out comes a fair and handsome
  lad*

(*the boy enters up center*)

*Whom they stop with great
  suspicion.
But when they scrutinize him closely
They see a coal-black neck*

(*the boy has been stopped at Gemba's
knee; Matsuō and Gemba look at him
slowly, with care*)

*And can't tell if he has moles there
  or ink-spots.
This isn't him, states Gemba*

(*the boy rises and goes to his waiting
father on the hanamichi*)

*And the lad is pushed away.
They've looked and looked*

(*the remaining fathers rise and go, one
after the other to the doorway and beck-
on to their children who come out in
fairly rapid succession, one for every line
of the gidayū*)

*At every child hereabouts
But none fits the description.
All the boys here in the country*

(*the last child enters and goes off on the
hanamichi with his father*)

*Look like potatoes so
They're all sent home again.*

GEMBA: (*As he rises, his stool is removed by
a stage assistant.*) Matsuomaru!

(*Gemba turns and enters the house, removes his thick-soled sandals, and slowly
crosses left where he stands with his back
to the audience.*)

MATSUOMARU: After you, after you.

(*He rises and his stool is removed. He
turns and enters the house where he removes his sandals. As he steps into the
room Genzō and Tonami enter from the
shōji yatai and come down center where
they note Gemba crossing past them as
he moves left. Genzō stares fearfully at
Gemba as he goes by. Still staring, Genzō
slowly moves right where he bumps into
the entering Matsuō and quickly crosses
left several steps posing with his sword as
if ready to draw it. Matsuō, at the same
time, strikes his sword on the ground,
looking steadily in the direction of stage
left. Matsuō now moves slowly left center, walking with his sword as a cane.
Tonami and Genzō countercross and sit
on their knees at the right, Genzō occu-
pying a position at right center with Tonami at his right. Matsuō arrives at Gemba's side and the two face front and sit
on high black stools brought on at this
moment by stage assistants. Matsuō is
holding his sword in the right hand
[point on the ground], eyes closed. Genzō*

places his sword on the floor to his left. The police enter and line up across the face of the upstage platform where they crouch, five on either side of the center step. Their leader, on entering, goes to down center and places the head box on the floor, then joins the others upstage. The last one in closes the door and straightens the sandals of Gemba and Matsuō.)

GIDAYŪ: (*During the above*)

Genzō and Tonami, man and wife,
Brace themselves as the fearsome
*   pair*
Now make their dreadful entrance.

GEMBA: Hey, Genzō, you remember me, Gemba. Hand over the head of Kan Shūsai so that we may inspect it! Brrring it here!

GIDAYŪ:

Gemba wastes no words
In his awesome request.
He shows not the slightest
Inkling of hesitation.

GENZŌ: The death of so important a personage as the young lord must be given more than the usual considerations. If you will kindly wait a moment I will see that the deed is done.

GIDAYŪ:

He rises to leave but...

(*Genzō picks up the sword at his side and begins to rise. When Matsuō speaks he puts the sword down again.*)

MATSUOMARU: That trick won't work!

(*He turns slightly to Genzō.*)

Don't think you can excuse yourself in order to delay and then sneak out the rear door. There are many men on guard out there and not even an ant could get past them.

(*Pause*)

Furthermore, you won't fool me by using a substitute head thinking I'll be confused by the difference between a dead face and a live one.

(*Genzō thrusts forth his chin, places his hands on his lap, and leans forward a bit in Matsuō's direction.*)

You'll regret using such old tricks on me!

(*This last is spoken very emphatically.*)

GENZŌ: What you say is absurd!!

(*Advances one step on his knees*)

But you'll soon see that a man as racked with illness as yourself will be uncertain about the head before him.

MATSUOMARU: Kill him now before your tongue dries up!

GEMBA: (*Leaning over in Genzō's direction and gesturing with his fan*) K-k-k-ill him!

GIDAYŪ:

Gemba spits out this command.

GENZŌ: (*Powerfully*) I will!

GIDAYŪ:

The schoolmaster shudders,

(*Genzō places his hands before him on the floor, lowers his head, raises it, lifts his sword, and puts it in his obi. He takes the box with his left hand under it and his right above, holds it to his left side against his armpit, rises, and, at a sharp note from the shamisen, quickly separates his legs in a pose, looks back, and moves to the platform*)

Then screws up his courage

(*he stands with his right foot on the edge of the platform, his other foot on the step, looks up center, and turns sharply to his left to look down at Tonami; she appears ready to follow Genzō and raises herself, stretches her body, puts her right hand forth on the floor, and looks up at him; he nods to her, then turns and faces up center, gripping the box firmly; pause*)

And leaves to do his deed.

(*He exits up center.*)

Tonami has been listening closely
And sits there gripped by fear

(*she sinks, hands before her, head lowered*)

As Matsuō, with callous eyes,

(*Matsuō looks up right in the direction of the desks*)

Surveys the classroom,
Counting all the desks.

(*Tonami has her hands on the floor before her, afraid to look up. She turns to face downstage right, away from Matsuō.*)

MATSUOMARU: Hold it! Something strange is going on here. We counted only eight brats but there is one extra desk here. Where is its owner?

GIDAYŪ:

This challenge startles Tonami.

(*Tonami is quite nervous and flustered in her replies. Her hand shakes and she shifts positions on her knees.*)

TONAMI: Why, uh, uh, that, that's the property of a new, uh...pupil...

MATSUOMARU: (*Loudly, coming right in on her line*) What's that?

TONAMI: (*Meekly*) A new pupil...

MATSUOMARU: (*Even louder*) What?

TONAMI: (*Quickly*) a new...

MATSUOMARU: (*Overriding her in a climactic shout*) What sort of foolishness is this?

(*He bangs his sword on the ground.*)

TONAMI: (*An idea comes to her and she slaps her thigh with her right hand.*) Er, well, you see, this desk is actually Kan Shūsai's.

(*She staggers to her feet, crosses to the platform at up right where the desk is situated with the book box on it, takes the desk and brings it left, placing it on the floor before Matsuō. She dusts off the top of the desk with her tenugui.*)

GIDAYŪ:

*She takes the lacquered wooden desk
Hoping to deceive her cruel enemy.*

(*Tonami bows low at the right of the box.*)

MATSUOMARU: Whatever it is, this business is taking far too long.

GEMBA: (*Sternly*) I agree.

(*Tonami carries the desk back to the platform up right.*)

GIDAYŪ:

They arise together.

(*Matsuō and Gemba rise from their stools and these are removed by stage assistants. Tonami, having returned the desk to its former place, puts the writing pad and copy book which were at the side of the book box on the box top. This is in preparation for a later piece of business by Chiyo. Matsuō walks slowly to center using his sword as a staff. Gemba turns his back on the audience.*)

But at this crucial moment

(*Matsuō has taken two or three steps to center; Tonami, having replaced the desk, rises; Matsuō turns his back to the audience*)

*From within there comes
The sound of decapitation.*

(*The offstage shout from Genzō, "Eiii!," coincides with the sharp smack of the tsuke which simulate the sound of Kotarō's head being severed by Genzō's sword. Matsuō starts as if an electric shock had gone through him, his knees seem to buckle, and he whirls around as his sword point, resting on the floor, appears to slide out from under him. He draws his body up with a great effort and steps to the right a bit. At the same time, Tonami, having heard the sound, tries to move, sinks, rises, and attempts to move center in order to go within. This all happens quite rapidly.*)

*It turns Tonami's blood to ice.
She rises to go within.*

(*Tonami's right shoulder bumps into Matsuō at center.*)

MATSUOMARU: (*Suddenly out of control, shouting*) Brazen woman!

(*Matsuō brings his sword down hard with his left hand, holding it with its tip on the floor near his right foot. He brings his right hand up in slow, choppy move-*

ments till it is near the side of his right cheek, holds his hand with fingers wide and thumb pointing to his cheek, and completes the mie by revolving his head and crossing one eye. Tonami, on bumping into him, falls to stage right, bowing very low. The tsuke accentuate the moment. At the completion of his mie, Matsuō mimes coughing as if to cover up for his state of distraction.)

GIDAYŪ:

Tonami is taken by surprise.
Genzō now emerges from within.

(Matsuō relaxes his pose, moves left, and turns to face the rear, as does Gemba. Genzō enters from up center, slowly, and stops at the edge of the platform with his right foot on the step. He holds the head box at his left side. He has removed his tabi. After a brief pause, he comes down center, and turns to Matsuō. Matsuō and Gemba turn front and sit on the stools, which once again are brought on by stage assistants. Matsuō now holds the sword in his left hand, using it as a staff. He closes his eyes.)

Carrying the head in its box.

(Genzō comes down center, a bit to the left, places the head box down on the floor, and sits on his knees at the right, with his body on a slight diagonal, facing upstage left.)

He seems quite calm
And heeds not those around him.

GENZŌ:

Here is the noble head of Kan
  Shūsai!
Severed by the force of
  circumstances.
Matsuomaru, you must not forget
The import of this moment—
When you inspect and verify

(slaps hand on right knee)

Its au-then-ti-ci-tyyy!

GIDAYŪ:

In silence, Genzō readies his sword

(Genzō removes his long sword from his obi, gripping it in his left hand)

And with bated breath, waits for the
  verdict.
If Matsuō declares the head is false
Genzō's blade will flash out boldly,
But if he says it's true
Genzō once more will breathe freely.

(Genzō moves forward a bit on his right knee, sharply pulling his kimono hem under his knee with his right hand as he does so. He raises his body off his heels, readjusts his body to the diagonal position facing up left, places both hands on his lap, and looks at Matsuō over his shoulder.)

MATSUOMARU: (Begins to recite a Buddhist prayer, spoken when in the presence of death) Our good and evil deeds are reflected in the crystal mirror of the King of Hades.

(*He laughs in an exaggerated, stylized manner, his laughter reaching a crescendo.*)

Ha, ha, ha, ha, ha, ha. Depending on whether our names are inscribed in his awesome registry with an iron stylus . . .

GEMBA: Or a golden one . . .

MATSUOMARU: (*Eyes downcast, looking at the head box*) We go to hell . . .

GEMBA: (*Powerfully*) Or to heaven!

MATSUOMARU: All right! Surround the schoolmaster and his wife!

POLICE: Yes sir! Don't move!

(*The policemen rise and line up across the stage holding their jitte in readiness and focusing on Genzō. Each one holds the jitte in his right hand just before his forehead with the tip pointed upward. Their left hands are held with fingers wide apart, palms facing downward, about seven or eight inches before the abdomen. Feet are together at the heels. Five police stand up right and, after a space of about three feet, the other five stand up left, above Matsuō and Gemba. The form is that of an open book, the interval between the two groups being where the binding would be.*)

GIDAYŪ:

The officers surround the helpless couple
Holding their weapons in readiness.
Tonami and Genzō brace themselves
To await the final verdict.

(*Genzō leans forward, perks up his shoulders, places his right hand on his knee, and then moves it to the tatami in time to two strokes from the shamisen.*)

GENZŌ: (*With great intensity*) Well, carry out your duties!

(*He sinks sharply on his heels, both hands on his upper thighs, his shoulders thrown back.*)

GIDAYŪ:

The moment of truth has at last arrived
For all concerned.
The police stand poised for action.
Gemba's eyes bore into Matsuō's face.
Matsuō pauses, then quickly approaches the fearful box.
If he sees that Kotarō's head is a mere substitute
Genzō's sword will fly from its sheath in a second.
Tonami silently prays: "Dear Gods and Buddhas,
I beg you for compassion in this, my hour of need."

(*Tonami mouths these words silently as the gidayū chants them. Matsuō and Genzō have been glaring at each other. Tonami is at Genzō's right, hands on the tatami before her, her face averted in the direction of stage right. Matsuō rises. His stool is taken offstage by a stage assistant. He takes his sword in his left hand,*

*gripping the sword's decorative cord
along with the hilt, takes two or three
steps toward center, sits on his knees before the box as a stage assistant slips a
small aibiki beneath him, and places his
sword on the floor at his left.)*

*Matsuō's eyes betray his thought
That Genzō may be lying.
He looks at the head from every
    angle.*

*(He lifts the cover and places it down
directly in front of him, places his hands
on the cover with the fingers of both
hands coming together like an arrow's
point, and with eyes closed, slowly brings
his face down to look at the head. He
opens his eyes wide, stares, starts for a
moment, and speaks.)*

MATSUOMARU: This is surely the head of the
young lord, Kan Shūsai! There can be no
doubt.

*(Unable to look any longer he rapidly re-
places the lid over the head. He then
raises his shaking right hand, fingers
wide apart, to a position at the side of his
head, slightly higher than his hairline,
and completes the facial expression of
this famous mie. His left hand is pointed
toward the closed head box, over which
it hovers. The tsuke accentuate the pose.)*

Well done, Genzō! You have done an
excellent job!

GIDAYŪ:

*These words stun the schoolmaster
    and his wife
Who stare at one another in
    astonishment.*

*(Genzō and Tonami turn and bow low to
Matsuō, heads near the floor.)*

*Gemba proclaims the deed of
    inspection done.*

*(Gemba has returned to his former posi-
tion at the left, where he stands. The
policemen have lowered their weapons
and are crouching on their haunches as
before.)*

GEMBA: Well done, Genzō! You have done
an excellent job. As a reward, all future
blame is removed from you. We must report
this to Lord Shihei as soon as possible,
Matsuomaru.

MATSUOMARU: Indeed!

*(His general attitude is now more relaxed
and he no longer seems under pressure.)*

He may think we have delayed too long.
Please allow me to be excused, however, as
I am ill and wish to rest.

GEMBA: Surely. Your duties are completed.
You may do as you please.

MATSUOMARU: Then, begging your pardon.

(*He takes his sword in his left hand, rises, nods to Gemba, takes the loose cord of his sword knot in his right hand, places it on the hilt, grips the hilt with his right hand, uses the sword as a staff, moves slowly to the doorway, puts on his sandals, takes the sword in his left hand, opens the door with his right, steps outside, takes the sword in his right hand again, and closes the door with his left.*)

GIDAYŪ:

Matsuō enters his palanquin and departs.

(*Holding the sword in his right hand, Motsuō "enters" the palanquin at the right. Actually, the actor exits into the wings, his entrance being hidden by a black curtain held up by two stage assistants. The policemen now rise and leave the room, lining up evenly at the right before the geza room in a curving line, their backs to the audience. They then turn and crouch on their haunches. The same policeman as before is holding the head box in his arms. When Gemba speaks, Genzō and Tonami, who have been bowing while facing center, turn to face right, on their knees.*)

GEMBA: (*Outside the doorway*) Well, Genzō.

(*Pause*)

I'll be leaving. You certainly talk a lot about loyalty but when *your* neck is threatened you go and cut your master's head off! You cling like a dog to your precious life!

(*Laughs viciously*)

Ha, ha, ha, ha!

GIDAYŪ:

Gemba leaves for the castle.

(*Gemba walks to the edge of the hanamichi, pauses a moment, and, standing with his heels together, moves his big sleeve grandly as he glares in a mie. He then moves on down the hanamichi slowly as the big drum in the geza begins to beat. The policemen rise and follow him off, their leader carrying the head box. Genzō and Tonami bow low to them as they depart. There is a long pause and when all are out of sight, they straighten up. Each is unable to talk as they are bursting with emotion. Genzō places his right hand on the floor. Tonami lifts her face and he gestures to the shōji yatai with his right hand. Understanding, Tonami rises and crosses to the shōji yatai, stumbling as she goes. She brings Kan Shūsai out from within and has him stand at up left center on the platform as she kneels, then bows, at his side. Genzō meanwhile goes to the door where he poses, holding the door post and looking about cautiously. He has left his sword on the floor. He shuts the door quickly, locking it, then stumbles to the center step overcome with emotion, and bows to the boy. He clasps his hands as if*) *thanking the gods and wipes a tear away. Tonami takes the boy off into the shōji yatai again. Genzō follows for a few steps then turns and moves to right center of the platform where he lifts a cylindrically shaped jug—some productions use an earthen tea-pot—lying on a small, round lacquer tray, and drinks the water in it. He drinks too quickly and is forced to cough sharply. He falls to the floor, coughing, at the top of the step center. Tonami has reemerged. She crosses to her husband and sits at his left side. As he straightens up he can barely talk for all the feeling welling up inside him. He is seated with one foot under him, the other on the step.)*

GIDAYŪ: (*During the above business*)

*Genzō sharply shuts the door.
No one speaks a word.
Genzō and Tonami sigh again and
    again
Glad to be rid of their great burden.
Their tension flees
And they thank the gods
Both those above and those below.*

GENZŌ: Praise be to the gods! The young lord's superior virtues shone forth and blinded Matsuō so that he was deceived by the substitution. We must rejoice, dear wife, that we have witnessed a miracle and that Kan Shūsai's blessed life will go on and on.

(*Makes a gesture of respect with his right hand in the direction of the shōji yatai, drops his hand, and raises his head*)

TONAMI: This was surely an extraordinary event! Do you suppose Lord Sugawara himself caused Matsuō to be deceived? Or maybe it was the glow from a golden Buddha that he saw instead of the head. Though the boys bore a resemblance it was like gilt to gold. How fortunate we are that this boy came our way. I'm so happy, so happy, so happy. I can't contain my tears.

(*She weeps, using her tenugui to wipe her tears and to gesture with. Genzō rises and they turn and kneel to pray to the altar hanging on the wall above the up center doorway.*)

GIDAYŪ:

At this moment of joy

(*Chiyo appears on the hanamichi*)

*And freedom from fear
Kotarō's mother, out of breath,
Comes knocking at the schoolhouse
    door.*

(*She runs down the hanamichi to the door of the schoolhouse. Her running is accented by the beating of the tsuke.*)

CHIYO: (*Trying to open the locked door. She looks nervously behind her to ascertain if she has been followed.*) Pardon me. It's me, the mother of the new boy. I've just returned. Please open up for me.

(*Genzō gestures to Tonami to leave. She crosses to the shōji yatai, stopping once or twice on her way to make sure that her husband is all right. He nods that he is. Tonami exits into the shōji yatai. Genzō comes down center, adjusts his kimono, smooths down his hair, picks up his sword, and holds it in his left hand. He steels himself and crosses to the door to let Chiyo in. The tension is building during this business. He begins to act slightly inebriated as if he drank too much at the headman's home.)*

GENZŌ: (*Readying himself*) I'll be right there, be right there.

CHIYO: Please open for me.

GENZŌ: Yes, yes, I'm coming now...

CHIYO: Please let me in.

GENZŌ: Yes, just a moment, just a moment.

(Genzō opens the door, holding his sword in his left hand. Chiyo enters and quickly closes the door behind her. She pauses at the door, Genzō to her left.)

CHIYO: (*Nervously*) Ha, ha.

GENZŌ: (*Countering in an equally phony laugh*) Ha, ha, ha, ha.

CHIYO: (*Continuing the attempt at casualness*) Ha, ha.

GENZŌ: (*Going along*) Ha, ha, ha, ha.

BOTH: Ha, ha, ha, ha, ha.

CHIYO: I am the mother of the new boy who entered your school earlier today.

GENZŌ: Oh, is that so? Well, please make yourself at home.

CHIYO: Thank you for your kindness.

GENZŌ: Please come right in.

(Genzō backs off to center where he kneels to bow to her. She removes her sandals, enters the room, and kneels, bowing, at right center. She places her fan on the floor before her, then looks at Genzō and he at her.)

I am Takebe Genzō.

CHIYO: I see. You are the schoolmaster himself, I take it? I've come for my naughty little boy. It's getting late so I'd appreciate it if I could take him home with me now.

GENZŌ: Surely. Please feel free to take him home with you, if you like.

CHIYO: (*Surprised*) Ah! It's all right for me to take him with me?

GENZŌ: Of course.

CHIYO: You mean I can... Then, where might he be?

GENZŌ: (*Thinking*) Why, he is inside having fun with the other children.

CHIYO: Ah! He is inside playing with the others? Er... Ko... Is he really? Well, if he is I'll just be taking him home with me.

GENZŌ: Yes, please do, if you like.

CHIYO: Kotarō, Kotarō, Kotarō...

(*Chiyo rises and moves toward center as if calling Kotarō, upstage. Genzō passes below her and makes as if he is going to draw his sword when her back is to him. He turns left and is going to draw but Chiyo senses this and looks back at him. They stare into each other's eyes and withdraw a step. He tries to cover by acting the innocent. He laughs, she laughs, he laughs, she laughs. They laugh together for several seconds. The laughter, like that when Chiyo entered the school, is obviously forced to cover the tension in the air. The timing of these laugh sequences is very difficult and can only be truly effective when done by seasoned performers.*)

GENZŌ: Ha, ha.

CHIYO: Ha, ha.

GENZŌ: Ha, ha.

CHIYO: Ha, ha.

BOTH: Ha, ha, ha, ha.

CHIYO: (*Turning once more to seek her son*) Well, I guess I'll take him home with me now. Where did you say he is?

GENZŌ: Within the house. Please do go in if you wish.

(*Indicates upstage center with his right hand*)

CHIYO: Pardon me.

(*They counter-cross, he to the left, she to the right. She faces upstage.*)

Kotarō, Kotarō.

GIDAYŪ:

> Genzō passes behind her
> And is about to end her life

(*Unseen by Chiyo, Genzō drops his right sleeve from his shoulder, then his left, revealing his under-kimono with its sleeves tied back by cords for action. He draws his sword, dropping the sheath, and attacks Chiyo.*)

With a single blow of his sword.

(*Genzō slices the air to either side of Chiyo three times as she dodges his blows. She wards him off and tosses her fan at him. He swings at it with his sword. She passes him and moves to Kotarō's desk and book box at right, takes the copy book placed there earlier by Tonami, and flings it at Genzō. It flies through the air, unfolding like a long scroll, and is caught on the outstretched sword. He throws the paper off and attacks again. Chiyo lifts the book box lid and moves to center. She sinks to the floor on one knee as he strikes at her but his blow falls on the lid which she holds up as a shield. They pose in a mie as the tsuke are struck. In this pose Chiyo is facing front on her left knee, the right one raised slightly. She holds the rectangular lid before her left shoulder, her right hand at its bottom edge and her left at its top. Genzō is at her left, his weight on his right foot leaning in toward the lid*) with his sword pointed on a diagonal toward the ground, its blade pressed against the lid.)

But Chiyo is no fool.
She deftly dodges to one side
And Genzō stands rooted to the spot.
Now he swings his blade with force
But Chiyo parries with her own
    child's desk
And Genzō's blow falls heavily on
    this.

CHIYO: Did my son prove worthy as a substitute for Kan Shūsai? Sa, sa, sa, saa, saa, saa.

(As she pronounces these stylized expletives, meaning something like "Well, well, well, etc.," she advances on her knees several steps to the left, forcing Genzō back with the lid of the desk. He moves backward one step on each "sa" with his sword held at his side. He lifts the sword again to strike. He pauses.)

Please tell me all that has transpired, as I am still unsure.

GIDAYŪ:

Genzō is startled by her words.

GENZŌ: It was with your consent?

(Chiyo runs to the book box where she places the lid. She lifts a prayer banner and shroud out of the box and crosses back to center with them, kneels, and shows them to Genzō. She holds them across both her outstretched arms.)

CHIYO: Indeed. Why else the shroud and prayer banner?

(Genzō looks inquiringly at her, sinks to his right knee, and lowers the point of his sword. Matsuō enters from right holding a pine branch with a poem card attached to it in his right hand. He carries a black hood in his left hand.)

GENZŌ: Then, to whose family do you belong?

GIDAYŪ:

At this point Matsuō
Appears in the doorway.

(Matsuō has changed his costume completely. He no longer wears elaborate, embroidered robes. He wears a black kimono, haori, and "outdoor" hakama [nobakama]. The purple headband is gone. His look is now refined and somewhat redolent of loneliness. He opens the door slightly but then closes it again. Matsuō opens the door with his left hand a bit, and tosses in the pine branch, then closes the door. The branch lands at right center. Genzō notices it, crosses below Chiyo to right, and picks it up, then sinks to his left knee to read it.)

GENZŌ:

The plum has flown
The cherry withered,
Wherefore should life

MATSUOMARU: (Completing the poem)

Be so heartless to the pine?

(He removes his long sword in its sheath and enters the room, removing his sandals and closing the door.)

Be heartened wife. Our boy has done his duty nobly.

(He throws the hood in the corner up right. Chiyo moves to stage left.)

GENZŌ: *(Moving quickly right)* It is Matsuō!

(Tosses branch to floor. Genzō attempts to strike at Matsuō but Matsuō holds him back by placing the tip of his sheathed sword against Genzō's chest, his right hand holding the hilt, his left on the sheathed portion. Matsuō faces front with the sword held across his body. Genzō, unable to move, poses with the sword held high in his right hand, his left hand high, palm forward. He stands facing the audience, mouth agape. He finds no opportunity to strike in this position.)

MATSUOMARU: Genzō, my friend, be patient. You will soon know all.

(Matsuō, crossing sideways, forces Genzō stage left. He removes the tip of his sheath from Genzō's chest, and moves past him, going below as Genzō countercrosses above. Genzō swings his sword at stage right while Matsuō at left switches the sword to his right hand, grips the hilt with his left, and places the point against Genzō's chest, forcing him right.)

GIDAYŪ:

Is this a dream?
Is this reality?
Are these man and wife?

(Matsuō removes his sword from Genzō's chest. He kneels on the floor before Genzō, then lets go of the hilt held in his left hand, takes it with his right, faces the hilt toward Genzō, places it on the floor before him, takes his short sword from his waist with his left hand, and turns it with his right hand so the hilt faces Genzō. It is placed alongside the long sword. During this Genzō once more swings his sword dramatically. He stands to Matsuō's right with the sword held in his right hand, pointed to the right, as he leans in on his left foot, the weight on it, toward Matsuō, his left hand held out to the left in a fist. Matsuō points emphatically to his swords with his right hand. He lifts his face sharply and he and Genzō stare at each other. Seated on his knees in a semierect posture, Matsuō holds the open palm of his right hand out toward Genzō in a kata of stopping him. Matsuō's left hand is on his lap. Pause. They perform a mie in these positions. They relax their postures and Genzō lowers his sword point. The tsuke are beaten for each emphatic movement during the sequence. Genzō, standing at Matsuō's right, seems very surprised. Matsuō moves backward a step or two and sits on a small boxlike stool placed behind him by a stage assistant. This is done to give the actor more height.)

*These thoughts race through
Genzō's baffled mind but
He speaks in measured tones.*

GENZŌ: Allow me to give you welcome.
Now, tell me, Matsuo, how you, whom up
to now I have considered my enemy, can have
made so abrupt an about-face.

GIDAYŪ:

And Matsuō replies.

MATSUOMARU: You are right to be
suspicious. As you well know, I and my two
brothers each served a different lord.
Unfortunately, I, Matsuomaru, entered the
service of Lord Shihei but when Shihei's thirst
for power grew uncontrollable I was forced
to become the enemy of my own father and
brothers. Even worse, I had to turn against
Lord Sugawara to whom my family has long
been indebted. At long last, thinking to be
rid of my attachment to the evil Shihei, I
feigned an illness and asked to be relieved
from service. This request was granted but
only on condition that I first come here and
identify the head of Kan Shūsai, Lord
Sugawara's son.

*(Genzō makes a threatening move but
Matsuō gestures to him to hear him out.)*

Knowing full well that you would never bring
yourself to slay your master's son, I imagined
that you would be willing to make use of a
substitute, if a suitable one could be found.
My wife agreed with me that we should now
pay back our debt of obligation to Lord
Sugawara and send our son here to be slain in

Kan Shūsai's stead. When I counted the
number of desks here before it was to see for
sure if my son had yet arrived. The world
knows me as the heartless Matsuo but would
one so heartless act as I have? Thus, the
poem's words should now be clear—
wherefore should life be so heartless to the
pine, the *matsu*?

GIDAYŪ:

*The world's opinion of him is
irksome indeed.*

*(Matsuō raises his left hand from his lap
and turns the palm upward, looking the
while at Genzō, then averts his eyes,
shuts them, waves his left hand, and
brings it down to his lap again.)*

MATSUOMARU: Can you imagine, Genzō?
My son has regained for me the esteem of
other men. A son *(closes eyes)* is man's
greatest blessing.

*(Genzō looks down, weeping. During the
following lines Genzō listens quietly
while unobtrusively removing the cords
tying back his under-kimono sleeves. He
slips the upper half of his kimono onto
his shoulders and adjusts his appearance
by smoothing out the kimono's folds. He
sheathes his sword after wiping its blade
with a wad of paper he also uses to dab
his tears.)*

GIDAYŪ:

*Chiyo tries in vain
To check her tears.*

CHIYO: "A son is man's greatest blessing."
These words are a fitting tribute to our boy.

(As she speaks she looks at the grave clothes lying on the ground before her.)

My heart pains me when I realize I scolded him for running after me before when we had to part.

(She dabs her tears with a small folded wad of paper held in her right hand.)

When I entered him into this fateful school he seemed to have a premonition of what lay in store for him. I said I was just going to the next village and, though I went as far as the road, I couldn't forget that I was leaving my child to be killed. I wanted to see his face once more, even if in death.

(Weeping, she places her right hand at her breast, her left on the floor. She then bows to Genzō and moves closer to her husband, behind him at his left shoulder, on a slight diagonal.)

GIDAYU:

*She mocks her feelings of lingering
   affection.
Was there ever in the world*

(she removes a purple wrapping cloth [furoshiki] from her sleeve)

*So sad a parting gift
As the steamed rice-cakes*

(crying freely, Chiyo tries to fight back her tears by taking the purple cloth and clenching it between her teeth, while pulling it with her hand; this conventional pose is held for several moments)

*She gave the little boy
On entering the school?*

CHIYO: If his birth and upbringing had been humble he would never have had to sacrifice his life for one he'd never met.

(She lifts his shroud and holds it to her as if it were a baby in her arms.)

GIDAYŪ:

*Her son, now dead,
Was born both fair and comely.
How sad his fate, how sad.*

CHIYO: They looked alike to the very smallpox marks upon their flesh.

(She smooths the shroud with her left hand.)

GIDAYŪ:

Overcome with grief

(she holds one side of the shroud to both cheeks, then places it before her on the floor.)

She gives in to her tears.

(Chiyo wipes her tears with the paper wad. Matsuō has sat through this with his eyes shut. Genzō has been sitting with

both hands on his lap, looking down. Toward the end he sheathes his sword, places it on the ground, and brings Matsuō's swords to him, placing them at Matsuō's right side. He then returns to right center. Tonami enters from the shōji yatai and crosses to Genzō's side, at his right. The stage is balanced with one man at either side of center, their wives behind them.)

Tonami now approaches
To console her.

(Before sitting, Tonami places a folded haori jacket on the floor below the platform, up right. Meanwhile, Matsuō puts his short sword in his obi and moves his long sword to his left side.)

TONAMI: My husband first got the idea of using your son as a substitute when he heard him say the words, "Dear master, I humbly beg your favor," at his side. I too was moved by the depths of his nobility. He was truly the son of noble parents.

(She bows, weeping.)

GIDAYŪ:

Their tears run freely
Along their cheeks.

MATSUOMARU: *(To his wife, with great feeling)* Please, my dear,

(he gestures with his right hand)

Do not grieve so. You have already given full vent to your tears in the confines of our home. I beg you to consider the feelings of Genzō and Tonami. Don't cry. I beg of you, don't cry. Genzō, my friend, I gave my boy instructions but tell me in your own words, please, how did he face his final moments?

(Matsuō sits with his hands on his lap, looking down. Chiyo's crying has gradually subsided.)

GENZŌ: *(Feelingly)* When he heard that he was to be slain as a substitute for the young lord, Kan Shūsai, he bravely stretched forth his neck.

MATSUOMARU: *(Struck by this, he lifts his face)* He didn't try to flee or hide?

GENZŌ: He even smiled a valiant little smile.

(His hands are clasped in his lap.)

MATSUOMARU: *(Overcome)* He smiled.

(Pause. He is amazed. He looks down, one hand on his lap, then says, to Chiyo)

He smiled. He smiled. Wife, Genzō says he smiled on meeting death.

(His right hand is shaking. He tries to laugh in his distinctively formalized manner, but sobs, equally formalized, break in.)

Well done, my son! Well done!

(*Pause*)

My clever lad, my splendid lad, my brave and upright little man.

(*With deep emotion*)

You have repaid your father's debt by your filial act and have performed most splendidly.

(*He stretches the last line, holding the vowels.*)

GIDAYŪ:

His thoughts lead back

(*Matsuō lifts the branch with the poem card, looks at it intently, moves his head sadly, and weeps quietly.*)

To Sakuramaru, his dead brother.

(*Holding the card in his hands, he closes his eyes.*)

MATSUOMARU: Even he who went before must feel envious of such a noble deed. My mind runs back to my poor dead brother, Sakuramaru, resting in his grave.

(*He takes a deep breath.*)

Sakuramaru.

(*Pause*)

Sakuramaru, Sakuramaru, Sakuramaru, Sakura, Sa, Sa, Sa, Sa...

(*His words get quicker and quicker as he chokes with emotion. Pause. He then bursts out, almost bawling, with his next line as he takes out the wad of paper from his bosom and slams it down at his right.*)

Genzō, my friend.

(*Pause*)

Forgive me!

(*He puts down the branch and, taking some sheets from the wad of paper, brings them to his face, looks up, and heaves his shoulders in great sobs.*)

GIDAYŪ:

*Unable to forget his sweet young
  brother
Matsuō cannot fight back the tears
  of sorrow.*

(*After some moments of weeping, Matsuō takes the paper from his face, dabs his eyes and nose, and replaces the paper in his kimono.*)

CHIYO: How tragic the fate of uncle and nephew.

GIDAYŪ:

*The sadness of these thoughts
Brings on a sudden outburst
And she sinks in tears of grief.
The sounds of grieving bring the
  prince,*

*Young Kan Shūsai, into their
presence.*

*(Kan Shūsai emerges from the shōji yatai
and crosses to center where he kneels, on
the platform. He is elaborately dressed
with a long red brocade overjacket, open
in the front to reveal trailing trousers
[nagabakama] and two front-tied obi,
one of white and one of turquoise. When
the others see him enter they restrain
their tears, adjust their postures, face
him, and bow their heads.)*

KAN SHŪSAI: Had I been told that someone
was to be killed in place of me I would not
have permitted it for I see how sad it makes
you all.

*(Matsuo lifts his face, brings both hands
to his eyes, wipes his tears. Genzō and
Tonami look at each other and bow.)*

GIDAYŪ:

*The tragic tears which drench
The sleeves of Matsuō and Chiyo
Now turn at once to tears
Of joy and heartfelt gratitude.*

MATSUOMARU: My lord, I have brought you
a present.

GIDAYŪ:

Matsuō gets to his feet.

*(He rises, crosses right, takes a whistle
from his left sleeve, opens the door,
walks out, blows the whistle once. He*

*raises his hand as a signal. From off
right, voices are heard.)*

PALANQUIN BEARERS: Coming!

GIDAYŪ:

*The bearers of the palanquin
Answer right away.*

*(Two palanquin bearers enter from right
with a palanquin. They place it about
midway between the doorway and the
wings at right, then leave.)*

*They carry on their burden
And place it by the school.
Its door is quickly opened
And from within emerges
The mother of the young lord,
The wife of Sugawara,
Lady Sono no Mae.*

*(Inside the room, Genzō and Tonami are
now facing right on their knees. When
the palanquin is in place Lady Sono no
Mae comes out from inside it and crosses
to the area of the door, below Matsuo.
During the entry of the palanquin the
doorway, which is portable, is moved
upstage to the side of the house wall by
two stage assistants. Another stage assistant removes all the sandals from the
doorway area. Lady Sono wears a long
purple overrobe [uchikake], a metallic
tiara in her hair, a white, red-lined kimono, and a black and gold brocade obi.
A purple patch is attached to the forepart
of her wig. She is a young and attractive
woman.)*

LADY SONO: Is that you, Kan Shūsai?

(*She speaks as she enters the room, acknowledging Genzō with a nod as she does so.*)

KAN SHŪSAI: Is that you, mother?

(*The boy moves a bit to his left. Lady Sono goes to him on the platform and stands next to him, then sits at his right. Matsuō enters after her and crosses left to his former position. Genzō and Tonami turn and bow low to the lady.*)

GIDAYŪ:

How strange this meeting of mother
   and child!
Genzō and his wife clasp their hands
   in thanks.

(*Genzō looks from Lady Sono to Matsuō.*)

GENZŌ: Though I asked everywhere, I could not discover Lady Sono's whereabouts.

MATSUOMARU: She was hidden in North Saga but when Shihei's men learned where she was and threatened to capture her I disguised myself as a mountain priest and helped her escape their clutches.

(*Genzō and Tonami nod. They bow and Tonami rises, goes to Chiyo, takes the burial materials from her, and exits up center.*)

We then made our way to Kawachi. Well, my wife, Kotarō's body will be laid in that palanquin and we will conduct his funeral services.

CHIYO: Yes.

(*As the gidayū chants, the funeral ceremonies are enacted. This pantomime takes about seven minutes in performance. After Tonami has left, stage assistants enter and help Matsuō and Chiyo remove their outer garments, revealing white satin mourning kimono and pale green obi beneath. Matsuō wears a pale green, stiff-winged vest [kataginu] and matching hakama over his kimono. Matsuō's small stool is removed. Chiyo takes off her hair ornaments.*)

GIDAYŪ:

As the noble Chiyo answers
The wise Tonami enters
Bearing in her arms
The sad remains.
She places these in the palanquin.

(*Tonami enters with the headless body. It is dressed in the clothes worn by Kotarō when he was admitted to the school. The white shroud is placed over the body. She carries it off to the palanquin and places it inside. She then takes the haori jacket she carried in earlier and helps Genzō into it. Tonami now exits up center but comes right on again, with props for the funeral service. These are a small metal*) pan and hemp reeds placed within it in a neat pyramid and a small flint box. The pan is placed near where the door formerly was.)

Kotarō's parents remove
Their outer garments,
Displaying as they do so
Their firm and grim resolve
Since underneath their robes of
    black
The white of mourning is disclosed.

(By now, Matsuō and Chiyo's change has been completed. Genzō turns his attention from Tonami to Matsuō and Chiyo and, seeing their change, is visibly surprised. Matsuō puts his short sword in his obi, takes a rosary out of his right sleeve, and holds it in his right hand. Genzō goes out up center. Tonami strikes a flint and takes a short stick, which is glowing from the sparks, to the pan, which she proceeds to light. The hemp flares up. Genzō comes out carrying lacquer-ware incense equipment which he places on Kotarō's desk. He lifts the desk, crosses center with it, and places it humbly before Lady Sono and Kan Shūsai. Genzō returns to his position at right while the lady takes a pinch of incense and drops it in the burner. She then clasps her hands in prayer. A similar action is performed in turn by the other characters. Tonami takes the incense from up center and places it before Matsuō, who bows, then does the action of placing incense in the burner. He wipes away his tears, then poses with his rosary as if in prayer. Weeping, he moves the desk to Chiyo, who first bows to Lady Sono, then rises, and moves closer to the desk. After putting incense in the burner, she sinks to her side, overcome. She keeps herself bent over during most of the rest of the scene. She holds a white rosary in her hands with which she prays, hands clasped, just before putting the incense in. Tonami crosses left, gets the desk, and brings it to Genzō, who rises and moves to it, holding the incense up in the direction of the palanquin. Tonami takes the desk and places it before the palanquin, does the business with the incense, and then places the desk with the burner on it inside the palanquin. She reenters the house and, together with Genzō, crosses left where she takes up a position on her knees before the shōji yatai, facing center with fingertips on the ground before her. Genzō stands at left center, right leg slightly bent at the knee, left one straight and to the left, holding his sword before him. Kan Shūsai and his mother have risen and Lady Sono stands behind her son and to his right with her hands placed on his shoulders. Matsuō and Chiyo cross left, meanwhile, and Chiyo sits on one knee, the right, the other being slightly raised. She faces down right on a slight diagonal. Matsuō, at left center, holds his sheathed sword in his right hand, his left leg slightly bent at the knee, his right leg straight. He slowly brings his left hand across in front of his body and brings it up to shoulder height,

*holding it out as if displaying Kan Shū-
sai, who stands just upstage above him.
The sword in his right hand is held just
below the hilt. Matsuō holds it in such a
way as to suggest that he is restraining
Chiyo from leaving her position to go to
the body in the palanquin. His eyes are
focused to the right, though his body
position leans toward the left. The tsuke
are beaten. This tableau is held until the
curtain is closed. During the above
action, the gidayū chants. Since some
productions allow these last lines to be
spoken by the actors, the usual break-
down of the lines is indicated by the
names in parentheses. The bracketed
words are those heard in productions
where the gidayū recites all the lines; they
are cut in other instances.)*

GIDAYŪ:

(*Lady Sono*) *The lad embarks upon
His journey to the school of Hades.*
(*Matsuō*) *His master speeds him on
   his way
With fervent prayers of*
(*Genzō*) *"Praise be to the Lord
   Buddha,*

Praise be to the Lord Buddha."
(*Tonami*) *His spirit is commended
Unto the god of children,*
(*Chiyo*) *Lord Jizō Bosatsu.
And in the waters of*
(*Matsuō*) *Death's fateful river*
(*All*) *He writes his final lesson.*
[*The child who practiced all his
   letters
Had a short and tragic life.
Now nothing can be done to bring
   him back.
Who, tomorrow night, will be at his
   side?
The grieving parents think
Of his journey down to Hades,
Of the treacherous Sword Mountain
He must climb along the way
As he passes on to Hades.
Are they dreaming?
Is this reality?
The parents soon depart
Taking their son home again.*]
(*The ki sound is heard. The striped
   curtain is pulled closed from left
   to right.*)

CURTAIN

Figure 28. Umeō and Sakuramaru meet at Yoshidaya Shrine (*Sakuramaru,* Sawamura Kiyoshirō; *Umeō,* Nakamura Tomijūrō).

Figure 29. Umeō lifts his hat slightly (*Umeō,* Nakamura Tomijūrō).

Figure 30.   Umeō reveals his face as he cuts a mie; since the photo was taken at a dress rehearsal, the stage assistant's face was uncovered (*Umeō,* Nakamura Tomijūrō).

Figure 31.   Umeō spreads his hands wide to stop the carriage (*Umeō,* Nakamura Tomijūrō).

Figure 32. Sugiomaru strikes a defiant mie (*Sugiomaru,* Oka-mura Seitarō).

Figure 33. Umeō prepares for battle as he spits into one hand, then the other (*Umeō,* Nakamura Tomijūrō).

Figure 34. Sakuramaru performs a mie without accompanying sound from the tsuke (*Sakuramaru,* Sawamura Kiyoshirō).

Figure 35. Umeō and Sakuramaru pose after knocking down two of Shihei's men (*Sakuramaru,* Sawamura Kiyoshirō; *Umeō,* Nakamura Tomijurō).

Figure 36. Matsuō executes a Genroku mie (*Matsuō,* Nakamura Kichiemon).

Figure 37. Matsuō does a "stone-throwing" mie (*Matsuō,* Nakamura Kichiemon).

Figure 38. The itsu no gashira pose (*Sakuramaru,* Nakamura Fukusuke; *Matsuō,* Ichikawa Omezō; *Umeō,* Nakamura Tomijūrō).

Figure 39. Ichikawa Yaozō as Shihei.

Figure 40. Matsuō moves in a shuffle step as he prepares to fight his brothers (*Matsuō,* Nakamura Kichiemon).

Figure 41. The triplets confront each other angrily, with Umeō and Matsuō almost nose to nose (*Sakuramaru,* Onoe Baikō; *Umeō,* Onoe Shōroku; *Matsuō,* Matsumoto Kōshirō).

Figure 42.   In the final tableau, Umeō
strikes a Genroku mie (*Umeō,* Nakamura
Tomijūrō).

Figure 43. Yodarekuri shows the other boys his cartoon of a priest.

Figure 44. Kotarō begs his mother not to leave him (*Chiyo,* Nakamura Ganjiro; *Kotarō,* Nakamura Kōji; *Tonami,* Nakamura Shikan).

Figure 45. Yodarekuri and Sansuke mimic their masters.

Figure 46. Genzō returns via the hanamichi (*Genzō*, Kataoka Nizaemon).

Figure 47. Genzō: "You're a splendid boy, aren't you?" (*Tonami,* Nakamura Shikan; *Kotarō,* Nakamura Kōji; *Genzō,* Kataoka Nizaemon).

Figure 48. Tonami puts her left hand on Genzō's lap, holding her tenugui in her right hand; he puts his arm around her shoulder (*Tonami,* Nakamura Shikan; *Genzō,* Kataoka Nizaemon).

Figure 49. Genzō holds his sheathed sword across Tonami's body, preventing her from going any farther (*Genzō,* Kataoka Nizaemon; *Tonami,* Nakamura Shikan).

Figure 50. Matsuō and Gemba inspect Yodarekuri; Gemba hits the boy on his head with a fan (*Matsuō,* Matsumoto Kōshirō; *Gemba,* Ichikawa Yaozō).

Figure 51. Genzō bumps into Matsuō and then withdraws several steps to the left, as if ready to draw (*Matsuō,* Matsumoto Kōshirō; *Genzō,* Kataoka Nizaemon; *Tonami,* Nakamura Shikan).

Figure 52. Matsuō does the bureimonome mie (*Tonami,* Nakamura Shikan; *Matsuō,* Matsumoto Kōshirō).

Figure 53. Ichikawa Sadanji as Genzō.

Figure 54. Matsuō begins the head inspection; he removes the lid from the box and cuts a mie (*Genzō,* Kataoka Nizaemon; *Matsuō,* Matsumoto Kōshirō).

Figure 55. Matsuō stares at the head (*Genzō,* Kataoka Nizaemon; *Matsuō,* Matsumoto Kōshirō).

Figure 56. Unable to look any longer, he replaces the lid on the box; he raises his shaking right hand and completes a mie (*Genzō,* Kataoka Nizaemon; *Matsuō,* Matsumoto Kōshirō).

Figure 57. Ichikawa Danjūrō as Matsuō performing his family's traditional kata for the moment depicted in Fig. 56 (*Genzō,* Ichikawa Sadanji; *Matsuō,* Ichikawa Danjūrō; *Gemba,* Nakamura Fukusuke).

Figure 58. Genzō and Chiyo laugh nervously as he prepares to strike at her (*Genzō,* Kataoka Nizaemon; *Chiyo,* Nakamura Ganjirō).

Figure 59. Genzō's blade is stopped by the lid of the book box held by Chiyo (*Chiyo,* Nakamura Ganjirō; *Genzō,* Kataoka Nizaemon).

Figure 60. Matsuō holds back the baffled Genzō with the tip of his sheath (*Matsuō,* Matsumoto Kōshirō; *Genzō,* Kataoka Nizaemon).

Figure 61. Placing his swords on the floor, Matsuō prevents Genzō from striking (*Genzō,* Kataoka Nizaemon; *Matsuō,* Matsumoto Kōshirō).

Figure 62. Matsuō bursts into tears (*Matsuō,* Matsumoto Kōshirō; *Chiyo,* Nakamura Ganjirō).

Figure 63. Tonami enters bearing the dead body of Kotarō (*Tonami,* Nakamura Shikan; *Lady Sono no Mae,* Nakamura Matsue; *Kan Shūsai,* Iwase Kōshirō; *Matsuō,* Matsumoto Kōshirō; *Chiyo,* Nakamura Ganjirō). Note the stage assistants helping Matsuō and Chiyo remove their outer garments as they prepare for the funeral ceremony.

Figure 64. Chiyo, having burned incense, prays for Kotarō's soul (*Lady Sono no Mae,* Nakamura Matsue; *Kan Shūsai,* Iwase Kōshirō; *Matsuō,* Matsumoto Kōshirō; *Chiyo,* Nakamura Ganjirō).

Figure 65.   The final tableau (*Lady Sono no Mae,* Nakamura Matsue; *Chiyo,* Nakamura Ganjirō; *Kan Shūsai,* Iwase Kōshirō; *Matsuō,* Matsumoto Kōshirō; *Genzō,* Kataoka Nizaemon; *Tonami,* Nakamura Shikan).

Shunkan

3

(*Heike Nyogo no Shima*)
A Kabuki Adaptation of a Puppet Play by
Chikamatsu Monzaemon
The Scene on Devil's Island (*Kikaigashima no ba*)

BACKGROUND TO THE PLAY

Shunkan is a title given to the scene at Kikai-gashima ("Devil's Island") in the five-act play called *The Heike and The Island of Women* (*Heike Nyogo no Shima*). Chikamatsu Monzaemon (1653-1724), generally conceded to be the greatest playwright in Japan's history, wrote the original version for the puppet theater in 1719. Its first performance was at Osaka's Takemoto Theatre but a year later it was produced in a Kabuki adaptation starring Anegawa Shinshirō at Osaka's Naka Theatre. Following Ichikawa Danzō III's (1709-1772) success with the role of Shunkan in the mid-eighteenth century, the Kikaigashima scene, which formed the major part of Act II, was separated from the rest of the play and became a frequently performed independent number. Full-length productions of the play are no longer given, though the National Theatre revived a long-neglected scene in its 1967 production—starring Nizaemon XIII. One or two other scenes have been revived since.

The subject matter of the Kikaigashima scene long had been familiar to the Japanese. It forms a chapter in the famous chronicle, *The Tale of the Heike* (*Heike Monogatari*) and was dramatized in a well-known Nō play, *Shunkan*. Chikamatsu's additions to the old story, which is based on historical fact, include the love affair of Naritsune and Chidori, unusual in that they are from entirely different social strata, and in the compassion shown them by Shunkan, whose sacrifice stems, in part, from his sympathy for their plight. In a way, the play is about the sublime love of Shunkan and his wife Azumaya for each other. Shunkan's sacrifice allows him to demonstrate the perfection of his love just as his wife was able to do the same by refusing the advances of the all-powerful Kiyomori. This material was treated by later playwrights but by none so effectively as Chikamatsu.

Shunkan was one of the works that was performed on Kabuki's recent European tours. Kawatake Toshio, who traveled with the actors, has written that it was, of all the plays performed, the most consistently successful, in Europe and the Soviet Union, receiving twelve or thirteen curtain calls at each performance. This he attributes to the play's universality and basic humanism. It was less taxing to understand than other Kabuki plays, where a fundamental knowledge of Japanese customs and attitudes seemed to have been more essential.

PLOT AND KATA

The Heike and the Island of Women tells the story of Taira no Kiyomori's last years as an arrogant ruler until his death. The reference to "the island of women" in the main title is an allusion to the third-act scene of the original in which the beautiful Lady Tokiwa lures man after man into her palace.

Depicted in *The Heike and The Island of Women* is the world of the Japanese middle ages when the Heike (or Taira) clan fought for supremacy with the Genji (or Minamoto). Woven into the play are such famous figures as Kiyomori, Lady Tokiwa, Shigemori, Ushiwakamaru (later called Yoshitsune), and, of course, Shunkan. Early scenes show the attempts of the powerful Lord Kiyomori to take as his mistress, Azumaya, wife of the exiled priest, Shunkan. Azumaya commits suicide rather than submit to Kiyomori. Shunkan and his cohorts have been sent to the distant island of Kikaigashima for their part in a plot against Kiyomori. The birth of a child to the Empress results in a general amnesty being granted but Kiyomori refuses to pardon Shunkan. Another powerful minister, Shigemori, the son of Kiyomori, takes it upon himself to grant the priest a pardon. *Shunkan* shows what happens when news of the pardons reaches the exiles.

Shunkan takes place on the desolate island of Kikaigashima (known today as Iwo Jima), where the exiles have been living for three years.

On the Gidayū and Sound Effect Music. As is normally the case with Kabuki adaptations of puppet plays, a gidayū chanter and shamisen player provide emotional background music throughout the performance. The play also makes frequent use of the large drum (ōdaiko), situated in the stage right music room, to simulate the sound of waves. *Sazanami* ("ripples") is the style of beating which accompanies emotional sequences whereas *namioto* ("sound of waves") is played for major exits and entrances and important moments of stage action.

When the main curtain is pulled aside, another curtain, the billowy light blue one called asagimaku, fills the inner proscenium. Some productions use a curtain with wave designs on it (the *namimaku* or "wave curtain"). When the asagimaku is removed the audience is shown the stage setting, a barren seashore backed by an expanse of blue sea. At center is Shunkan's pathetic hut.

After some preliminary gidayū recitatif, Shunkan makes his entrance from behind a cluster of rocks upstage right.

Shunkan's Entrance and Appearance. Depending on the actor playing the title role, his entrance manner takes a variety of forms. Nakamura Kanzaburō XVII, upon whom the description in the translation is based, varied his entrance method in the course of the May 1975 Kabuki Theatre production. During the early days of the run he entered as described in the text but later in the month he made his entrance down right, below the rocks. Certain actors like to enter from stage left while others prefer to come in on the hanamichi. The old method, no longer used, had Shunkan appear on the small elevator trap (seridashi) at center. A few actors experimented with several of these entrance possibilities. Thus, Kichiemon's early productions had him entering on the hanamichi, but later years saw him make his entry from stage left. Ichikawa En'ō (1888-1963) sometimes entered on the hanamichi, sometimes entered from stage right, and sometimes was discovered when the curtain opened. A variation of the latter is played by Nakamura Kan'emon III (1901-) who, instead of being seated within his hut at the opening, as is usual, sits on a rock before the hut with his staff propped against a shoulder. The variations in this small matter of Shunkan's first entrance offer clear evidence of the wide lattitude in the selection of kata of which Kabuki actors may avail themselves.

The setting itself may vary somewhat from one production to another. Ganjirō I provided the most radical departure in his version. He did away with the hut entirely, though the other scenic elements were for the most part retained.

Shunkan appears wearing a bedraggled kimono. He is bearded. The costume used to be quite stylized, in the manner of the grand history plays (ōjidai) set in the years prior to the rise of the Minamoto and Heike factions. In this old style, Shunkan wore a brocade patchwork kimono padded with cotton and a thick maruguke obi (like that worn by the triplets in *Pulling the Carriage Apart*), tied in front with a large bow. His wig and beard were of long, white hair. Ichikawa Danzō VII made the costume more realistic, having Shunkan dress in a kimono supposedly made of paper (the *kamiko*) from discarded sutras. Another realistic garment modern actors wear in the role is of rough hemp torn here and there to suggest the character's suffering.[1]

Matsumoto Kōshirō VIII has these interesting things to say of the character's costume:

The costuming of the role creates a problem for me as I have recently put on weight. The character of Shunkan, though, must be made to appear emaciated and weak. Thus, I don't follow the costume approach of my teacher, Kichiemon I. I have changed from his conventional robe of tatters and wear a slightly more realistic kimono. I also do not make up the face to look emaciated, according to custom, and may, perhaps, create too strong an effect as a result.... A realistic, thin-type face would be of little use for me.[2]

Kōshirō goes on to note that the role of Shunkan is very demanding and, even in November, he is drenched with sweat in mid-performance. Kichiemon perspired profusely and, during Chidori's big scene later in the play, used to go offstage to change his costume. Kōshirō states that he does not sweat as much as Kichiemon and keeps the same costume on throughout. "Further," he writes, "if the costume looks thoroughly worn out at the very end it will probably be quite effective-looking, won't it?"[3]

With regard to Shunkan's makeup, some realistically inclined actors allow their teeth to look slightly soiled, the result of three years of privation on a barren island. Kan'emon, though, feels the teeth should be clean. Then, he notes, when the teeth glisten faintly at the end of the play as Shunkan smiles (in his interpretation), the play's theme of hope and love will be enhanced.[4]

1. See Kawajiri Seitan, *Engi no Densō* (*Acting Traditions*) (Tokyo, 1956).

2. *Jōen Shiryōshū* (n.d.), p. 38.
3. Ibid., p. 39.
4. *Omocha Bako* (*The Toy Box*) (Tokyo, 1970), pp. 204-205.

Shunkan's age has been a frequent source of controversy. According to the historical accounts, he was only in his mid-thirties when he died. Yet many actors play him as if he were aged. This was emphasized in the old productions by a white wig and beard. Among actors who play Shunkan as relatively young are Kan'emon and Nizaemon. The latter points out that Shunkan resigns all hope of returning to the world upon hearing of his wife's death. His obvious passion for her would be inappropriate for an elderly man.[5] Though Kan'emon feels Shunkan is still in his early thirties, he acts the role with a certain feeling of increased age which he justifies on the basis of the three years of bitter suffering Shunkan has endured.[6]

Shunkan enters his hut and begins to cook some seaweed in an abalone shell (some versions use an iron pot). The gidayū informs the audience that his friends, Naritsune and Yasuyori, are coming to see him. Although most productions today omit it, Shunkan has a long soliloquy (*jūkai*), which he delivers prior to the entrance of his friends. A number of critics bewail the omission though it has been restored by the Zenshin-za company in their production.

Acting Shunkan. The role of Shunkan has been a specialty of actors in the Ichi-

kawa Danzō line ever since the 1764 production of Danzō III. Actors in this line were responsible for most of the play's important kata. Kichiemon I, himself a master player of the role, freely admitted to his reliance on the standard Danzō kata. Other famous modern actors of Shunkan were Ichikawa Danshirō II (1857-1922), Chūsha VII, and En'ō I. Among living actors, Kōshirō VIII, Kanzaburō XVII, Nizaemon XIII, and Kan'emon III are famous for their portrayals. The latter, a member of the progressive Zenshin-za company for many years, has written prolifically about his experiences in creating the role.[7]

Dōmoto Masaki, a contemporary critic, provides an extremely detailed comparison of the Zenshin-za production starring Kan'emon with that of Kōshirō VIII. He views Kōshirō's work as typical of most Kabuki productions presented at the major Kabuki theaters. Masaki criticizes such presentations as being overly conservative and hidebound by their adherence to kata that are insufficiently understood by the actors who go on performing them year after year. On the other hand, the Zenshin-za's work is seen as a vital, refreshing, and altogether necessary reexamination of the classics in light of contemporary realities. Its careful attention to detail can be seen in Dōmoto's thorough account. In justifying his contempt for the Kōshirō production and his delight with that of the Zenshin-za, Dōmoto points to a number of factors, including these:

---

5. See Koike Shōtarō, "Heike Nyogo no Shima Saiken" ("A Close Look at 'The Heike and The Island of Women'"), *Kabuki,* XVI (1972), 145.

6. *Kabuki no Engi* (*Kabuki Acting*) (Tokyo, 1974), pp. 105-106.

7. Ibid.

1. The Zenshin-za uses a director to provide a unifying approach; the Kōshirō version (performed with the Kichiemon troupe), as is common in Kabuki, does not.

2. The Zenshin-za bases its entire approach on carefully established classically oriented criteria; the Kōshirō production has no discernible standards to go by.

3. The Zenshin-za, in returning to the classical piece, determined its contemporary significance and developed the production with this idea at its core; the Kōshirō version was completely lacking in its grasp of the play's classical or contemporary significance.[8]

Dōmoto's comments, made almost two decades ago, still bear the ring of truth. A recent Zenshin-za production of *Shunkan* clearly had improved on the play's staging possibilities by incorporating a more dynamic tempo and a greater attention to ensemble playing. Especially exciting was the fight scene between Shunkan and Senō. Whereas the battle in the Kanzaburō version had a stately, almost perfunctory quality to it, the Zenshin-za had captured something of the excitement and sense of danger that must once have prevailed in such Kabuki encounters. Another sign of the progressive Zenshin-za approach was in their use, at alternating performances, of a male and female performer to play the role of Chidori. Actresses are still taboo in the more conservative Kabuki troupes.

Yasuyori and Naritsune enter on the hanamichi. They carry baskets suggesting that they have been gathering shells.

Two Hanamichi. In some productions two hanamichi are employed, with Yasuyori entering on the temporary hanamichi and Naritsune on the regular one. In such productions they engage in dialogue (cut in the present version) from the hanamichi with Shunkan on the stage so that their words are spoken from three widely separated sections of the theater, creating an interesting effect. In the Zenshin-za production and that directed by Takechi Tetsuji, Yasuyori appears by entering over the rocks at right while Naritsune enters on the hanamichi holding a bunch of seaweed. The first lines are spoken with Yasuyori on top of the rock and Naritsune on the hanamichi.

After the three men have greeted one another happily, Yasuyori announces that Lord Naritsune has taken a local diver-girl, Chidori, for his wife. Yasuyori moves to the hanamichi to call the girl.

A Variant Kata. There is also a kata wherein Naritsune goes to call Chidori rather than Yasuyori. A few critics feel this is more appropriate, given the relationship between the couple.

Chidori comes in on the hanamichi bashfully, runs out again, and then returns. She is

8. See *Koten to no Taiketsu* (*Confrontation With the Classics*) (Tokyo, 1959), pp. 330-331.

introduced to Shunkan and the group prepares to hold a nuptial ceremony. Water will replace the traditional wine and an abalone shell will serve for a cup of lapis lazuli. Shunkan rises to do a ceremonial dance but, overcome with weakness, falls laughing to the ground. He uses a pine branch lying on the floor as a fan during his dance.

The Dance "Fan." Some actors use a branch of the "eight-fingered-leaf shrub" (*yatsude*). In Takechi's experimental production, Naritsune carried a tattered chūkei-style fan. Shunkan borrowed this fan for his dance. The Zenshin-za completely omits Shunkan's dance. Instead, Yasuyori performs a lively one, using a bamboo tube and a shell borrowed from Chidori, while everyone else claps and enjoys themselves.

As they are celebrating, Yasuyori notices a large boat approaching the island. The boat (a miniature maneuvered by unseen stage hands) soon appears on the horizon and moves across the rear of the stage.

Appearance of the Boat. At this point in some productions the stage makes a half-revolve, taking the characters out of the audience's sightlines. The Zenshin-za method is to have Yasuyori stumble while dancing, then notice the boat at the same moment. Instead of the boat moving across the rear of the stage, it arrives immediately at left. In the old days a small boat actually appeared out in the audience, moving along the edge of the balcony seats, but Danzō VII, believing that this small property diverted the spectators' eyes from the actors, had the business cut and merely acted as if the boat could be seen off in the distance beyond the audience. En'ō I revived the old business, but when the audience laughed, being unfamiliar with the convention, he cut it out again, midway in the play's run.

The overjoyed group goes behind some rocks at right to await the boat, which they hope is carrying their pardons. At stage left, the large prow of the boat moves into view and the sailors on it jump off and use a hawser to secure the boat to a rock.

Arrival of the Boat. A few productions (Chūsha, Danshirō, En'o, etc.) have had the boat enter from the right, instead. In such cases the actors enter from the boat but take up their usual positions at the left. One criticism of this method is that the progress across the stage looks unattractive and takes up too much time.[9]

The chief envoy, Senō, descends from the boat and takes a position at left.

Appearance of the Envoys. The original version of *Shunkan* has the two envoys, Senō and Tanzaemon, enter here together. Nowadays, though, the usual method is to have Tanzaemon enter later in the play when Shunkan is already in

9. Miyake, *Kabuki o Mirume*, p. 162.

dire distress. Since it would be too difficult, says one critic, for the actor of Tanzaemon to sit motionless during Shunkan's torment, it seems the kata was changed accordingly.[10]

Senō calls for Naritsune and Yasuyori, who come forth from behind the rocks. Shunkan, though not summoned, comes out too. Senō announces the pardon of Naritsune and Yasuyori. Shunkan, not hearing his name, is dazed. He demands to see the official document and peruses it closely. Terribly upset, he realizes he alone has been refused a pardon.

Examining the Pardon. Shunkan's acting as he examines the document is a high point of the role. The kata for the perusal range from the relatively complex, such as that described in the text, to the artlessness of Ichimura Takenojō IV, who merely took the papers and wept. Kan'emon as Shunkan looks at the pardon, then demands the wrapping paper in which it was carried; Senō throws the paper at him. Shunkan places the two papers side by side comparing them, puts them together, and examines them again. On his "nothing" lines he shows them to his friends and, while repeating the word, allows his hands to tremble violently.

Finally, the other envoy, Tanzaemon, descends from the boat.

Tanzaemon Enters. The actor, Arashi Yoshisaburō V, claimed that in his view,

Tanzaemon does not appear until this point because he feels his function to be an unsavory one, having no exact knowledge of the message he bears. According to this interpretation, it is only when he breaks the seal that he learns of the message's contents.[11]

Tanzaemon reads a pardon from Lord Shigemori in which Shunkan is permitted to return to the mainland, though not to the capital itself. The exiles are beyond themselves with joy and proceed to move toward the ship, taking Chidori with them. Senō sees her going and cruelly stops her. He says only three persons are authorized to leave the island and that the girl may not go. Naritsune begs Senō to allow the girl to accompany him at least as far as the first port of call but this is refused. Naritsune resolves to stay behind with his wife and the other exiles demand to be left behind with him. If one can't go, then none will go. Tanzaemon intercedes on the exiles' behalf but Senō is adamant.

Senō tells Shunkan that the latter's wife, Azumaya, was killed for refusing Lord Kiyomori's advances.

Senō's Disclosure. Longer versions of the play than that translated here relate that Shunkan's mother committed suicide and his son disappeared because of Kiyomori's pressure. Actors of Shunkan vary in the degree to which Senō's disclosure prompts their subsequent sacrificial gesture to remain behind on the island. Some actors justify the sacrifice

---

10. Koike, "Heike Nyogo no Shima Saiken," p. 149.

11. Ibid.

on the basis of a deep feeling of sympathy for Chidori, combined with a feeling of desperation following Senō's remarks. Kichiemon I wrote, however, that "it is because of his feeling of sympathy and pity that Shunkan [subsequently] slays Senō. If this is not the way it is done, Shunkan appears to murder Senō purely out of desperation, which is inappropriate to his character and uninteresting."[12]

The Zenshin-za, wishing to stress that the motive for Shunkan's decision to kill Senō is the death of Azumaya, without whom life for the priest has no purpose, added several new lines to the work to clarify this point. These lines relate that Senō himself was ultimately responsible for Shunkan's wife's death, thus making it requisite that Senō be killed by Shunkan in revenge. Senō's new dialogue reveals that Azumaya had taken sanctuary at a temple but that he, Senō, learning of this, forcibly removed her and presented her to Kiyomori as a "gift." This precipitated Azumaya's secretly drawing her dagger and stabbing herself to death.[13]

The three exiles are now forced on board the boat. Senō injures Chidori by jabbing her with his elbow.

Chidori's Injury. In an alternate kata, Senō pulls Chidori away from the boat so sharply that she falls and strikes her side on a rock. In the Zenshin-za production she is kicked off the boarding plank by Senō and falls to the ground.

After all have gone on board, Chidori has the stage to herself as she bewails her lot.

The Kudoki. Chidori's solo is technically known as *kudoki* or *sawari,* terms which refer to a scene, usually of a female's lamentation, in a Kabuki version of a puppet play. In such scenes the actor speaks and moves in time to the rhythm of the gidayū shamisen. This specific example is called *ama nagori* ("the diver's farewell"). The basic kata for the sequence are fairly standard, regardless of the actors, but those used by Arashi Yoshio and others who play the role for the Zenshin-za differ to some degree.[14]

Shunkan makes his way off the boat and entreats the girl to take his place. He begs the envoys to allow the substitution but Senō, of course, strongly refuses. Shunkan sneaks up to Senō and grabs one of his swords.

Stealing the Sword. Actors are divided on whether Shunkan should draw the long sword or the short sword. Takechi has written,

> Those who support the use of the long sword say that Shunkan is very weak so he would take his adversary's greatest weapon whereas those who back the short sword say that there is no reason

12. Kawatake, *Nakamura Kichiemon,* p. 387.
13. *Koten to no Taiketsu,* pp. 343-344.

14. Ibid., p. 345.

for Shunkan to be able to take a long sword from one as formidable as Senō. Also, pulling out the long sword is difficult but removing the short sword is simple; moreover, the weakened Shunkan would be able to use a short sword with ease.... However, the short sword theory is not conclusive and since there is also a basis for those who favor the long sword, it would be best to follow the original script's indication and have Shunkan use the long sword.[15]

Senō is immediately wounded in the right shoulder in the present version though there are actors who wound Senō in the left shoulder instead. Wounding him in the right is better as it allows him to battle while holding his right shoulder with his left hand.

During the ensuing battle Senō asks Tanzaemon for help. Tanzaemon refuses on the grounds that to do so would be to overstep his authority. Since Senō gave a similar reason for his own behavior earlier in the play, Tanzaemon's remark is seen as an example of ōmu or "parroting," a conventional device for adding irony to a play. The present ōmu is not in Chikamatsu's original play but was added by Kabuki actors.

The Fight Scene Kata. The kata for the battle between Senō and Shunkan differ somewhat according to the performers.

This is especially true of Chidori's business. In some versions she interferes by using her rake (as in the translation), her apron (by throwing it over Senō's head), her basket (by tossing it in his face), and her teeth (by biting his hand).

Shunkan finally overcomes Senō and is about to execute the *coup de grace* when Tanzaemon interrupts and pleads with him not to do so.

The Kan'u Mie. On the gidayū speech, "I will once again become/An exile on Kikaigashima," many actors of Shunkan perform a famous mie pose. It was omitted, however, in the version described in the translation. Kichiemon I also did not perform this mie. The pose involves Shunkan's thrusting the point of his sword into the ground, one foot extended, while gripping his beard in one hand. The variations of the pose basically depend on which hand holds the sword, which the beard. It is called the *Kan'u mie* and is almost identical with the kan'u mie performed in Chikamatsu's *The Battles of Coxinga* (*Kokusenya Kassen*), from which it is derived. Kan'u is the Japanese name for a famous Chinese general about whom an old Kabuki play, *Kan'u,* was written. Kōshirō and Kan'emon are among actors who still perform the mie. When it is executed the words spoken here by the gidayū are said by Shunkan.

Shunkan disregards Tanzaemon's plea and kills the evil envoy. Chidori refuses to let

15. *Kari no Tayori,* p. 176.

Shunkan stay behind in her place. He has to force her to board the boat. The boat is prepared for departure as Shunkan calls out farewells to his friends. Tanzaemon raises his fan in a gesture of respect for Shunkan.

Tanzaemon's Gesture. Arashi Yoshisaburō V changed this business. He made the change after noticing in the course of rehearsals that Tanzaemon must demonstrate how moved he is by Shunkan's humanity and, wishing to make him some gesture of respect, passed the fan to Naritsune, sensing the father-son relationship between the pair.[16]

The boat moves off left. Shunkan sadly follows the path of the departing boat with his eyes. He tries to run after it but is repulsed by the waves. The stage revolves and a huge rock comes into position at center. Shunkan climbs to its top and looks off over the spectators' heads at the vanishing boat.

Shunkan's Final Moments. The manner in which Shunkan's final moments are played differs from actor to actor. Kichiemon's version, in which Shunkan seems unable to give up his attachment to the world, is famous. This great star wrote,

> I have created a new way of playing the final curtain where up to now Shunkan has climbed the rock with deep sadness and looked off after

the boat. I have no room for sadness, being simply blank, vacant, the mere shell of a man as I look off at the departing ship.

> Previous actors have climbed the rock as in a dream, the stage revolved and came to a stop, they leaned on a pine branch, it broke, they stumbled forward, the sound of the final blow of the ki clappers being struck was heard, they recovered their senses, and sadly looked off as the curtain closed. In my case, the stage revolves while I am climbing and, even though I lean on the pine branch, I do not recover my senses but merely hold out both my hands and, while I make swimming motions, the curtain closes. In my early days I also did such things as have the stage go on slowly moving toward stage left as the curtain closed or play the ending without the sound of the ki.[17]

Kan'emon, in the Zenshin-za production, after breaking the branch and tumbling forward, remains motionless for several seconds, then lifts himself and looks off, overcome by misery and anguish. Presently, though, a dim smile comes to his lips as, filled with his deed of self-sacrifice and renewed awareness of his own humanity and love for mankind, he conveys an attitude of faith in the future. Amidst the sounds of the

16. Koike, "Heike Nyogo no Shima Saiken," p. 168.

17. Kawatake, *Nakamura Kichiemon*, p. 388.

crashing surf Shunkan's beard and hair flap in the wind (helped by an electric fan) as the flute begins to play and the curtain closes.[18]

The full-length play goes on to depict various other events, including the death of Chidori, for which Kiyomori is reponsible, and the return of both her angry spirit and that of Azumaya to plague Kiyomori. Kiyomori eventually burns in hell for his misdeeds.

THE PLAYWRIGHT

Chikamatsu Monzaemon was born the son of a samurai family. He began writing puppet plays in the mid-1670s in Kyoto. After several successes in the 1680s his position was firmly established. He wrote Kabuki plays from about 1693 to 1704, most of them for the great actor, Sakata Tōjūrō (1647-1709). Chikamatsu was superb at infusing a sense of humanity into plays that, to satisfy popular demand, had to treat of outlandish characters and situations. He is also famed as the creator of the double-suicide (*shinjū*) play in which two young lovers, unable to reconcile their love affair with their social duties, kill themselves as the only possible alternative to living without each other. Among his numerous respected works are *The Battles of Coxinga*, *The Love Suicides at Amijima* (*Shinjū Ten no Amijima*), *Gonza the Lancer* (*Yari no Gonza Kasanu Katabira*), and others.

The present translation uses the text of the National Theatre production, found in *Kokuritsu Gekijō Jōen Taihonshū,* Vol. II, Tokyo, 1968, and in the *Meisaku Kabuki Zenshū,* Vol. I, Tokyo, 1969. In the production upon which the stage business described in the text was based, Nakamura Kanzaburō XVII played Shunkan, Nakamura Tomijūrō V played Yasuyori, Nakamura Fukusuke VIII (1946-) played Naritsune, Jitsukawa Enjaku III (1921-) played Senō, Kataoka Nizaemon XIII acted Tanzaemon, and Nakamura Shikan VII played Chidori (Kabuki Theatre, Tokyo, May, 1975).

I do not know of any available recording of this play.

18. Koike, "Heike Nyogo no Shima Saiken," p. 172.

THE SCENE ON DEVIL'S ISLAND

(After a preparatory interval of about ten minutes, punctuated at increasingly briefer gaps of time by the muffled crack of the ki, heard from offstage, issei *music of flute and drums begins to play in the geza. Then there is a crack of the ki, the sound of the ōdaiko beating out a wave pattern, another crack of the ki, more wave sounds from the drum, several cracks beat faster and faster and the standard Kabuki striped curtain is pulled across the stage from right to left. After a brief pause, a final crack of the ki is heard. Discovered at extreme stage left, at the edge of the proscenium arch, are the gidayū chanter and shamisen player, seated on the conventional gidayū platform backed by a gold single leaf screen, framed in black. The entire width of the stage within the proscenium is occupied by the large light blue billowy curtain called the asagimaku. The shamisen player begins to play; a moment later we hear the resonant recitative of the chanter.)*

GIDAYŪ: *(Very slowly)*

From time immemorial
This island's fearful name
Has been Kikaigashima
    —Devil's Island—
A place where demons live.
It is indeed a hell on earth.

(The wave pattern is beat loudly in the geza. At the sound of the ki being struck, the asagimaku *suddenly falls, revealing the setting for the action to follow. The place represented is a spot near the shore on the exiles' island of Kikaigashima. The hanamichi and forepart of the stage are covered with loose, gray ground cloths. At center is a small, ramshackle, four-post hut, open at the front. Its low thatched roof, too low for a man to stand under, is of rush, with several long strips of seaweed hanging loosely from its edges. Within is a makeshift tripodlike fireplace made from sticks of wood. Hanging on the hut's rear wall is an abalone shell, used as a cooking pot. At stage right is a man-sized boulder. An especially large rock, like a small hill, is immediately upstage of this boulder. A small pine tree tops this rock. The rocks are lightly covered with vines of ivy. Another rock sits upstage of the hut. A number of shells lie loosely scattered before the rocks and at several other areas around the stage. At left is a small rock, about the size of a man, rising perpendicularly off the stage floor. It is later used to secure a ship's hawser. Yet another rock, flat topped, with a step built into its downstage side, is to the left of this. A ground row of dry grass is up center, near the water's edge. A pine tree stands to either side and slightly upstage of the hut. A pine branch lies on the floor at center, below the hut. To the left of the perpendicular rock a ground cloth bearing a painted pattern of waves emerges from the wings. Wave cloths line the upstage area of the stage as well. Waves are also painted on the backdrop*

*that runs along the rear of the stage to a
height of about seven feet. The blue sky
is depicted on another drop [actually a
series of flat panels abutting one an-
other] immediately behind this. As the
drums recede, the gidayū begins reciting
again.)*

*The only things to remind one
Of bygone days in the capital
Are the sun and moon
Shining in the sky.*

*(The geza drum beats out the wave pat-
tern. Shunkan, the former priest, now an
exile, enters slowly from upstage right,
behind the rock cluster there. He leans
on a long staff of withered wood, held in
his right hand. In his left is a small
wooden ring from which hangs a meager
meal of limp seaweed [arame]. He wears
a patched and ragged old kimono of light
brown, zōri sandals, and an obi, tied in
front. His hair is combed straight back
from his forehead and hangs in a pony-
tail behind. Its color is brown with flecks
of gray. He wears a thin, drooping mustache and goatee. His movements suggest
weakness and despondency. An air of extreme melancholy and grief clings to him
as he slowly comes to right center, while
the gidayū chants.)*

*Shunkan, the exiled priest,
Having exchanged some sulfur
From the mountaintop
For a fisherman's meager haul*

(he stumbles)

*Comes stumbling, tottering,
Staggering along*

*(having stumbled, Shunkan rights him-
self and poses, leaning on his gnarled
staff which he presses to his right shoulder as he straightens up. This is done
rhythmically, to the sound of the shamisen. It is performed gently, to express the
great pathos we must feel at once on seeing the formerly proud Shunkan in his
present state of misery)*

*With his wretched, scraggly walking
  stick,
He is surely a sight to be pitied.*

*(During these last lines, he looks pitifully
at the seaweed in his hand, then crosses
to the right of the hut, leans his staff
there, removes his sandals, enters the
hut, and kneels, exhausted. He takes the
seaweed from the ring, puts the seaweed
in the shell which he takes off the wall,
lifts a palm leaf and fans the embers beneath the pot. A red glow can soon be
seen under the pot. Shunkan breaks a
nearby twig or two and puts them on the
fire. He busies himself with his cooking,
stirring the food with a stick, during the
following narration. His friends and fellow exiles, Yasuyori and Naritsune, enter
on the hanamichi and move to the shichi-
san.)*

*The same may be said of Yasuyori,
  Lord of Hei,
Bedecked in rotting rags
And of Naritsune, Lord of Tamba,*

*Who come walking along the sandy
 beach.*

(*Naritsune stands on the hanamichi several feet closer to the stage than Yasuyori. He turns to address his friend. He is
played in the soft, romantic wagoto style
which suggests his youthfulness and deli-
cacy. He and Yasuyori wear costumes
similar to Shunkan's except that the color
is rather grayish. They each carry wicker
baskets in their right hands.*)

NARITSUNE: Lord Yasuyori! I can see Lord
Shunkan where he sits within his hut.

(*Yasuyori is not so obviously a wagoto
type as Naritsune, though he too is quite
young. He speaks and moves with definite grace and refinement. This is necessary to suggest his former position as a
highly placed aristocrat in Kyoto. Yet,
since it is Naritsune about whom the
play's romantic subplot revolves, only
Naritsune wears the traditional wagoto
stark white makeup on face and limbs.
Yasuyori's makeup is more realistic and,
like Shunkan's, uses flesh tones.*)

YASUYORI: Fortunately, the weather today
is fine so we can gather at our ease...

NARITSUNE: And seek relief...

YASUYORI: From our melancholy burdens.

GIDAYŪ:

*Friends to the waves which
Lap at the lonely house
Are the plovers, circling o'er the
 crests.*

(*Wave drumbeats. Naritsune and Yasuyori cross to the stage right area, below
the rocks, at the right of the hut.*)

NARITSUNA: Fortunately, Lord Shunkan...

YASUYORI: May be found...

BOTH: At home.

SHUNKAN: (*Noticing them*) Ah! Lord
Naritsune! Lord Yasuyori! Welcome! Come,
come!

(*Though obviously glad to see his friends,
Shunkan barely has the strength to rise
and greet them.*)

GIDAYŪ:

*Though his means are scanty
His welcome is sincere
Showing how truly close
Their friendship is.*

(*Naritsune and Yasuyori put their baskets
on the ground to the right of the hut. A
stage assistant appears from behind the
rocks and removes them. The two men
stand at right center, Naritsune being
closer to center. Shunkan, meanwhile,
rises slowly and moves down to left center, sits, and gestures to them to sit,
which they do. They then bow very low
to him and sit up.*)

YASUYORI: Well, well! We haven't met
together recently, so I hope things are well
with you.

NARITSUNE: It's been at least four or five days since we last met; we've missed you a great deal.

SHUNKAN: My friends, Lord Yasuyori and Lord Naritsune, though we are usually together, it has been some time since I heard anything of either of you.

(He slowly lifts his right hand, within its full sleeve, to his eyes, and lightly mimes weeping and dabbing at his tears.)

YASUYORI: It is only natural for you to be upset but let me explain. Together with Naritsune I have been praying daily to the gods of the three shrines of Kumano and simply have not had time to visit you.

(The geza shamisen begins to play background music during this speech.)

NARITSUNE: As Yasuyori has said, we have been praying everyday that we may be granted a pardon from the capital which will let us return to our loved ones there.

(Bows low)

YASUYORI: Therefore, we have had no occasion to get in touch with you.

(Both bow low.)

But, leaving that aside, what you still don't know, Lord Shunkan, is that we three friends have recently become four.

SHUNKAN: We've become four? Do you mean another exile from the capital has joined us?

YASUYORI: *(Smiling)* No, no! Not at all! Lord Naritsune has fallen in love with a charming island diver-girl and has taken her for his wife.

(Naritsune makes an expression of bashfulness and lowers his face.)

SHUNKAN: *(Coming to life a bit)* He has? Wonderful, wonderful! Do you know this is the first time in three years any of us has uttered the word "love"? It is also the first time I've seen a smiling face. It reminds me of the love affair of the fabled Prince Yukihira, who fell in love with a fisher-girl at Suma Beach. I myself constantly long for my darling wife, Azumaya, whom I had to leave behind in the capital. Though she is my wife, it is as though she were my lover. So not only is the speaker in love, you see, but so is his listener. I beg you, then, to tell me your story.

(Shunkan gestures with his right hand for Naritsune to begin.)

GIDAYŪ:

Implored to tell his tale
The Lord of Tamba's face reddens.

(Naritsune acts as if embarrassed.)

NARITSUNE: The three of us share the same lot so there is no reason to conceal anything from one another. Thus, I will tell you the story of my love for the humble diving-girl, the vessel of all my delights.

(*He holds the final vowel for effect. Shunkan places his raised knee on the ground.*)

GIDAYŪ:

Though it embarrasses me to say . . .

NARITSUNE: The girl I love is named Chidori. She is the daughter of a Kiri Island fisherman and works on the beach wearing a sea-stained robe, gathering in the seawater and drying it for its salt.

GIDAYŪ:

*When the tide is right
She reveals her lovely body*

(*Naritsune adjusts his position to mime the words of the narrative; he rises on his right knee, points off in the distance with his right hand, and slowly folds his arms across his body as if bashfully hiding his nakedness.*)

NARITSUNE: As she takes a bucket and scythe . . .

GIDAYŪ:

*And plunges into the bottomless
  depths
To gather many kinds of seaweed
Too busy even to keep her hair back
  with
A boxwood comb.*

(*As the gidayū sings, Naritsune makes dancelike gestures of parting the waters and cutting the seaweed with a scythe. He then makes a gesture of combing his hair with his right hand, gestures by lightly waving his hand before him, then sinks to his knees again.*)

NARITSUNE: In no time at all, the god of marriage swept down on this very island and caused us to fall in love. We are now living as man and wife in my humble cottage. Chidori has only the deepest feelings of devotion and love for me. She told me, in her charming island accent, that she is overwhelmed with gratitude for having been shown kindness and sympathy, though she is but a poor island girl. I have no family, she said, so I pray that my husband's good friend Yasuyori will be my elder brother and that Lord Shunkan will act as my father. I will be a most devoted daughter and sister in return, she said. As she spoke, the tears falling freely from her eyes, her charm was just like that of a woman from the capital. She begged us to take care of her.

(*Bows low, head near ground, as gidayū sings*)

GIDAYŪ:

*Her words have penetrated to my
  very soul.
Hearing this tale, Lord Shunkan
Is overcome with delight.*

SHUNKAN: This is just wonderful! Your love story is fascinating yet tinged with pathos, dazzling yet commendable. Yours is a truly precious love. I want to meet this girl. Shall we go to your hut?

YASUYORI: No, no, that won't be necessary. She's come along with us to your place. Wait a moment.

(Rises and crosses to edge of hanamichi. Beckons to rear of hanamichi with right hand. Japanese beckoning gestures are somewhat similar to the Western wave of farewell. The hand is extended slightly and, palm downward, the fingers are waved in the direction of the one doing the beckoning. Wave drum begins to beat.)

Chidori! Chidori! Please come here! Lord Shunkan wishes to meet you. Come on over, Chidori! Chidori!

CHIDORI: *(From the room at the rear of the hanamichi)* Coming!

GIDAYŪ:

*Chidori responds and comes
Running through the weeds
Carrying a basket of bamboo.*

*(As the wave drum beats Chidori runs in along the hanamichi, carrying a wooden rake on her left shoulder and a wicker-work basket in her right hand. In the basket, tied to it with a string, is a bamboo tube supposedly carrying drinking water. She comes to the shichi-san but, overcome by shyness, turns around and runs out again. Yasuyori turns to the others and laughs when she does this. He then moves again to the edge of the hana-*michi. *She soon runs in again. When she reaches the stage, bashfulness strikes her once more and she turns to flee, but Yasuyori stops her, holding on to her rake, and pulls her back. He takes the rake and places it upstage near one of the rocks, and resumes his former position. Chidori, meanwhile, sits between Yasuyori and Naritsune at right center and bows low but, still shy, to the right, away from Shunkan who is seated at left center. All this entrance business, when properly performed, is brimming with light-hearted charm and humor. Meanwhile, the gidayū continues.)*

*Her beauty is such that,
Though she be clad in rags,
It were as if her garments
Were of silk and silver threads.
Why in the world was she born
A lowly maker of salt?*

(Chidori wears a bright green kimono with medium-length hanging sleeves. A seaweed design decorates her pink front-tied obi. Her kimono has an octopus pattern adorning it. She wears a straw apron around her waist. Her feet are bare.)

YASUYORI: Allow me to introduce Chidori.

GIDAYŪ:

Shunkan extends his greetings.

SHUNKAN: I must say I have been quite impressed by all the charming things I've heard about you. You've already met with Yasuyori, I know, and I know also that you wish me to act as your father from this day forward. We three men are already virtually related. Since we are to be parent and child, from now on you are my daughter. If a pardon were to be granted to us we would all four return to the capital together; you would be acknowledged the wife of Naritsune, Lord of Tamba, and would wear long, trailing, scarlet hakama trousers, like any other noblewoman. But what I find terribly annoying is that even if we were to dig through all the rocks and earth on this island (*he looks around and makes grabbing gestures at the sand*) we would not find one drop of wine nor even a cup to drink it from. After all, we should perform the congratulatory wedding rites.

GIDAYŪ:

Hearing this, Chidori answers.

CHIDORI: Dear Lord Shunkan, if a lowly saltmaker like me were to wear long, scarlet trousers she would surely be punished.

(*Bows low quickly*)

I am happy enough merely to be married to a gentleman from the capital. A sacred hermit lived 700 years by drinking water in which chrysanthemums were floated.

(*Takes the bamboo tube from her basket*)

We should follow his example and drink fresh water from an island stream as if it were wine. This abalone shell will serve as a wine-cup.

(*Takes shell from basket and holds it out as if a cup*)

We shall thus be parent and child from this day on. How delightful it will be to call each other "father" and "daughter."

(*She takes the tube and runs over to Shunkan, places the shell and tube down by him, turns back, almost stumbles into the seated Naritsune, makes a revolving move around him to his rear, and sits at his right, very bashfully, her hand on his. As she makes her first move toward Shunkan, Yasuyori puts her basket upstage right by the rock.*)

GIDAYŪ:

The men all laugh at her
Charming island accent.

YASUYORI: Congratulations! Congratulations!

(*Rises*)

Then, I will act as go-between.

(*Wave drum plays during the following.*)

Naritsune, you must sit in the groom's seat.

(*Yasuyori takes Naritsune to stage left, where Naritsune sits. Yasuyori crosses to Chidori.*)

You, Chidori, must take the bridal seat.

(Chidori, at the beginning of this speech, turns to face upstage. She removes her straw apron and gives it to a stage assistant who takes it with him. Yasuyori now comes to her and takes her to the left where she sits upstage of Naritsune, on a diagonal, facing right.)

We will have to skip a lot of the formalities, of course. As the groom's father-in-law, Shunkan, you take the seat of honor.

(Shunkan is seated up center, below the hut. Yasuyori goes to Shunkan's right, takes the abalone shell, brings it to the couple at left, and hands it to Chidori. Yasuyori pours water from the tube; she drinks it, bashfully. She hands the cup to Naritsune, Yasuyori pours water into it, he drinks, then returns it to Chidori. Yasuyori pours, she drinks again. Yasuyori brings the shell to Shunkan, pours for him—at Shunkan's right—and Shunkan drinks. The couple, meanwhile, bow low. During all this, the gidayū recites the following.)

GIDAYŪ:

*The abalone shell is a wine cup of
    lapis lazuli
As they pretend to be drinking wine.
The three—no—four friends
Celebrate the nuptials.*

(Yasuyori gives a stage assistant up right the tube and shell. These are removed. Yasuyori then takes his former seat at the right, where he bows once to Shunkan.)

SHUNKAN: I will whet your appetites.

(He nods to each side, then picks up the pine branch lying nearby on the ground. He dusts it off on his hand and knee.)

GIDAYŪ:

*Thoughts of their sulfur-belching
    island fade
As their hearts drift to an enchanted
    world of make-believe.*

(The following is a traditional wedding ceremony dance and song performed in Nō theater style. It is derived from the Nō play Shōjō [The Orangutan]. The movements are stately and ceremonious and the chanting is deep and sonorous, though, of course, the emaciated Shunkan can barely move or speak with any vigor. He holds both hands wide apart, pine branch in the right, then brings them toward his lap. He begins to chant as he rises on his right knee, stumbles slightly, and with sliding steps moves downstage slightly. He holds the branch out to the right, stumbles a step forward, raises the branch high, then falls down on his back. He laughs delightedly, though weakly, a technique demanding great ability on the actor's part. The words he chants are as follows.)

SHUNKAN:

*They revel in the never ceasing flow
    of wine
From the inexhaustable wine-fount.*

(When he bursts into laughter after falling, the others laugh too, then bow low.)

GIDAYŪ:

They all make merry.

(Laughing, Yasuyori happens to look off into the distance, towards the rear of the theater. He seems startled by what he sees.)

YASUYORI: My god! There's a large boat out there. I've never seen it before. It's headed in this direction.

(Shunkan shields his eyes with both hands as he looks off. All rise on their knees, looking off.)

NARITSUNE: Maybe it's another exile.

SHUNKAN: *(Now using only his right hand to shield his eyes)* No, no! Its sails are spread and one can clearly see it's a ship from the capital.

YASUYORI: Look, look! It's coming closer and closer!

NARITSUNE: There's no doubt it's an official ship from the capital!

SHUNKAN: It's surely a reception boat!

CHIDORI: Look, look! It's almost here!

(They form a tight group with Yasuyori holding onto Shunkan at the right and Naritsune at the left, Chidori, in turn, clinging to Naritsune. All are looking off into the distance. Moving as a unit, they cross up right near the farthest downstage rock as if looking at the boat, now on the up right horizon. They point to it as it appears there. They then go behind the rock and crouch there, out of sight, as the boat moves slowly across the backdrop. A miniature boat is moved along the horizon line at the rear of the stage, from right to left, as utai music using ōdaiko and kotaiko drums is played in the geza.)

GIDAYŪ:

As they chatter in excitement
A Kyoto government ship
Makes its berth at the shore.

(Several seconds after the miniature boat passes off to the left the prow of a large wooden boat thrusts its nose onto the stage from the wings at left. Only the prow is shown but the impression is of the entire boat's presence. As the boat rolls to a stop five or six boatmen, dressed alike, appear on the prow. One jumps off and ties the ship's thick rope to the nearby perpendicular rock on the shore. Several others lay a gangplank from the side of the prow to a rock downstage left. The rock has a step built into it to help the actors walk off the boat. Several men sit cross-legged up stage right. Two men support the gangplank, kneeling one on either side. One bears a small black folding camp stool, which he places on the ground near him.)

GIDAYŪ:

> The boat's anchor is dropped
> At the dry and sandy beach

A VOICE: (*Offstage*) We have arrived at Kikaigashima!

VOICES: (*Offstage*) At last!

GIDAYŪ:

> The Heike samurai, Senō Tarō
>   Kaneyasu,
> Descends from the boat
> And calmly walks along the beach.

(*During this narrative four of Senō's men appear on the prow and sit on their haunches. A moment later, Senō appears and walks down the plank to the shore. His men stand and follow him off, then stand in a row before the eight boatmen. The two men holding the plank exit left. Senō is dressed in the highly stylized costume called the ryūjin maki, often worn by important envoys in Kabuki. The left sleeve of his black overjacket* [suo] *is stiffened with splints and looks like a large black kite. His other sleeve is folded in a shape similar to that in which abalone is often gift-wrapped and is placed behind his right shoulder. His hakama are tucked up in balloonlike puffs at his thighs. He wears a small yellow pad* [the sanriate] *on each knee, yellow tabi, and thick-soled straw sandals. His white wig is the conventional curly hairstyle worn by these exaggerated envoys. A black lacquer cone-shaped cover is placed on the bushy topknot. Senō carries a chūkei-*type fan in his right hand. He is made up with a red face and ferocious black eyebrows and mouth. He is rough and overbearing and should be as cruel and nasty as possible. He stands at left center and bellows.*)

SENŌ: Hear ye! Year ye! Are the exiles, Naritsune, Lord of Tamba, and Yasuyori, Lord of Hei, sent here three years ago, present?

(*Senō's four samurai sit on their haunches. Naritsune, then Yasuyori and Chidori, appear from behind the rock and prostrate themselves. Shunkan emerges last but goes farthest toward center and prostrates himself.*)

NARITSUNE: (*As he enters*) I am Naritsune.

YASUYORI: (*Emerging in his turn*) And I am Yasuyori.

SHUNKAN: And I, Shunkan, am here as well.

(*Chidori is nearest the rock, stage right. Yasuyori is a bit below her and to her left. Naritsune is a bit to the left of Yasuyori and Shunkan is several feet left of Naritsune, toward center. Senō balances the stage at left center.*)

GIDAYŪ:

> They bow formally, their heads low.

(*Senō removes a folded slip of paper from his breast. He takes off the outer wrapper of blank white paper, turns to*

the exiles, and, unfolding the message
and holding it before him with both
hands in a ceremonious manner, reads.)

Senō takes the letter of pardon
From his breast and reads it
With great show of ceremony.

SENŌ:

"Because of the recent birth of a son
   to their reverend majesties,
The Emperor and Empress,
A general amnesty has been declared
   throughout the land.
The two exiles to Kikaigashima,
Naritsune, Lord of Tamba, and
   Yasuyori, Lord of Hei,
Are hereby ordered to leave their
   place of exile
And to return to the capital with all
   due haste!"
You have heard this from the
   Imperial Envoy,
Senō Tarō Kaneyasu!

(*During the reading, Shunkan, not hearing his name, lifts his head, raises himself
a bit, and crawls forward a step or two.
Senō, on finishing the reading, turns the
page so it may be seen by the pardoned
exiles, then holds it in his right hand at
his side.*)

GIDAYŪ:

Even before the reading is completed
The two stunned exiles
Are groveling with thanks.

SHUNKAN: I beg to ask why the name of
Shunkan was omitted from the reading?

SENŌ: Be quiet, Shunkan! How dare you
accuse a person such as myself of omitting
your name?

(*He walks toward Shunkan. His steps
are broad and heavy, a convention for
such roles.*)

If you think there is any other name than the
two I read, you can look at this for yourself!

(*With this, Senō, facing front, thrusts
the papers at Shunkan's breast. He poses
like this for a moment, his right leg bent
at the knee, Shunkan gripping the papers
desperately.*)

GIDAYŪ:

Senō thrusts the papers at Shunkan.

SHUNKAN: Let me see!

GIDAYŪ:

Naritsune and Yasuyori also
Marvel at this paper as Shunkan
Reads it over and over,
This way and that.
Even when he reads the wrapping
   sheet
No sign of Shunkan's name or title
   can be found.

(*During the narration Senō straightens
up, leaving the papers in Shunkan's
hands. Shunkan puts down the wrapping
paper, then reads the sheet with the writing on it. He soon puts this down and*

lifts the wrapping paper, a sheet that is precisely the same size as that of the formal written pardon. He examines it and sees that it has nothing written on it. He picks up the pardon again, his hands trembling. He raises his left knee a bit, then drops it and, holding the papers up to the light with both hands, turns on his knees in a circle to the right until he faces front again.)

SHUNKAN: Nothing.

(Pause)

Nothing.

(Pause)

Nothing, nothing.

(He speaks these words faster and faster, his voice fading in a sob, pathetically.)

GIDAYŪ:

Shunkan faces Senō . . .

(Shunkan throws the papers down, slaps his hands on his lap, and addresses Senō. As he begins to speak he holds the papers down with his right hand, pointing to the names on it. The others are all bowing low at right.)

SHUNKAN: I wish to say something to Lord Senō. Only the names of Naritsune and Yasuyori appear on this official pardon

(he points to the names)

but neither my name nor my title is here. Perhaps it is because Lord Kiyomori forgot to add it or maybe the scribe merely made an error.

SENŌ: Shut up, Shunkan! You have been ordered to remain behind alone as the overseer of this island.

SHUNKAN: *(Stunned)* What? Overseer of this island?

SENŌ: That is the order of Lord Kiyomori!

SHUNKAN: We have committed the same crime and have been exiled to the same place. We should then receive the same pardon!

GIDAYŪ:

*Only two of us have been pardoned
And I alone have slipped
Through the net of Buddha's grace.*

(Makes a gesture of weeping)

*Even Buddha's great love and mercy
    is discriminatory!*

(Shunkan slaps the paper lying on the ground at his right.)

SHUNKAN: If I had killed myself long ago I would not have to face this grief I feel.

(He is bent low over the paper, weeping. As the gidayū slowly delivers its narration, Shunkan turns front, picks up the pardon from the floor in his right hand, and holds it out to his friends, his hands

trembling. He grabs the other paper with his left hand and angrily crushes the papers together into a ball. Senō comes over and grabs them away from him and walks back left three steps where he puts the papers in his roomy left kimono sleeve. Shunkan, wailing, lies in a heap on the ground.)

GIDAYŪ:

*He loudly bemoans his lengthened
  life
A life of misery and grief.
A voice is now heard from the boat.*

TANZAEMON: Lord Shunkan. Cease your weaping! It is I, Tanzaemon Motoyasu!

(The sound of waves is beat on the ōdaiko. Yasuyori and Naritsune move to Shunkan to comfort him but run back right and bow low when Tanzaemon appears. Two men come in from the left to support the gangplank. Following Tanzaemon are his four retainers. Tanzaemon walks to the prow and walks down the plank. He bows to Senō, Senō bows back. Tanzaemon stands to Senō's left. The four Tanzaemon retainers walk in unison to the area immediately below the shamisen player and gidayū chanter and sit there on their right knees. The two men supporting the plank join the group up right, where they sit. A boatman brings the folding camp stool to Senō, who sits on it, by the hawser. The boatman kneels on one knee behind Senō. During this action, the gidayū chants.)

GIDAYŪ:

*With these words, Tanzaemon now
  enters.*

TANZAEMON: I should have announced it earlier but I have held back till now so that you may know to your very marrow the beneficence and goodwill of Lord Shigemori, Councillor to Lord Kiyomori. Therefore, listen to me well.

(Tanzaemon is dressed in a light blue ryūjin maki envoy's costume. His appearance is refined-looking. On his head is a black lacquered hat. He stands left of center and removes the formal document sticking out of his kimono at the breast. Shunkan bows respectfully in the presence of this paper.)

GIDAYŪ:

*From his breast fold
He removes a document.*

(Tanzaemon reads the document, holding it out ceremoniously with both hands.)

TANZAEMON:

*"Hear ye! Hear ye! Be it known that
Lord Shigemori, Keeper of the Privy
  Seal,
Out of his great compassion
Has seen fit to allow the exiled
  prisoner,
Lord Shunkan, to return as far as
  Bizen,*

Though not to the capital itself,
Signed, Notto no Kami no Ritsune,
Nephew to Lord Kiyomori."

(*As this is read, Shunkan sits up, a sudden change having come over his face. The other exiles, too, look up with joyous expressions.*)

GIDAYŪ:

Even before the reading is over...

SHUNKAN: What? Then all three of us are pardoned?

(*Shunkan tries to move forward to the left, but is too overcome to make any progress. He crawls a step or two, then his friends come to help him, supporting him as, in time to the shamisen, he struggles several steps to Tanzaemon.*)

TANZAEMON: Indeed!

(*He turns the paper so the writing can be seen by the exiles.*)

SHUNKAN: Ah! Ah! Ah!

GIDAYŪ:

He scrapes his head against the sand
Bowing deeper and deeper,
Overcome with tears of joy.

(*Shunkan raises himself on his left knee and holds his hands up in gratitude, then bows low again, raises his face, and wipes his tears. Tanzaemon folds the paper neatly and puts it back in its wrap-*

per, then inserts it in his kimono at the breast.)

GIDAYŪ:

Tanzaemon faces Senō.

TANZAEMON: We have no reason to remain here any longer. Let us embark and leave this island quickly.

SENŌ: Fortunately, the wind is just right.

TANZAEMON: Attention! The guards will please escort the pardoned exiles on to the boat!

BOATMEN: Aye, aye!

TANZAEMON'S RETAINERS: Come now!

ALL THE RETAINERS: To the boat!

(*Tanzaemon turns to board the boat. He bows to Senō, Senō to him, Senō crosses right a bit, Tanzaemon crosses left. The three exiles and Chidori form a line at right center to go on board, Shunkan at the head.*)

GIDAYŪ:

Exchanging joyful words
The pardoned company approach
The boarding plank.
But Senō now raises his voice
To stop them.

(*As the foursome moves left Senō steps in front of them and makes a gesture of striking Shunkan with his fan. The tsuke accent the blow. The line instantly falls in disarray to the ground, right. Shunkan is at right center, several feet to his right is Naritsune, Chidori is at Naritsune's right, and Yasuyori is even farther right. Tanzaemon, who had put one foot on the rock under the plank, turns and moves to the right of the gangplank.*)

SENŌ: Hold it, you shabby creatures!

(*Addressing Chidori*)

If you're seeing someone off you can go no farther since you're not fit to board this boat. You'd better get out of here right now if you know what's good for you!

NARITSUNE: No! It's all right! Leave her alone! During my period of exile I have become greatly indebted to this girl and have recently been wed to her. I have made an unbreakable promise to her that if I was allowed to return to the capital she could surely return there with me. Please be kind enough to take us with you to the first port of call. We will be eternally indebted to you for this kindness.

SENŌ: (*Raising his fan threateningly*) Shut up! Shut up! Shut up! The very idea of taking this woman along in addition to you exiles is preposterous! Men! Get rid of this filthy creature!

SENŌ'S RETAINERS: Yes, sir!

GIDAYŪ:

A jangle of harsh sounds is heard.

(*Seno's men cross behind the exiles and stand there like a wall, hands spread apart, fingers splayed, legs wide. Naritsune turns to them with outstretched arms to keep them back and then takes Chidori in his arms and rises on one knee, protecting her.*)

NARITSUNE: Wait, wait, wait! Wait! Since you refuse to honor my request I can do nothing. Therefore, you must leave me behind on this island and return to the capital without me.

(*Shunkan looks at him.*)

My friends, Shunkan and Yasuyori, please board the boat.

(*As he speaks, Chidori wipes away her tears. He is on his right knee, embracing her, his left hand on his raised left knee.*)

SHUNKAN: No, no! We have no intention of leaving this place without you.

YASUYORI: As Shunkan has said, we are one and will return only as one.

SHUNKAN, YASUYORI, NARITSUNE: We won't go! We won't go! We won't go!

(*Shunkan rises and joins the group at right in a huddle, all of them bent over, on their knees. This is a famous kata [the* kai no kata *or "shell" kata] and the image of the four bent low, heads near each other, is supposed to represent a shell. The four retainers kneel on their left knees up right, nearby.*)

GIDAYŪ:

> They set their resolute wills
> Against Senō and Tanzaemon.

TANZAEMON: (*Approaches Senō*) Lord Senō, don't you see that this sort of action on your part will constitute an impediment to the prayers offered in the name of the Imperial infant? Though you do not permit the girl aboard the boat perhaps a stay here of one or two days will soften your heart and you will allow everyone to embark. Since this will be an act of charity on your part it will undoubtedly have a strong effect on the prayers for the Emperor's baby.

SENŌ: (*In disgust*) Aaach! That would be an act of insubordination on the part of an official! I am not happy about the fact that Lord Notto altered our official document of passage so that the number two would be a three, but by whose permission can we further alter it to be a four? Until we hand the exiles over to Lord Kiyomori they are my responsibility. I don't give a damn if they say they won't board! Yai, yai, yai, yai!

(*He walks to the group, strikes Shunkan lightly on the shoulder with his fan as the tsuke are struck. Shunkan falls forward, the "shell" breaks to the right, in a line, with Naritsune and Chidori at center, Yasuyori at the right. Senō stands over Shunkan.*)

Shunkan, I'll bet you didn't know that Lord Kiyomori had your wife, Azumaya, killed for refusing his advances, did you?

SHUNKAN: Wha...?

(*Senō places his fan at Shunkan's neck, stretches his left leg until it is straight, leans his weight on his right, and poses, menacingly.*)

SENŌ: Her head was then chopped clean off!

SHUNKAN: What are you saying? My wife, Azumaya—I...

SENŌ: (*Violently*) And there's even more to learn! The hated priest, Shunkan, will be beheaded in the capital like a common criminal.

(*Strikes Shunkan sharply on the back of the neck with his fan as the tsuke are beat. Shunkan falls forward.*)

Take these three prisoners and put them in the bottom of the ship. Tie them so they can't move! That's an order!

(*Everyone rises. The large group of boatmen go off up left, above the boat. During the following, Senō's retainers escort the exiles onto the boat and exit left.*)

SENŌ'S RETAINERS: We understand, sir!

GIDAYŪ:

> The four retainers roughly
> Thrust Chidori aside.
> The pardoned exiles are brusquely
> Led aboard the ship.

(*Two men take Shunkan by either arm and lead him onto the boat. One retainer herds Naritsune and Yasuyori on board. Tanzaemon crosses to left center, below*)

Senō. A fourth retainer holds Chidori back, standing over her, his left leg bent at the knee, weight on the right, gripping her right arm. Tanzaemon's men kneel at left on their right knees.)

TANZAEMON: Although I feel great pity for you, young lady, your presence on the boat will simply cause too many problems when we reach the checkpoint for inspection. After we return to the capital, Lord Naritsune will petition for your person and I am sure a boat will be sent to bring you back. But for now, you simply must be patient.

SENŌ: See here, Tanzaemon. We are officials, entrusted with the simple task of bringing back these exiles. Even if we should see the suffering and misery of others we must act as if we were blind and ignorant!

TANZAEMON: That is simply too cruel a way to be.

SENŌ: I know neither compassion nor sympathy. Entrusted with an important mission I may not permit my private feelings to occupy my time. Fast now, make it fast!

(Tanzaemon turns and boards the boat, followed by his men. Chidori breaks loose and tries to get past the guard. He moves to block her. She gets by him and then falls at Senō's side, taking his hand, pleading. He suddenly jabs her sharply in the side with his elbow. The tsuke accompany the move. Senō, after laughing cruelly to himself, boards the boat, followed by the retainer. The gidayū has been chanting.)

GIDAYŪ:

*Pressed to embark, the kindly Tanzaemon
Resignedly boards the boat.*

(Chidori, in pain, slowly struggles to her feet, then falls in a heap before the hut. She rises and falls again, clutching her breast. Again she rises and again she falls, weeping and wiping her tears with her right sleeve. She does this during the narrative portion. All her movements are in a rhythmic dance-mime.)

*Left alone, a pitiful figure, on the beach
The friendless Chidori, bewailing her lot,
Slowly lifts her tear-stained face.*

CHIDORI: *(Lying on her side, right hand on the ground)*

A samurai is said to know the meaning of compassion.

(Struggles to rise, weeps)

GIDAYŪ:

It is a lie! It is a falsehood!

CHIDORI:

There are no devils on Devils Island.

(Left hand on her breast, right on the ground)

GIDAYŪ:

The devils are all in the capital.

(*Chidori rises to her knees and slowly gestures off into the distance with her right hand, falls to the ground on her right hand, grabs her breast with her left, shakes her head sadly.*)

From the very day we first exchanged
    vows

(*crosses arms from shoulder to shoulder, sways from right to left*)

CHIDORI:

    Wishing a letter of pardon from
        Kyoto

(*falls to left side*)

GIDAYŪ:

    I worshiped the sun and the moon

(*she makes a praying gesture, hands clasped*)

    And fervently prayed to the Dragon
        God,
    Not because I wanted

CHIDORI:

    To return with my husband to the
        capital

(*crosses arms, shoulder to shoulder*)

    To live a life of splendor
    But because I wanted to sleep
    With him there at least one night.

(*Holds her left breast with her right hand, leans on her left hand*)

GIDAYŪ:

    That would have been
    My sole delight.

(*She wipes tears with sleeve.*)

CHIDORI: You evil devil! You fiend! Will a single girl make your flimsy boat too heavy?

(*Turns to rear to face hut*)

Have you no eyes to see the misery of others? Have you no ears with which to hear? Hear me! I want to go on board. I want to go!

(*Turns front, right hand on breast*)

GIDAYŪ:

    She screams and cries

(*leaning on her left hand, she stumbles to her feet*)

    Stamps her feet and rolls in the sand

(*she climbs the small perpendicular rock, stretches for a glimpse of the passengers, sinks down and poses, revolving her head in time to the music of the shamisen*)

    Wailing and weeping shamelessly
    Regardless of who may be watching.

(*Chidori gets off rock, runs about on shore, seeking a glimpse of Naritsune on the boat. She comes to center, right hand raised, removes the tenugui towel from her obi, sinks to her knees and weeps, pressing the towel to her face. She takes the towel and ties it around her waist from the rear, knotting it in front, above her obi.)*

She is a diving-girl
So a one or two-league swim

(she rises)

Is not unthinkable for her.

(She runs about at center, gesturing with the loose ends of the tenugui, looking to the boat, then sinks to her right knee, arms folded across her breast, shaking her head sadly. She looks at both palms)

But even she cannot swim
The hundreds and hundreds of
    leagues
From here to the capital.

(She rises on one knee, hands outstretched, making light swimming movements. She makes a gesture of counting the leagues on the fingers of both hands, Japanese-style, beginning with open palms and then closing in one finger after another, starting with the little finger. She then makes gestures of swimming with her arms outspread. She rises, moves about with difficulty, falls against the hut's left front post, brings her right sleeve to her mouth, moves forward a bit, and weeps.)

CHIDORI:

>*I will beat my head against this rock*
>   *and end my life.*

(She gestures to her head with her right hand.)

GIDAYŪ:

>*Dying for Lord Naritsune.*

CHIDORI:

>*Unable to bear parting from my lord,*
>*I will pray to Buddha for salvation.*
>*Dear God, please remember this*
>   *poor island maid.*

(She bows low before the hut, facing front, wipes her tears as the wave drum begins beating. Shunkan runs in off the boat, falls at the rock, goes to her, and takes her left hand. She struggles, trying to flee to the right. They sink to their knees. He continues to hold her hand. These actions go on during the following.)

GIDAYŪ:

>*Seeing her about to die, Lord*
>   *Shunkan cries.*

SHUNKAN: *(Coming off the boat)* No, no! Wait, Chidori, wait!

GIDAYŪ:

>*Stumbling, staggering, Lord*
>   *Shunkan,*
>*With great difficulty,*
>*Leaves the boat and goes to the girl.*

SHUNKAN: (*Desperately*) Board the boat! Go to the capital! Board the boat and go to Kyoto! I have been told that my darling wife, Azumaya, was slain after refusing Lord Kiyomori's advances. Now that my beloved is gone, what joy can I find in Kyoto where I would have to view the moon and flowers with only myself for company? Rather than face grief again in the capital I will remain here on the island and you will board the boat in my place. The number of people listed on the pardon will remain the same so there will be no trouble at the checkpoint. The envoys will not be doubted. Please board the boat and leave me, Shunkan, who is all alone in the world, here on this island where I will devote myself to Buddha. Please board the boat!

(*He rises, one knee at a time, still holding her hand. He pulls her a few steps with him to the left, then they sink to their knees again.*)

GIDAYŪ:

His tears flow copiously
As he takes the girl's hand
And leads her to the boat.

SHUNKAN: Honored sirs, I beg you to grant my request. Please allow this girl to embark with you.

GIDAYŪ:

Hearing this humble plea
Senō boils over with rage
And leaps down from the boat.

(*Wave drum beats. Senō, fuming, comes down the gangplank. The couple on the beach rise but he pushes them roughly. They fall as the tsuke beat, Senō leans his weight on his right foot and speaks.*)

SENŌ: No! Never, never! You dumb priest! When did you crawl down there? How dare you ask me to let this girl go on board? What use would the pardon or we envoys be if we merely did as we pleased? Aach! You're too dumb to even understand!

SHUNKAN: (*On his knees*) Sa, sa, sa! I, Shunkan, who have nothing left to live for, am asking you to have some pity! Leave me here and take this girl in my place!

SENŌ: How dare you? You impudent, conniving priest! Your pleas are useless! If you want to die, you'll have to do it in the capital!

(*Senō lifts his right foot in a kicking gesture and the tsuke accent the move. He glares as Shunkan falls down.*)

GIDAYŪ:

He kicks and tramples on the priest.

SHUNKAN: Then, no matter what I say...

SENŌ: I will refuse!

(*As the wave drum begins to beat Shunkan starts to crawl on his knees closer to Senō, as if praying for leniency, his hands pressed together.*)

SHUNKAN: Even if I beg you...

SENŌ: Shut your mouth!

SHUNKAN: For compassion!

GIDAYŪ:

Shunkan stealthily makes his way
To the side of Senō, where his
Sword can be reached.

(*Shunkan reaches over and draws the un-*
suspecting Senō's short sword with his
right hand and, rising, makes a gesture
of slicing Senō's right shoulder with it.
The tsuke beat. At the moment of con-
tact two seagulls rise from behind the hut
and fly off into the upper reaches of the
stage. They are rigged on a wire that is
practically invisible from the audito-
rium.)

As quick as lightning
He pulls it out
And wounds the startled envoy.

(*Shunken falls weakly to the right near*
Chidori. A stage assistant enters to aid
Senō, who has fallen below the perpen-
dicular rock at left. Senō drops his fan
and removes his sandals. He sits cross-
legged as the assistant helps him remove
his outer jacket and to drop his over-
kimono from his shoulders, revealing a
yellow under-kimono with a red cloth
sewn on the right shoulder to signify
blood. The assistant removes the black
lacquer cup from Senō's topknot, reveal-
ing a bushy white topknot beneath. Senō
ties his sleeves down securely by strings
at his abdomen. He places his left hand
on his right shoulder as if in pain.)

A SENŌ RETAINER: (*Appearing on the boat*)
Hey! The exile is running riot!

ALL ON BOAT: (*Offstage*) Part them!

GIDAYŪ:

Tanzaemon speaks amidst the
*   confusion.*

(*Tanzaemon enters on the boat and sends*
Senō's man off left. Tanzaemon sits on a
camp stool set up on the prow by a boat-
man. His retainers enter and crouch on
their haunches behind him in a row.)

TANZAEMON: Hold it! This is strictly their
affair. Every detail of this quarrel between
the exile and the envoy must be ascertained
and reported to the authorities. No one must
interfere on either of their behalfs!

SENŌ: Wait, wait! What are you saying,
Tanzaemon! Why do you side with this
criminal and refuse to grant me any aid?

TANZAEMON: My duties extend only to the
release of the exiles. I have no other duties.
I am just a bystander here.

SENŌ: Well, let that be an end to it then.

GIDAYŪ:

Senō, taken by surprise, rights
*   himself*
And draws his other sword.

(*Senō draws his long sword and, on his*
knees, crawls toward Shunkan. The stage
assistant removes his sandals, fan, and
sheath, and goes out up left.)

He swings his sword as best he can
But staggers like a willow on
*   unsteady legs.*

(*The two opponents cross swords at cen-*
ter and remain with swords crossed as
they struggle to their feet, then fall down.
Shunkan is on the floor at the right, pos-
ing with his sword held over his head.
Senō is at the left, holding his sword out
to the right. They struggle on their knees
to center, slice at each other, cross
swords, struggle for control, and rise
with locked swords. Shunkan forces Senō
back by moving backward, facing the
audience, his back against Senō. Senō
falls to the left. Shunkan poses at the
right of the hut, holding his sword over-
head. Senō rises, crosses swords with
Shunkan at center, and Shunkan falls to
the right. Senō is about to strike at the
fallen man but Chidori knocks Senō over
to the left with her rake.)

Shunkan totters like a withered pine.
Pitting all their strength against the
*   other*
The two antagonists breathlessly face
The moment of truth
As they stagger to and fro
On the strand.
Unable to bear the strain
Chidori too strikes out but
Shunkan's angry voice cuts in.

SHUNKAN: Get away! Get away! I'll consider
you my enemy if you so much as hand me a
stick! If you interfere I'll never forgive you!

GIDAYŪ:

Startled by his harshness
Chidori withdraws her proferred aid.

(*Upset at being reprimanded, Chidori*
pouts and shuffles away to the right. This
movement of hers has great charm and
often gets a laugh. Once again Shunkan
and Senō cross swords, then rise. Chidori
interferes and parts them, pulling Senō
left with her rake on his shoulder. Senō
slices, misses, then knocks Shunkan
down on his back at center. Meanwhile,
the gidayū sings.)

The weakened priest, bloody, worn
*   from hunger,*
Slashes out valiantly as he staggers
And falters in the sand.
The heavy sword hangs loosely
In his tired hands.
The flying sand clogs their lungs
And danger seems an equal threat to
*   both.*

(*Senō stands over the fallen Shunkan,*
facing the audience, about to kill his
adversary.)

Finally, Senō, used to looking down
*   on men*
As though he were an eagle

(*Chidori runs over and tosses sand in*
Senō's eyes, once, then again. Blinded,
he falters, and the fallen Shunkan thrusts
home. Senō grimaces and twists, then
falls forward slowly and lies with his

*head toward the audience, his arms out-
spread, on his back*)

*Is felled by a fatal blow
As the pitiless waves
Beat here and there
Upon the shore.*

(*Shunkan kneels with his sword by
Senō's head, at his right.*)

*As Shunkan raises his blade
To give the* coup de grace . . .

TANZAEMON: No! Wait a moment! You have
clearly won the battle. It will be a mistake to
give him the finishing blow. It will only
increase the number of charges against you
and invalidate your pardon. It is not worth
the trouble.

SHUNKAN: It is all one with me as I wish to
remain on this island.

TANZAEMON: How can I let you? Leaving
you behind would simply negate the kindness
shown you by Lords Shigemori and Notto.
It would also mar the celebrations for the
Imperial infant. I would be held responsible
for such an offense. Moreover, if we don't
have three exiles on board we will surely have
difficulties with the inspectors at the
checkpoint.

SHUNKAN: I understand, I understand. But
if this girl boards with Yasuyori and
Naritsune, there will be no discrepancy in the
number of passengers and you can't possibly
have any trouble at the checkpoint. As for
receiving the clemency of Lords Shigemori
and Notto for my former offense, I will

negate it by killing this envoy and thus
become guilty of a new offense.

GIDAYŪ:

*I will once again become
An exile on Kikaigashima.*

(*Shunkan makes a slow sweeping gesture
from left to up right with the blade of his
sword and puts the point down on the
stage for his first line.*)

SHUNKAN:

*And we'll pass beyond the bounds
Of the great Imperial amnesty.
Not a bit of blame
Will fall to you.*

(*He places his left hand on Senō's breast
to steady himself.*)

GIDAYŪ:

*Making firm his heart
Shunkan delivers the mortal blow.*

SHUNKAN: Senō!

(*Pause*)

Take for your sins

(*he thrusts the sword into Senō's throat;
Senō's arms and legs flail up for a
moment and then lie still*)

GIDAYŪ:

My vengeful sword!

(*The tsuke accent the move. Five boat-men enter immediately from up left and remove the body. One takes the sword with him. Shunkan falls to his face, weeping. Naritsune and Yasuyori run in on the boat and kneel at Tanzaemon's left.*)

All those on board
Burst into tears.
Naritsune and Yasuyori
Join their hands in prayer.
Chidori, hearing and seeing
All that has transpired
Is overcome with grief.

CHIDORI: Husband and wife will be together in the next world. Therefore, I will remain alone on this bitter island, never forgetting you. But I will not brazenly board the boat in your stead. Farewell everyone, farewell!

(*She tries to go right but Shunkan holds her back by her left arm. He is on the floor, on his knees. She stands at his side, then sinks to her knees.*)

SHUNKAN: (*Holding her left hand as she weeps*) Wait a moment! Listen to me. I have already passed through the three evil hells— the hell of hunger, the hell of battle, as you've just seen, and the hell of brimstone, which is always being burned on this island. I will surely be given salvation in the next world. The boat in which Shunkan will ride will be Buddha's noble craft bringing me to the shores of enlightenment.

GIDAYŪ:

I have no desire to take a boat
Back to the floating world.

SHUNKAN: Please, leave me here and board the boat, quickly, quickly!

GIDAYŪ:

He takes her by the sleeve
Pulls her by the hand
And puts her on the royal boat.

(*Wave drum beats. Shunkan pushes Chidori left. A Tanzaemon retainer comes off the boat and holds the gangplank steady. Chidori boards and sits on the prow between Naritsune and Yasuyori, who are at the left of Tanzaemon. The retainer boards and exits left.*)

GIDAYŪ:

Naritsune and his bride,
Yasuyori, too . . .

YASUYORI: Are loath to leave you . . .

NARITSUNE AND YASUYORI: Lord Shunkan.

TANZAEMON: Keep up your spirits!

SHUNKAN: (*Standing at center, weakly*) Farewell!

(*A boatman appears from up left, unties the rope from the rock, and tosses it onto the boat. The plank is pulled up on board by a boatman and removed stage left. Tanzaemon stands.*)

GIDAYŪ:

> Farewell tears cloud their eyes.
> The rope is loosened
> And the oars emerge.
> On board a fan is raised.

(*Tanzaemon snaps open his chūkei fan
and slowly raises it aloft in his right
hand. Shunkan raises his right hand in
response. Naritsune, Yasuyori, and Chidori weep.*)

> On shore a hand.

(*The boat slowly begins to move off left.*)

SHUNKAN: In the next life!

YASUYORI AND NARITSUNE: In the next life!

SHUNKAN: In the next life!

GIDAYŪ:

> Their calls grow faint
> As a heartless wind
> Fills out the sails
> And pushes the boat
> Farther and farther
> Into the offing.
> Soon, the ship is lost to sight.
> Only a glimpse of it
> Can now and then be caught
> Beyond the rolling waves.

(*Shunkan goes to the boat and grabs the
rope, pulling it across the stage to the left
in a long line. Then, waving to the departing boat, he moves right as the rope
begins to move left, pulled by the boat. It
moves under his feet and trips him,
throwing him to the floor. He crawls
after the moving rope and grabs it but it
is yanked from his hands at the water's
edge.*)

> Though he is resolved to stay
> His heart, after all, is just
> Like yours or mine.

(*By now the boat is out of sight. Geza
music, called* Chidori no aikata [*"Chidori's accompaniment"*], *using ōdaiko,
ōtsuzumi, and kotsuzumi drums as well
as the shamisen, accompanies the action,
a wave pattern being beaten on the ōdaiko. Waving to the distant boat, Shunkan
mounts the perpendicular rock, leans on
it, and sadly waves. His eyes seem to be
watching the boat as it slowly moves
away behind the audience from left to
right.*)

> He climbs up to the highest shore
>   point
> And, waving, stretches his frame
> As tall as he can,
> Then breaks down, weeping,
> In the pure white sand.
> Though he burns with longing
> And shouts with despair
> Not a soul is there to comfort him.
> Only the cries of the gulls
> And the wild geese flying overhead
> Answer his lonely calls.

(During this passage Shunkan comes to the edge of the stage down left, waving and calling "Farewell, farewell" in a tone which is half laughing, half crying. He moves to center, still watching the imaginary boat, then stops, walks to his hut, weeps, turns back to face the audience, suddenly runs to the hanamichi, and goes several feet onto it. A few moments earlier the gray ground cloth on the hanamichi was removed, revealing a wave cloth covering half its length. Pulled by unseen strings this cloth now moves toward the stage. When it comes to his feet, Shunkan stops. The waves pursue him, chasing him back to the stage. Meanwhile, the ground cloths on stage are whisked away by unseen hands, the cloths being pulled underneath the flats standing at either side of the stage, including those fronting the geza. The entire stage surface is soon seen to be covered with wave cloths. As Shunkan moves back from the hanamichi, the revolving stage begins to move slowly from right to left. The large rock that was upstage right now comes into the foreground at down right.)

His only friends are the chidori,
The plovers, which he lures to his
  side.
The tide rushes in to cut him off
  from those
Who have left him behind.

(A camouflaged ramp is built into this rock and this ramp now faces the audience. Shunkan begins to struggle up the ramp as if trying to climb to the top of the rock for a better view. As he does so the stage continues to revolve slowly until the rock is at center. He stumbles but clings to a vine of ivy. He turns to gaze off into the distance, holding the ivy over his shoulder, as the rock revolves. He then pulls himself to the top. At the peak is a small pine tree. Shunkan comes up behind this and strains for a glimpse of the boat through the branches. He leans too heavily on a branch and it snaps off suddenly as the wave drum beats loudly. He falls forward roughly, almost toppling off the front of the rock. He lifts his hands to his face, calling, them waving, "Ahoy! Ahoy!" He is in the spotlight, the other lights having been dimmed.)

His sleeves are drenched
By his falling tears.

(The sound of the final crack of the ki is heard. Shunkan stops calling, slowly lowers his hand, his body sinks lower, he places his right hand on his right knee and looks off. All hope has fled from his face and he is now, for the first time, truly aware of the loneliness that henceforth must always be his. The wave pattern is beaten on the geza drum as a flute's plaintive notes are heard and the curtain closes.)

CURTAIN

Figure 66. Shunkan enters and stands before his hut holding a bit of seaweed in his hand (*Shunkan,* Nakamura Kanzaburō).

Figure 67. Shunkan peruses Senō's orders but cannot find his name (*Shunkan,* Kataoka Nizaemon).

Figure 68. Shunkan's friends commiserate with him on his tragic news (*Yasuyori,* Kawarazaki Gonjūrō; *Naritsune,* Kataoka Gatō; *Shunkan,* Kataoka Nizaemon).

Figure 69. Tanzaemon shows his document to Shunkan (*Yasuyori,* Kawarazaki Gonjūrō; *Shunkan,* Kataoka Nizaemon; *Naritsune,* Kataoka Gatō; *Tanzaemon,* Ichimura Uzaemon).

Figure 70. Nakamura Fukusuke as Senō.

Figure 71. Senō viciously strikes Shunkan with his fan (*Shunkan,* Nakamura Kan'emon; *Senō,* Ichikawa Yoshinosuke). Note Senō's white wig as compared with that worn by Fukusuke in Fig. 70.

Figure 72. Shunkan gains the upper hand for a moment in his fight with Senō (*Chidori,* Nakamura Tanosuke; *Shunkan,* Ichikawa Ennosuke; *Senō,* Kataoka Takao).

Figure 73. The Kan'u mie (*Shunkan,* Ichikawa Somegorō).

Figure 74. Shunkan begs Chidori to board the boat in his place (*Chidori,* Nakamura Senjaku; *Shunkan,* Kataoka Nizaemon).

Figure 75. Tanzaemon raises his fan to Shunkan (*Naritsune,* Kataoka Gatō; *Yasuyori,* Kawarazaki Gonjūrō; *Tanzaemon,* Ichimura Uzaemon).

Figure 76.   Shunkan waves farewell from the top of
the rock (*Shunkan,* Nakamura Kanzaburō).

Naozamurai

4

(*Kumo ni Magō Ueno no Hatsuhana*)
A Kabuki Play by
Kawatake Mokuami
The Soba Shop Scene (*Soba-ya no ba*)
The Ōguchi Hostel Scene (*Ōguchi-ryō no ba*)

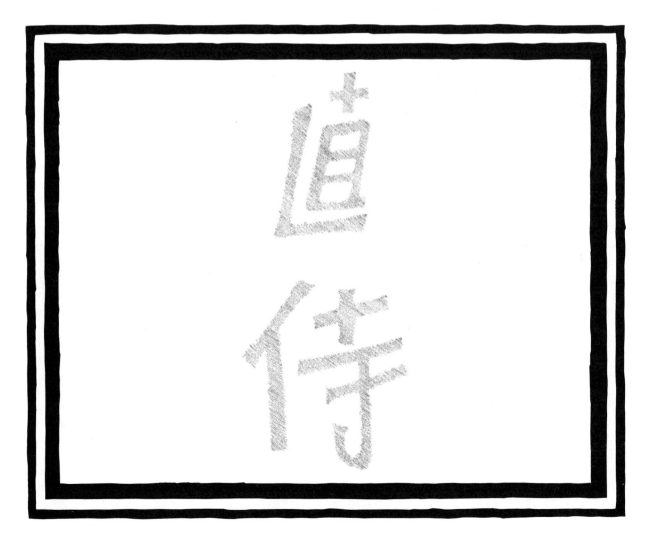

BACKGROUND TO THE PLAY

Naozamurai is the name given to a section of Kawatake Mokuami's long domestic play, *The First Flowers of Ueno* (*Kumo ni Magō Ueno no Hatsuhana*), often performed as an independent play. It was first detached from the longer work and played separately in 1910 at Tokyo's Kabuki Theatre. Ichimura Uzaemon XV starred as Naozamurai and Baikō VI played Michitose.

The story was derived from the storyteller's tale (*kodan*) titled *Six Poets of the Tempō Era* (*Tempō Rokkasen*), by the famous Matsubayashi Hakuen, popularly known as "Thief" Hakuen because of his expertise at creating robber-stories. The "six poets" alluded to in the title of the kodan were the six chief demimonde characters in the tale. When the play was first performed, at the Kawarazaki Theatre (Kawarazaki-za) in 1874, only part of the full-length play as it now exists was produced. It dealt with an extortion carried out on a samurai lord by the sacrilegious priest, Kochiyama, and was titled *The Clouds of Ueno* (*Kumo no Ueno Sane no Sakumae*). This plot forms the basis for the part of the play now popularly known as *Kochiyama,* also often performed as a separate drama. In 1881 the play was expanded to include the dramatic action dealing with the character of the romantic rascal, Naojirō, commonly called Naozamurai. This was staged at the Shintomi Theatre (Shintomi-za) with Kikugorō as Naojirō and Iwai Hanshirō VIII as Michitose. Following the 1910 performance of *Naozamurai* and the 1913 presentation of *Kochiyama,* producers had the option of presenting the two parts together on one bill as a full-length production or of doing either part separately.

Another title for the Naozamurai section dealing specifically with the Naojirō-Michitose love story is *A Narrow Road in Iriya on a Snowy Evening* (*Yuki no Yube Iriya no Azemichi*). This title, which applies to the scenes translated here, makes up the sixth act of the original play, which is in seven acts.

Naozamurai is famous as an example of the type of writing which led to Mokuami's being labeled the "bandit play" dramatist. Like *Benten Kozō* it is a "bandit play" or shiranami mono; similarly, it is classed as a kizewamono play, one which depicts quite vividly the lives and activities of colorful figures from Edo's underworld. In conventional Western terms, the play is "realistic"; it lacks the spectacular pyrotechnics associated with such Kabuki fare as *Pulling the Carriage Apart* and concentrates on the closely observed behavior of its leading characters. The scenic environment and costumes evoke the illusion of real life in their attention to naturalistic details. Yet, Kabuki "realism" is far from what most Westerners think of in connection with the term; despite certain outward displays of naturalistic technique, the acting is constantly informed by a fundamental rhythmic premise of which the audience is frequently reminded by the almost constant background accompaniment of shamisen music. In the second of the scenes given here, the actual onstage presence of a group of musicians acts to remove the events transpiring in Michitose's room from the realm of actuality and to raise them to a plane where they can be appreciated for their aesthetic value.

The Ōguchi hostel scene is considered a representative Kabuki love scene or *nureba* ("moist scene"). The hauntingly romantic and melancholy kiyomoto singing and shamisen playing of the onstage musicians are one reason this scene has become so well known as an example of Kabuki eroticism.

PLOT AND KATA

The long and complex play from which the present scenes are taken tells of a scheme devised by the clever but rascally priest, Kochiyama, to extort money from a powerful samurai, Lord Matsue. Matsue has been keeping one of his young ladies-in-waiting at his mansion against her will. Kochiyama disguises himself as a well-known abbot's emissary, enters Matsue's mansion, and manages to extort a nice sum of money from Matsue and to secure the girl's release as well. Meanwhile, another plot development presents the love story of the dashing former samurai, Naojirō, nicknamed Naozamurai because of his earlier position, and the beautiful courtesan, Michitose. Naozamurai is Kochiyama's close friend. Nao (as he is affectionately called) has had his hand in a number of illegal pies, including gambling. He also participates in Kochiyama's deception of Lord Matsue. Ultimately, the law becomes aware of Nao's misdeeds and sets out after him. He decides to leave Edo until things cool down. It is at this point that the first scene translated here begins. The curtain opens, revealing a snowy April night. Desolate, snow-covered rice fields and the soba shop to which they are adjacent are shown.

Soba is a kind of long noodle, usually eaten in a special broth. Hot soba is a favorite dish during the cold winter months. Iriya, where the soba shop is located, was a part of greater Edo during the Edo era and was not far from the famed pleasure quarters, the Yoshiwara.

Two men are being served soba by the proprietors. These men are police spies. They have been asking questions regarding a nearby house, the Ōguchi, used as a hostel by a Yoshiwara brothel. After they leave, the proprietors, Nihachi and Okayo, reveal their ill feelings regarding the two. They surmise that their best customer, a blind masseur named Joga, has been delayed by the storm.

As drums beating out a rhythm suggestive of a snowstorm begin, the dashing figure of Naozamurai appears on the hanamichi. Aware that the police are on his trail, he is seeking to get out of Edo. However, he is resolved, whatever the danger, to see his girlfriend, Michitose, once more before leaving.

Acting Naozamurai. The two representative styles for playing this role were created by Kikugorō VI and Uzaemon XV, the same actors whose Benten Kozō kata form the main traditions for that play. Uzaemon is said to have displayed a casual, carefree elegance in this scene whereas Kikugorō's Naozamurai had a tense, edgy quality. As Kagayama Naozō writes, the nervousness is explicit in the text itself, so Kikugorō's depiction, though less visually beautiful, was probably superior. Uzaemon relied too heavily on his "form," and his personal sparkle and bravado detracted from the lonely mood the scene is meant to convey.

It was part of Kikugorō's approach for the houselights to be dimmed during the scene; this technique, though not used during the greater part of his career, was adopted by Uzaemon in his later years when his approach to the role veered more toward the Kikugorō style. According to Kagayama, his performance was thereby improved.[1]

Among later actors, one of the most popular players of Naozamurai was Danjūrō XI, who performed in a style mixing the best kata of Kikugorō and Uzaemon, as he had done in his interpretation of Benten Kozō. His son, Ebizō X, upon whom the present stage directions are based, follows his father's kata in most essentials. He says he never did see his father's performance, though, and learned the role from Kawarazaki Gonjūrō III (1915-), who also has performed it successfully in recent years. Danjūrō once related his ideas on acting the role of Naozamurai; his words are instructive:

> In the soba shop scene, I have selected what I felt was best from the styles of both Uzaemon and Kikugoro, creating a compromise between the two. Since my physical appearance is closer to that of Uzaemon than to that of Kikugoro my approach may seem closer to Uzaemon's but my own inner point of view attempts to blend the two.

In so far as my makeup and costume is concerned I never saw Kikugorō V do the role so I can only guess at his emotional qualities but they say he changed his facial appearance from the soba shop to the hostel scene. From a theoretical point of view this is a bit odd since the scenes follow one another directly but, according to Kikugorō's inner approach, the soba shop scene emphasizes a conservative, realistic mood, while the scene at the hostel is more romantic and is even backed by kiyomoto music. Therefore, he used more flesh tones in his soba shop makeup and added more white for the [more romantic] hostel scene. Thus, they say that when the soba shop scene was over Kikugorō V changed his entire makeup. Since he was so diligent, they say the curtain for the next scene was always late; in the old days, when things were more relaxed, the audience took this in its stride but it would be absolutely out of the question today; further, it would probably destroy the continuity between the soba shop and hostel scenes. Therefore, when I exit on the hanamichi from the shop I don't return to my dressing room. I adjust my facial makeup in the agemaku room by simply adding a slight amount of facial whitener.[2]

---

1. *Kabuki* (Tokyo, 1968), pp. 113-114.

2. "Geidan" ("Chats on Art"), *Engekikai,* no. 2 (1956), p. 103.

Kikugorō VI wrote that a difficult feature of the role is that Naozamurai is not the average samurai. Even though he is seen here as a gambler, he must communicate the quality of a stylish character once in the employ of a noble house. His father, the creator of the role, said,

> It is very difficult to act the part of a samurai if one isn't wearing one's swords; to show that, even though he is now a gambler who was once a samurai, it is important to act the role as if there were swords at his side; if this technique is carried out thoroughly, the samurai quality will be retained, even if he is only wearing a simple obi.... Furthermore, the left hand should be placed on the obi as if there were two swords there. If this is remembered the "look" of a samurai will be conveyed.[3]

Nao's costume, created by Kikugorō V, became quite popular in Tokyo at the time of the play's first presentations. Many lower-class elements in the city took it up as a badge but Kikugorō asserted that this was not his purpose in creating it. He merely wanted a costume that suggested the gentleness of a strong character.[4]

Nao is carrying an umbrella over one shoulder. It was Kikugorō V's kata to come to the shop with the umbrella on his right shoulder and to go to the hostel with it on his left. Uzaemon also did this but Danjūrō had it on his right shoulder both times. Ebizō, though, enters with it on his left shoulder here and on his right when going to the hostel. In his book, *Gei,* Kikugorō VI mentions that he bore it on his left shoulder in the present scene. Switching the shoulder used provides visual variety and helps, though subtly, to suggest the contrasting tone of the two scenes.

Nao decides to stop for a bowl of soba on his way out of town. He enters the shop, takes off his clogs, and seats himself on the upstage platform used by customers in the shop.

Kikugorō's Clog Kata. Kikugorō V had a distinctive way of taking off and putting on his clogs or sandals, off stage and on. He would remove them so that one sandal faced outward, the other inward. Then, when he stepped into one he would wheel about and put on the other. He used this method in the soba shop scene when Nao gets ready to make his exit.[5]

Nao runs to the hibachi upstage left and warms himself around the thighs.

The Thigh-Warming Kata. This is an Uzaemon kata. Often criticized for being too lighthearted for the scene, the audience does indeed laugh when Ebizō performs it. Kikugorō VI was much more

3. Quoted in Kikugorō VI, *Gei,* p. 196.
4. See Endō Tameharu, "Naozamurai," *Engei Gahō,* no. 1 (1921), p. 284.
5. *Jōen Shiryōshū* (October 1968), p. 101.

toned down here and did not play up the coldness for comic effect as much as Uzaemon, who even ad-libbed, "It's cold, it's cold" as he ran to the hibachi. Kikugorō suggested the cold through subtle gestures and tone of voice. He was more successful than Uzaemon at transmitting the idea of a fugitive on the run.[6]

Danjūrō XI, who followed the Uzaemon kata in this section, wrote,

> I feel this business emphasizes
> Naozamurai's rakish character. I
> therefore follow the Uzaemon kata
> here even though Kikugorō felt it
> would be better to suggest
> Naozamurai's nature as a former
> low-grade samurai by behaving
> more modestly. As I see it, Nao
> enters freezing; he sees the hibachi,
> which makes him feel even colder
> and, shivering, he wants to run over
> to get near it. This is the same as
> when one is walking outdoors on a
> cold day and sees a fire or such
> burning and wants to run over
> quickly and warm oneself.
> Therefore, at this point, I dash over
> to the fire with my clogs going
> clip-clop, clip-clop. This too is an
> Uzaemon technique.[7]

Sitting at the hibachi he loosens his scarf, allowing its ends to hang down past his cheeks.

6. An interesting discussion of these points is in ibid., pp. 72-79.
7. "Geidan," p. 104.

The Scarf Kata. A good deal of critical ink has been devoted to discussions of the scarf business in this scene. Critics are fond of comparing those actors who left the scarf knot tied while eating and those who first loosened it. Uzaemon was the leader of the faction in favor of keeping the knot tied whereas Kikugorō VI always untied it. Also, though most actors wear the knot tied under the chin, Kikugorō V, according to extant photos, wore it a bit to the left side. As far as the actor's justification for keeping the knot tied or untied is concerned, some feel that it is a nuisance to untie the knot just so that they may eat their soba. (Soba, it should be noted, is eaten by holding the bowl near one's face and scooping the noodles into one's mouth with chopsticks.) Others argue that a petty crook like Nao would not eat his soba without first untying his scarf as was the way with members of his class. Which of the two ways is better is, of course, a moot point. There are some actor's tricks concerned with the wearing of this scarf. Danjūrō IX summed them up succinctly (he followed Kikugorō's kata of untying the scarf):

> Since the scarf is twisted around at
> both sides and, when untied, hangs
> down at either ear, it would
> normally unwind and look awful; it
> would also hamper one's acting.
> Further, it would be a bother to fix
> correctly at the point where it has to
> be retied. Therefore, a thread is

sewn into the scarf at precisely that place just before the temples where the side twists hang down, to hold them in place. Also, Nao is an outlaw and wears a wig with the topknot slightly awry, but since he merely unties his knot in the soba shop and doesn't remove the scarf completely, the topknot is worn straight in this scene to make the scarf style more flattering. An off-center topknot would not look good here. Thus, a pin is stuck in the scarf at the topknot, holding it in place. Moreover, in order to make the knot at the chin look good it is tied tightly. Since the scarf is removed in the following scene, however, the pin can't be there to hold back the topknot nor can the knot under the chin be too tight for fear of ruining the topknot. The knot must now be tied lightly and not sewn in at either side; accordingly, a different scarf is used for each scene, though they look the same.[8]

In addition, actors of Naozamurai have a white thread sewn into the pleat at the center of the forehead. This preserves the dashing look of the scarf, even when it is retied later in the scene. Kikugorō VI was the first to use this device.

8. Ibid., p. 103.

Nao chats with the proprietors and learns of the two who were here before he arrived. As he begins to drink his sake he notices a mote in it and flicks it out swiftly with a chopstick.

The Dust in the Sake Kata. The "dust in the sake" kata was created by Uzaemon and is not performed by those who follow the Kikugorō tradition. Audiences used to greet this minute piece of business with shouts of "infinitesimal!" (*komakai*). Although it often gets a laugh, it has been criticized for weakening the dramatic mood.

Nao begins to eat his soba while drinking warm sake.

Eating the Soba. Being a true "son of Edo" Nao eats his noodles the way any Edokko would, even today. In other words, he slurps its, sucking up the noodles noisily and, to the average Westerner, rudely. However, the two spies seen earlier in the scene do not eat their noodles in this way but chew them silently as is the manner with out-of-towners and country folk. This difference in the manner of eating the soba is always maintained in performances of the play.

The drinking of the sake is usually done with the actor holding the cup in his left hand and the bottle in his right; Kikugorō V drank while still holding the bottle, in order to make Nao's manners seem slightly vulgar.

Nao listens surreptitiously and learns from Joga's remarks that his sweetheart, Michitose, is ailing from Nao's not having visited her for a very long time. Nao calls for a brush and ink and begins to quietly write Michitose a letter.

The Brush-Tip Kata. An interesting kata, no longer performed, had the tip of the brush falling off when Naozamurai went to write with it. Superstition held this to be a bad omen years ago but contemporary audiences do not share the superstition and would not understand the kata's significance if performed. At any rate, this is the reason offered by present-day actors for their not performing it. The kata was created by Kikugorō V, who followed it up by another interesting piece of business. Not having a brush to write with, Kikugorō took a toothpick he had in his kimono collar, chewed its end to make it soft, and used it in lieu of a brush to write his letter. In one modern interpretation, that of the late Ichikawa Jukai III (1887-1971), the brush was brought to Naozamurai already missing its head; Jukai then did the kata with the toothpick. Uzaemon XV is said never to have done the toothpick kata and even Kikugorō V abandoned it in his later years. Kikugorō VI noted that his own reason for not doing the toothpick kata was that one has no use for a toothpick when eating soba. He states that his father told him that this reason eventually prompted him to abandon the business.[9]

Nao finishes eating and pays his bill. He rises, puts on his clogs, takes his umbrella, and quickly leaves the shop. As he walks to stage right, the set revolves to stage left. He waits in the shadows for Joga, who soon appears. Nao convinces Joga to deliver his note to Michitose. As Nao is about to leave he is confronted by his fellow gang member, Ushimatsu, whose voice stops him in his tracks.

Encounter with Ushimatsu. Miyake Saburō, the critic, recalls that when Uzaemon and Jukai played Naozamurai they paused upon first hearing Ushimatsu's voice, seemed to give the matter some thought, then turned to face him. Danjūrō XI, he says, was a little vague here but Kikugorō VI was excellent. He did not show his face to Ushimatsu right away but looked carefully at his friend's feet from behind his umbrella, suggesting his precautionary attitude.[10]

The two fugitives discuss how dangerous the situation is in Edo and wonder what they should do to escape. They part sadly, Nao calling out, with a sniffle, "Take care!" as he moves on down the hanamichi.

Parting of the Fugitives. Ushimatsu's parting call to Nao must be timed exactly. His words, "And so, dear friend..." must be spoken at precisely that moment when Nao is extending his right foot. If Ushimatsu's timing is one breath late Nao will end up in a position with his left foot extended. This will

9. *Gei*, p. 181.

10. *Kabuki o Mirume*, pp. 23-24.

force him to take an extra step in order to turn back to his left to speak his final line and will throw off the timing of the sequence. Kikugorō V was very strict about this matter with the actors who played Ushimatsu to his Naozamurai. Iguchi Seiji tells an amusing story concerning this business. The actor, Kozō, had been in disfavor with Kikugorō and was finally allowed back into the master's good graces when he played Ushimatsu in a performance at the Kabuki Theatre in 1900. Because he was extremely concerned about getting the timing of Ushimatsu's line down perfectly so as not to rile Kikugorō, he prepared as diligently as he could. On opening day, when he successfully finished the scene, he returned home delighted with himself. After eating dinner and calming down, it suddenly dawned on him that he had forgotten to make his entry in the following scene, where he appears for a brief but important moment of pantomime business. His heart pounding with fear he went to Kikugorō's house in the middle of the night to beg the master's forgiveness. The next day, even though he made the proper entrance in the hostel scene, the kiyomoto singers who accompany the scene's action failed to sing their customary line about his entrance. Instead, they were silent during his business and then thrust in the improvised line, "Oh, did he make his entrance today?"[11]

As mentioned, Nao speaks his final line as he sniffs his nose, suggesting that he is weeping inwardly at having to leave his good friend. Not all actors perform this kata. Among those who did were Danjūrō XI, Kikugorō V, and Uzaemon XV. Kikugorō VI ignored it because, in his words, "Nao is leaving in order to have a rendezvous with the beautiful Michitose and sniffing his running nose has no romantic overtones."[12]

Danjūrō, though, had this to say:

As I see it, the moment when Nao says, "Take care!" and wipes his nose derives from the fact that, though they are both petty crooks, he and Ushimatsu share a bond of brotherly affection. Each must leave Edo. When Nao is stopped by Ushi's cry, "dear friend," he is thinking they may never meet again and a feeling of compassion comes over him, causing him to wipe his running nose, after which he delivers his line, "Take care!"[13]

After Nao has gone, Ushimatsu reveals that he can save his own neck by turning Nao in to the police. He debates the ethics of the matter with himself and then resolves to betray his friend. The curtain closes as he moves off to accomplish his task.

The following scene is at the Ōguchi hostel where Michitose is pining for her lover. At the right of the stage is a gateway leading to the hostel; at center is a reception room within the hostel; at left is a pavilion in which sit a group of kiyomoto musicians and singers behind a closed bamboo blind. Snow blankets

11. *Jōen Shiryōshū* (October 1968), p. 103.

12. *Gei*, p. 185.
13. "Geidan," p. 104.

all outside areas, including the roofs of hostel and pavilion.

The Kiyomoto Accompaniment. The kiyomoto musicians provide narrative accompaniment to the action, much like the gidayū in other plays included in this book. However, the main purpose of kiyomoto, unlike the gidayū, is not so much to describe the actions of the play in detail as it is to fill in the mood and atmosphere—to enhance the reverberations of feeling evoked by the acting.

Though the acting style in this scene is not as naturalistic as in the soba shop scene, it is still fairly realistic when compared with that used in other Kabuki plays. In other words, the vocal and physical emphases are relatively subdued; the histrionic focus is, on the whole, more internal than external and there is a good deal of attention to the minutiae of quotidian existence. Nevertheless, the existence of the kiyomoto musicians on their raised platform would seem to call for a more overtly theatricalized mode of performance. In order to rationalize their presence and bring it into line with the basically illusionistic acting format, several lines were inserted in the script stating that the people in the home neighboring the hostel are practicing kiyomoto this evening. Though some of these lines are in segments no longer performed and, consequently, not translated here, a line later in the scene still remains to justify the musicians being there. The placement of the kiyomoto pavilion, though, is actually contrary to

convention. Normally, kiyomoto (and *tokiwazu*) musicians are seated stage right, nagauta at center, and gidayū at left.

The kiyomoto in this scene is one of Kabuki's most famous examples. Its great beauty so thrilled audiences at its first performances that the number of kiyomoto pupils is said to have increased greatly.

After a mood-setting passage of kiyomoto music, Naozamurai enters on the snow-covered hanamichi.

Uzaemon versus Kikugorō. Most critics feel that Uzaemon XV's Naozamurai was superior to Kikugorō VI's in the hostel scene, though they say the contrary was true for the preceding scene. Obviously, the scene's romantic qualities were perfectly suited to the handsome Uzaemon's personal style.[14]

At one point during his entrance, Nao seems to stumble; he whirls around in a beautiful pose with his umbrella over his shoulder. He then moves along and comes to the gateway at stage right.

The Snow Trick. There is a good deal of paper and cotton on the eaves over the gateway to simulate snow. Hidden beneath the artificial snow at the center is a sheet of material attached to a thin string leading off right into the wings. When

14. See, for example, Shino Hatarō, "Naozamurai," *Engekikai,* no. 2 (1972), pp. 98-101.

Nao strikes the bamboo clapper on the gateway the sound-effects musicians beat a large drum to signify the sound of snow and a hidden stage assistant in the wings at right pulls the string, causing a pile of "snow" to fall heavily from the eaves onto Nao's shoulders.

Michitose's maids hear Nao at the gate and cautiously let him in. Shivering from the cold, Nao enters the room and soon begins to warm himself at an elegant wooden brazier. At this moment, Ushimatsu enters from the wings at right and indicates in pantomime (the business alluded to above) that he will go and fetch the police now that his friend's location is assured. The courtesan, Michitose, summoned by a maid, enters upstage center and rushes to her lover.

Acting Michitose. Prior to today's generation of actors, the great performers of Michitose included Iwai Hanshirō VIII, who created the role, Onoe Baikō VI, Kataoka Nizaemon XII, and Sawamura Gennosuke IV (1859-1936). Popular actors of the role in today's theater include Baikō VII, Utaemon VI (1917-), and Nakamura Jakuemon IV (1920-). Kikugorō VII, upon whose performance the stage directions in the translation are based, has not played the role many times but his work shows excellent promise for the future.

Baikō VI said that Michitose must not come rushing into the room on her entrance nor should she merely stand at the doorway. The actor should, instead, first look to the doorway on the right,

then, looking left, see that Naozamurai is there and rush to him. It is a test of the actor's skill, he said, to see how fully he can convey the proper emotional tone at this moment. He also pointed out that

Naozamurai has stopped by to see his love on his flight to Jōshu, so he should not be filled with joy at this meeting. Therefore, his speech and acting with Michitose must be as moderate as possible. Michitose, for her part, not having seen her beloved Naojirō for some time, has become ill and has even had to come to the hostel for a rest. So she, too, is melancholic. Her sole expression of joy is when, having heard that Nao has come to see her, she flies into the room; when she learns that they must soon be parted she, like her disconsolate lover, must not fail to sink into a quiet and sad melancholy. She must never appear to the audience as gay and flashy....[15]

Sawamura Gennosuke IV, who often played the role of Michitose against Kikugorō VI's Naozamurai, left the following instructions for playing the role:

The role of a courtesan is often played with the kata of having one knee raised while sitting and, among today's young actors, there are those who deliberately raise their

15. *Jōen Shiryōshū* (October 1968), pp. 68-69.

knee high. However, a far better form than this intentional assumption of the one-knee-raised posture is produced by neither raising the knee nor keeping it flat on the floor but by lifting the leg very slightly, letting it appear at the side of the body to the rear, with the side of the big toe on the floor, the robe covering the feet. The feet are not seen in this kata but it looks fine nevertheless. Still, if this is not performed correctly and does not come from the center of the body, it will look like a rather queer slumping position that actors must be careful to avoid.[16]

The lovers are left alone and, as the kiyomoto accompanies their movement, enact in a sort of dance-mime their feelings of longing and despair.

The Kudoki. The dance-mime in this scene is within the framework of a convention known as kudoki or "lamentation," an example of which we have seen performed by Chidori in *Shunkan.* Kudoki scenes are most frequently performed as solos by female impersonators but in the present instance both a male and female performer participate in it. It stands out from the more naturalistically acted portions of the scene in its evident musicality and almost dance-like nature. Though surely a *pas de deux* in its lyrical evocation through movement of passion-

ate emotions, Kikugorō VI was very insistent that it not be danced. He said it must be a kind of "non-dance dancing." It was originally choreographed by the nineteenth-century dance master, Hanayagi Jusuke, his inspiration being a woodblock print by Utamaro in which Michitose stood posing with her left hand holding up her collar from within her robe, looking down at Naozamurai seated beneath her on the floor. Though the choreography is somewhat different, a pose similar to this is still performed during the sequence and the general outline of the original choreography remains.

This love scene is considered one of Kabuki's most erotic. Although it is performed in a beautiful, languid pattern of elegantly graceful movements, a tone of intense sensuality runs strongly throughout it. The degree of overt sensuality in the scene is apparently less today than formerly. There is said to have been a production where Naozamurai, played by Kikugorō VI, lay on his belly playing with Michitose's feet but the Metropolitan Police put a stop to it and it was never repeated.[17]

Nao tells Michitose he must leave Edo and may not see her again for years. To his surprise, she reveals a knowledge of his crimes and begs him to take her with him or kill her. He refuses both requests. A clerk named Yoshibei enters and entreats the two to

16. Ibid.

17. Kikugorō VI provides a detailed description of his performance during this sequence in *Gei*. It differs in a number of small details from the manner described in the text.

flee together. In fuller versions of the scene another character, Kaneko Ichinojō, enters here. He is a wealthy patron of Michitose's who has long sought to have her break off with Naozamurai. Since Ichinojō suffers from night blindness he does not see Nao and mocks him sharply, as if he were not there. He tosses Michitose her bond of indenture, freeing her from a life of prostitution, and departs. Only later do the lovers learn that this man is really Michitose's brother. The section was cut from the performance used as a model for this translation and is not included here.

The two police spies from the opening scene burst into the room but Nao throws them off and escapes, calling out to Michitose that they will never meet again.

The Final Moments. This closing sequence used to be performed with a bit more action than is presently the case. A larger number of pursuers was used. Nao would run to the hanamichi and be attacked there by a policeman; he would then turn around swiftly and his jacket would come off in the attacker's hands. The battle between Nao and the police was more complex and interesting than the rather perfunctory staging it now receives.

In productions where Ichinojō is not cut, the final tableau differs from that described in the text. In such productions the two maids are likely to be on stage at the end of the scene. When the National Theatre staged the play several years ago, Yoshibei was on the platform and Michitose posed at the center step, held back from pursuing Naozamurai by the maids kneeling at her sides.

Ultimately, both Naozamurai and his confederate, Kochiyama, are taken by the police. When the play ends, it appears likely that they will eventually be released from prison.

The exquisite kiyomoto music of *Naozamurai* can be heard on a recording that does not include the scene's spoken dialogue. This is on Japan Victor album JL-18. The music is titled *Secret Rendezvous During the Spring Thaw* (*Shinobiau Haru no Yukidoke*). It is also called, simply, *Michitose*.

Texts used in preparing the translation may be found in the *Kokuritsu Gekijō Jōen Taihonshū,* Vol. IV, and the *Meisaku Kabuki Zenshū,* Vol. XI.

The production from which the stage directions were derived starred Ichikawa Ebizō X as Naozamurai, Onoe Kikugorō VII as Michitose, and Bandō Minosuke VII (1929-) as Ushimatsu (Kabuki Theatre, Tokyo, March 1975).

THE SOBA SHOP SCENE

(*The Iriya Village soba shop, near Edo. A conventional Kabuki indoor-outdoor setting, the better part of the stage from left to right center being occupied by the soba shop. Upstage a platform about eighteen inches high occupies most of the interior. A price list hangs on the wall upstage left. The stage right area within the shop, off the platform, contains a brick stove on which soba is prepared. Steam pours out over the top of the stove when fanned by the proprietor, Nihachi, a middle-aged man. In the upper right corner of the platform is a low, latticed screen that denotes the area as an "office." An abacus and writing utensils, including ledger, inkstone, and brush are placed above this screen. A latticed wooden standing screen is at the rear of the platform. On the wall above the "office" area is a paper window. The area above the stove contains a row of shelves with bowls and cups. The door to the shop is at right and consists of a sliding door, the upper half of which is made of latticed frames filled with paper. A gray cloth covers the floor below the platform. Below the stove is a large barrel stuffed with straw. When the curtain opens Nihachi is standing above the stove, tending to its fire. His wife, Okayo, is seated on her knees below the office screen, slicing onions on a board. She faces right. Seated on the edge of the platform at right center are two men, eating soba. They wear black kimono and "rain" haori as well as slacks of the same material. They also wear wooden clogs. A single umbrella rests against the platform, at the left. The scene outside the shop is one of a snowy evening. Background scenery depicts the snow-covered fields nearby. The wall covering the musicians' room at right shows trees with snow-laden branches. White sheeting lies over the entire stage area outside the shop, including the hanamichi. Snow drifts down from overhead on this portion of the stage proper. It is about eight in the evening and the roads are deserted. The two men eating soba, Kanji and Senda, are actually police spies, searching for Kataoka Naojirō, better known as Naozamurai. Drumbeats from the geza suggest the falling snow. As the ki clappers are smacked together faster and faster the curtain opens. As is typical of such scenes the first few lines are spoken quite realistically, almost as though ad-libbed. The scene is played in a rather realistic style but this "realism" is always tempered by the rhythm of the dialogue and the shamisen music accompanying the action. The scene progresses at a fairly smooth and "nondramatic" tempo until the entry of Naozamurai.*)

KANJI: (*Speaks as soon as the curtain opens; he is seated to the left of his partner.*) Hey waitress, I'll have another bowl of soba here.

OKAYO: Yes, yes. Certainly.

(*To Nihachi*)

Another portion, please.

NIHACHI: Sure.

KANJI: Hey, boss, the Yoshiwara district's Ōguchi hostel is around here somewhere, isn't it?

(*Nihachi crosses down a few steps to the right edge of the platform. He holds a flat utensil, something like a fan, used for fanning the flames on the stove. He gestures with it off right as he talks.*)

NIHACHI: Yes, you'll get there if you go left at the next side street. It's the second house from the corner.

SENDA: They say that Michitose, the popular courtesan is staying at the Ōguchi, right?

NIHACHI: Yes. She's been there with her servants ever since she became ill.

KANJI: I understand there's a gardener there who's been looking after the place.

NIHACHI: (*Crossing back to stove*) Yes, that's true. His name is Yoshibei and he's a good man.

KANJI: (*Places right hand on edge of platform and leans over, talking over his shoulder*) They've got a pretty fancy front gate over there, I hear. Where would their back entrance be, I wonder?

NIHACHI: It's on the new road behind the charcoal shop.

KANJI: (*Quietly, to Senda*) We can enter from there, huh?

(*They raise their bowls, drink the broth, and put down a coin or two in payment.*

Okayo crosses down, takes the money, and bows to the men, who rise. She sits by the tray holding their empty bowls.)

SENDA: (*As they rise*) Now that this soba's warmed us, let's get moving.

(*They cross to the door, Kanji taking the umbrella.*)

NIHACHI: (*Coming to them as they cross*) The bridge is damaged up ahead so please be careful crossing it.

KANJI: (*At door*) Right. Thanks.

OKAYO: Thank you and come again.

(*Nihachi bows slightly. Okayo moves to the right of the platform bowing to the men on her knees. Kanji opens the door, then opens the umbrella outside the door.*)

KANJI: Brrr. It sure is cold. That wind goes right through you.

SENDA: Let's not waste any time.

(*The ōdaiko drum in the geza beats out the sound effect of snow. The men step out under the single umbrella, huddled together. As they begin to go out right, Senda sharply flips back the downstage fold of his jacket, revealing a jitte stuck through his obi. This is an immediate signal to the audience that the men are policemen. They exit right. Nihachi comes to the door and closes it. Okayo moves to the tray, brings it to the right of the platform, and sits there on her knees, talking to her husband, who comes down to the right of the platform.)*

NIHACHI: I wonder who those two were. They sure didn't look honest. Why do you think they were asking so many questions about the Ōguchi?

OKAYO: They asked about the back entrance. You don't think they're robbers, do you?

NIHACHI: What? If they were robbers do you think they'd show their faces like that and speak about such things so openly?

OKAYO: Whatever they are I don't trust them. Don't you think we should close up early tonight?

NIHACHI: No one is out in this snowstorm nor is anyone sending out for deliveries. Maybe we should close up but Joga, the blind masseur, still hasn't come. He always stops here every day on his way to the Ōguchi.

(He crosses back to the stove with the tray. Okayo goes back to the onions. She places them behind the screen and then busies herself entering accounts in the ledger. She uses an inkstone and brush.)

OKAYO: Maybe he's not coming today because of the snow. If he were passing by he would certainly drop in.

NIHACHI: He's our best customer. No one likes soba as much as he does.

(Tends to soba fire)

OKAYO: That's true.

(Shamisen music begins to play, snow falls, drums for the sound effect begin, and the lights on the hanamichi come up. After a few moments, Naozamurai enters. He wears a short coat [hanten] and his blue, lined kimono [awase] is tucked up at the rear, leaving his hand-some legs exposed. His kimono's fine criss-cross pattern is called aimijin. *He wears the* fukuro tsuki no mushiri *wig that shows the hair grown in, but not too thickly, on the usually shaved crown of the head. His hair and cheeks are covered by a polka-dotted towel [tenugui], used as a scarf. On his bare feet are geta clogs. He carries a cream-white umbrella with cotton fluff and paper attached to it to look like snow. He walks slowly, lifting each foot high before putting it down, suggesting that he is walking through snow. He comes to the shichi-san, looks back to where he has come from, then turns to face the audience at the center of the theater. The umbrella rests on his left shoulder. His right hand is in his sleeve, held before his left shoulder. This is a posture known as the* yazō kata, *signify-ing a kind of popular stance taken by gamblers in the late Edo era. He speaks slowly, with deep feeling.)*

NAOZAMURAI: This morning's southerly wind has gone and that which now is blowing comes from out of the northeast. The snow has not fallen so thickly in years. Not a soul has passed me on the road, which suits me very well.

(*Pause; then looks off to the main stage*)

I think I'll have a bowl of soba.

(*Drums play and snow falls as he comes to the main stage. He stops about seven feet from the door of the soba shop, turns to face front, looks around cautiously, moves to the door, turns with his back to the door, bends over and taps the edge of his open umbrella on the ground to shake off loose snow, straightens up, closes the umbrella, stands with his left hand on the door, facing right, opens the door, looks into the shop cautiously, sees no one, steps quickly in, closes the door with his left hand, takes the umbrella in his left hand, and speaks. The next few lines are in a very rapid tempo.*)

Excuse me.

NIHACHI: Welcome, welcome. Can I help you?

NAOZAMURAI: One tempura soba please.

NIHACHI: I'm really very sorry but we haven't got tempura.

NAOZAMURAI: (*Speaking in the crisp, stacatto style of the Edokko*) Well, just give it to me plain. And some sake, too.

(*He is very cold and cannot bear it any longer. He runs quickly over to the left, puts his umbrella against the platform, removes his clogs, steps up onto the platform, and drops the hitched-up portion of his kimono so that it falls to his*

ankles. *He straddles a hibachi which is there, heating his frozen legs and thighs. He then unties the knot of his scarf, allowing it to remain on his head with the loose ends hanging down past his cheeks. He takes each of the front hems of his kimono and holds them for several moments over the hibachi, as if wringing them out. He then does the same for his sleeves, first the left, then the right. He holds his hands over the hibachi, warming them. Meanwhile, Okayo comes over, turns his clogs around to face away from the platform for his later ease in putting them on, and returns to her place up right. During this, the dialogue continues.*)

NIHACHI: Fine, fine.

(*Takes a bowl and begins to prepare soba. His wife warms a small sake bottle.*)

NAOZAMURAI: Waitress, can you bring me some hot charcoal?

OKAYO: Of course. It certainly is cold.

(*She brings some warm charcoal to the brazier on a small steel shovel and dumps it in.*)

NAOZAMURAI: The wind out there on the road through the rice fields is as sharp as a knife.

NIHACHI: The road is in bad condition. It must be a real bother walking on it. Ah! Your soba is ready.

(*Hands tray to Okayo*)

OKAYO: (*Going to Nihachi to get the tray*) Sorry to keep you waiting.

(*She brings a small tray with soba, sake bottle, and sake cup to Naozamurai. He picks up the cup, pours some sake into it, brings it near his lips, notices something in it, slowly reaches over, picks up a chopstick, brings it very slowly to the cup, then quickly flicks away the speck of dust he spotted and immediately downs the sake. He pours two more cups and drinks them down, saying "Ahhh!" as the warm sake hits his insides. Then, using chopsticks, he puts the chopped onions, served on a small dish with the soba, into the soba bowl, mixes them in, and, lifting a few strands of soba, begins to eat. Since he has been so cold, the eating of the hot noodles and drinking of the warm sake should suggest the need of the character to warm himself, as well as to fill his belly. Meanwhile, Okayo is grating radish up right and Nihachi is tending his fire. Naozamurai, after eating several mouthfuls, relaxes.*)

NAOZAMURAI: Errr...the Yoshiwara's Ōguchi hostel is around here, isn't it?

NIHACHI: Yes, you turn at the next side street.

NAOZAMURAI: Ah! The next side street, hm?

OKAYO: A couple of other men were just here asking the same thing.

NAOZAMURAI: What sort of men, may I ask?

OKAYO: Two rough-looking characters, dressed in rainjackets.

NAOZAMURAI: (*Slightly taken aback at the news*) Oh. I see.

(*Long pause as he thinks. He pours sake, drinks. The sake is cold so he turns to Okayo.*)

Waitress.

(*Gestures to sake bottle*)

Could you warm this please?

OKAYO: Certainly. I'm so sorry.

(*She crosses to Naozamurai, takes bottle, crosses up right, hands it to Nihachi. He heats the sake in a small pot in the up right corner. Naozamurai slowly eats his soba, a little at a time. Snow falls outside and the drums beat out the snow effect. Joga, a blind masseur, enters on the hanamichi. He wears dark slacks, a dark kimono, and a matching haori. A hood covers his head. He walks with a blind man's staff in his right hand, his umbrella over his left shoulder. On his feet are tabi and geta clogs. He comes to the shichi-san, stops, and faces the audience. His eyes are closed like a blind man's. Naozamurai pauses in his eating while Joga talks though the masseur is not aware of his presence.*)

JOGA: It just keeps snowing. It's hard walking when your clogs keep getting stuck in the snow. It sure isn't good weather for the masseur business.

(*Joga turns and walks slowly to the main stage, tapping before him with his cane. Nihachi goes to the sake, removes it, and hands it to Okayo on Joga's last line. Okayo brings the warm sake to Naozamurai.*)

OKAYO: Here you are. Sorry to take so long.

(*She crosses back to her vegetables up right. Naozamurai pours several cups of sake during the next few moments. When he hears Joga's voice in the shop he pulls the standing screen closer to him with his right hand, placing it so it shields him from view.*)

JOGA: (*Touching the door to the soba shop with his cane*) Hello in there.

(*Nihachi and Okayo see him and happily go to greet him. Okayo opens the door fully and lets him in.*)

NIHACHI: Ah! It's you, Joga, eh? Welcome, welcome.

(*Closes door*)

OKAYO: It's so good to see you.

(*Joga crosses to the platform where he sits on the edge, at right. Okayo steps on to the platform, gets a hibachi, places it near the old man at his left, and sits on her knees above him at his right. He warms his hands over the coals.*)

JOGA: I'm lucky you stayed open tonight, eh, Nihachi-san?

NIHACHI: Joga-san, we were just before talking about you.

(*Naozamurai, having recognized Joga, breathes a sigh of relief and begins to drink his sake again.*)

JOGA: Ahh. You flatter me. I'll have a nice hot bowl of soba, please. The usual way.

NIHACHI: Coming right up.

(*Returns to stove*)

OKAYO: You were late tonight so we thought you might have been taking the night off.

(*At this point, Naozamurai puts his hand in his right sleeve and takes out a tobacco pouch and pipe. He sits for a few moments with his left hand in his right sleeve, holding the pipe in his right hand. He is sitting on a slight angle, facing downstage left. He stuffs some tobacco in his pipe and lights it in the hibachi, takes a puff, and sits holding the pipe near his lap. When he hears mention of Michitose's name he strains his ears to listen to the conversation.*)

JOGA: Why's that? Why's that? I haven't taken even a single night off since Michitose became ill and left the pleasure quarters to stay at the Ōguchi hostel.

(*Naozamurai starts slightly at this. He has been staying away from the Yoshiwara because of his fear of being caught.*)

She asks for my services every night. I send my son on ahead for me but never fail to make my trip there after sunset.

(*Nihachi brings a bowl of soba on a tray to Joga. Okayo rises and takes it from her husband at right, and brings it to Joga herself. She takes the bowl and places it in his hands, then returns up right. The following is spoken during the sequence.*)

NIHACHI: She's certainly a good customer, eh? Here comes your soba!

OKAYO: Good. Here you are, Joga-san. The seasoning is already in it. Here are your chopsticks.

JOGA: (*Eating*) Ah! This is really hot. Mmmm. Good! Good!

NIHACHI: Thank you very much.

OKAYO: Tell me, Joga-san, what is the matter with this courtesan, Michitose?

JOGA: (*Stops eating momentarily*) Well, when a courtesan gets sick, seven out of ten times she's got syphilis. But Michitose's illness comes from the fact that her boyfriend, Nao-san, as she calls him, has done something awful and hasn't been able to visit

her in quite some time so she's suffering pretty badly from love sickness.

(*When he hears his name, Naozamurai turns away to face left on a diagonal.*)

Since she's a pretty important courtesan, she's been allowed to come out here for a change of environment at the hostel, in the hope that she'll soon recover.

(*During this Nihachi moves down from his stove a bit, stands at right of the platform, and smokes his pipe. Naozamurai is leaning against the screen, his left hand in his right sleeve, his right hand holding the pipe. Okayo moves to about two feet behind Joga.*)

NIHACHI: This Nao-san—I don't know him, of course, but if he can make a courtesan suffer like this, he must be quite a man.

JOGA: (*Laughs*) I wish I was lucky enough to have the same opportunity.

(*Nihachi laughs. Naozamurai quietly taps the ashes of his pipe into the receptacle on the hibachi; he then places the right hanging end of his scarf in his mouth, in order to muffle his voice. He leans over slightly to the right.*)

NAOZAMURAI: Pardon me, but could I have an inkstone and brush, please?

OKAYO: (*Crossing to him and bowing*) Surely. I'm afraid the brush is pretty poor, though.

NAOZAMURAI: That's all right. Anything will do.

OKAYO: I'll bring it right away.

(*Okayo brings the inkstone and brush, then returns stage right to Joga. Naozamurai pulls the nearby lamp closer at his left. He takes a folded piece of paper from his wallet, unfolds it, holds it in his left hand, rubs the inkstone to make ink with his right hand, dips the brush, thinks hard, and writes lightly holding the paper before him. Nihachi has crossed back to the stove. Naozamurai writes during the following.*)

OKAYO: If you go there every night you're probably being treated to all sorts of delicious things, eh?

JOGA: I'm afraid that's not the case. There's rarely any sake served and I was once served broiled eels three days in a row. One can get fed up with the same food, even if it's something tasty.

NIHACHI: If you can get delicious foods there why bother with soba?

JOGA: I'm so crazy about soba that I only have to sniff the stuff and I can't rest until my craving is satisfied.

NIHACHI: You really do like soba, don't you?

OKAYO: I don't know anyone . . .

BOTH: Who likes it as much as you do.

(*Naozamurai has finished his letter. He folds it and sharpens the creases by rubbing the letter against the edge of the hibachi. He then ties it into a knot and places it in his sleeve. He pushes the inkstone and brush away with his right hand.*)

JOGA: Can you bring me some of the soba broth?

(*Nihachi hands Okayo a red pitcher with the broth; she takes it and pours broth into Joga's bowl, then returns the pitcher.*)

NAOZAMURAI: (*A long pause as he puts a coin down on the tray and says with the cloth in his mouth*) Here you are.

(*He puts his tobacco and pipe away in his right sleeve and ties the scarf under his chin. He adjusts the crease above his forehead. Okayo comes over and removes the inkstone and brush and returns with it up right. Naozamurai rises, steps off the platform into his clogs, hitches up his kimono so that his legs are exposed, picks up his umbrella in his right hand, holding it at the top, and begins to go right. He sees Joga, pauses, then walks right very softly so as not to give himself away. He stops at the door, takes the umbrella in his left hand, opens the door slowly with his right, steps out quickly, turns to the shop, and says, quickly*)

Thanks a lot.

NIHACHI: Thank you, thank you. Please come back again.

(*Naozamurai closes the door and opens his umbrella which he does by holding it out then snapping his wrist back, forcing the umbrella to pop open by itself. Snow falls and the snow effect is beaten on the drums. The stage begins to revolve slowly to the left as Naozamurai walks carefully through the snow to the right. He lifts his feet high before putting them down. His umbrella rests on his left shoulder, his left hand being held within its sleeve. As the soba shop revolves to the left, a long black fence comes into view, a continuation of the shop's side wall that, shortly before, was perpendicular to the front of the stage. At up right center is a large black box with the character for "water" written on it. A naked white tree stands at up left center. The side window of the soba shop faces the audience. A lit sign hangs there with the words, "Nihachi Soba" written on it. At the center of the fence is a small wooden door that is open. Spikes line the top of the fence. A house with a snow-covered roof is painted on the backdrop upstage of the fence. Naozamurai stops at center and turns to face the audience. He places the umbrella on his left shoulder and withdraws his right hand into its sleeve, holding it at his chest in the* yazō *kata. Pause.*)

NAOZAMURAI: I'm really in luck that this masseur, Joga, who came to eat soba just now, is going to see Michitose tonight. I must see if I can get him to deliver my letter for me.

(*He crosses up to the fence, left of the box, and turns his back to the audience, as if hiding in the shadows. The door of the shop opens. Snow drum beats.*)

NIHACHI: The snow is letting up a bit.

(*He opens Joga's umbrella for him.*)

OKAYO: (*At door*) Well, I'll see you again tomorrow.

(*Leaves shop. The door is closed by Nihachi. As he walks slowly right Joga speaks. He carries his umbrella over his left shoulder.*)

There are many good soba shops from Yamashita to Sakamoto but none of them give you a good portion. The taste may be only so-so but when it comes to getting a heaping bowlful, there isn't a place that can beat Nihachi's.

(*As Joga approaches center Naozamurai turns and moves down to his left. The drums stop.*)

NAOZAMURAI: (*Stealthily*) Hey, Joga-san! Joga-san!

JOGA: (*Stops*) Yes? Who is it?

NAOZAMURAI: It's me.

JOGA: Eh? Who is that?

NAOZAMURAI: Don't tell me you've forgotten my voice?

JOGA: Ah! Please forgive me if I'm mistaken but the person speaking wouldn't by any chance be Michitose's friend, Kataoka Nao-san, would it?

NAOZAMURAI: You've got it.

JOGA: Ah! It is you, Naojirō, sir? Oh, sir . . .

(*He puts his open umbrella down right and crosses closer to Naozamurai at center.*)

NAOZAMURAI: Here now, keep your voice down, okay?

(*Gestures with right hand, then puts it in his kimono at the chest*)

JOGA: Yes sir, yes. Whatever you say, sir. Oh, master, sir, what have you been doing? Ever since you stopped coming to visit Michitose last month, she's been in a terrible state of depression and has even had to come out here to Iriya to recuperate.

NAOZAMURAI: I know. That's what I heard you say in the soba shop.

JOGA: Oh? Were you there?

NAOZAMURAI: I was right behind you and heard everything you said.

JOGA: It's too bad I don't have eyes in back of my head.

(*Points to his eyes*)

NAOZAMURAI: Hah! That's a good one. You haven't even got eyes in the front of your head.

JOGA: A masseur doesn't need eyes to practice acupuncture. Get the point?

NAOZAMURAI: That's an old one, isn't it?

JOGA: Joga, the jokester, that's me.

NAOZAMURAI: (*Forced smile*) Listen, Joga,

(*he closes his umbrella and holds it with the tip of the handle on his left clog between the toes*)

I had a different purpose in calling you. I'd like you to do me a favor, if you don't mind.

JOGA: What would you like me to do?

NAOZAMURAI: I want you

(*pause*)

to deliver a letter to Michitose for me.

JOGA: Certainly. I'll slip it to her secretly while I'm giving her a massage.

NAOZAMURAI: If you can get it to her I'll be very grateful.

(*Takes letter from his wallet, which he removes from his kimono at the breast*)

Well, here it is. Give me your hand.

(*Puts the letter in Joga's hand*)

All right, the rest is up to you.

JOGA: Fine. I'll do what I can.

(*Puts the letter in his sleeve*)

NAOZAMURAI: Now, give me your hand again.

(*Naozamurai takes out a coin from his right sleeve and hands it to Joga.*)

It's not much, but it's for delivering the letter.

JOGA: Thank you very much for your kindness but I'm afraid I . . .

(*Tries to give the money back*)

NAOZAMURAI: It's the least I can do for you. Even though it's not much, take it, will you?

JOGA: Thank you very much.

(*Puts it in his purse*)

Now listen, Nao-san, since Michitose wants to see you very badly I would take you along with me but Kubei the clerk is there to visit his girlfriend, the seamstress, so you'd better stay away.

NAOZAMURAI: So Kubei is there, hmm? What I've written is pretty important so you've got to be very careful with it. I don't want it to fall into the wrong hands.

JOGA: Don't worry. It's as safe as can be.

(*He looks up, puts out his right hand, feels a drop of snow, and picks up his umbrella. Naozamurai opens his umbrella. Snow falls, sound effect is beaten on the drum. Joga leaves right as if stepping in very deep snow.*)

NAOZAMURAI: (*Looking off after him*) Be careful, watch your step!

(*Gestures off right with right hand*)

Watch it! Be careful.

(*He continues saying such things until Joga has been off stage for a few seconds. He then puts his hand back at his breast and faces front.*)

Maybe now that I was lucky enough to run across this Joga and get him to deliver my message

(*pause*)

I'll be able to see Michitose whom I thought

(*pause*)

I'd never see again.

(*Snow falls and the drum beats out the snow effect. Naozamurai begins to go out right, slowly. From right comes his fellow gang member, Ushimatsu, but neither recognizes the other at first as each attempts to hide his face. Naozamurai hides behind his umbrella and Ushimatsu behind his broad straw hat [manjugasa]. Ushimatsu is also on the run from the police. As Ushimatsu approaches, Naozamurai places his open umbrella before his face and feints to either side. Ushimatsu does likewise. Naozamurai then moves sharply left one step, opens up to*) *face the audience, his back to Ushimatsu, then turns slowly to go right. Meanwhile, Ushimatsu crosses above Naozamurai to his left and turns to peer at him in the darkness. Naozamurai keeps his umbrella over his shoulder, hiding his face. Ushimatsu wears a scarf around his head. He has on straw sandals, a red rainjacket [akagappa], and a dark kimono hitched up to free his legs for walking. He removes his scarf.)*

USHIMATSU: That's not you, is it, my old buddy?

NAOZAMURAI: It's the voice of . . .

USHIMATSU: Me, Ushimatsu.

NAOZAMURAI: I didn't know if it was a good imitation or if it was really you.

USHIMATSU: Where are you heading for?

NAOZAMURAI: I thought I'd cut across the rice fields and head for Asakusa.

USHIMATSU: I don't know if that's such a good idea.

NAOZAMURAI: What? Why do you say that?

(Shamisen music begins and the characters' realistic style of dialogue slips into a more formal tone.)

USHIMATSU: Your crimes have been found out and a posse has been formed on orders from the authorities. They are spreading a net for you from Asakusa

(gestures with hat)

to the Yoshiwara so you'd be better off heading for Yamanote and hiding out there for awhile.

NAOZAMURAI: *(Standing as before, right hand at his breast in the yazō kata)* Maybe I'll take your advice and not go to Asakusa. What about you? Where are you going to go?

USHIMATSU: I think I'll take advantage of tonight's snow and go as far as Sōka and then head for Jōshū. So, my friend, what will you do?

NAOZAMURAI: I can't remain in Edo either so I guess I'll wait things out in the Kyoto-Osaka area.

USHIMATSU: I imagine we may never see each other again. We will have to abide in unfamiliar places.

NAOZAMURAI: We should leave the city in the dead of night. And not wait until the morrow comes . . .

USHIMATSU: Yet we should at least have one last drink . . .

NAOZAMURAI:

*But out here in Iriya, away from
The town, a simple soba shop . . .*

USHIMATSU:

*Must serve us with our parting feast,
Garnished with cheap eggs and fish,
   a sorry state . . .*

NAOZAMURAI:

*Still, we must postpone our rites of
   parting.*

*The snow which falls at our
    departure...*

USHIMATSU:

Is not so highly piled as our crimes.

NAOZAMURAI:

*Will we be slain by spears like
    icicles...*

USHIMATSU:

Or will it be by blades of ice?

NAOZAMURAI:

The chill wind blows upon our necks

(*stretching these words in a mournful
tone*)

USHIMATSU:

An unseen blizzard...

NAOZAMURAI:

Blows us to our destiny.

(*He turns and slowly walks to the shichi-
san. As he reaches it Ushimatsu speaks.*)

USHIMATSU: And so, dear friend...

(*Pause. Ushimatsu takes a step right.*)

NAOZAMURAI: Ushi.

(*Pause. He brings his right hand to his
nose, sniffs lightly, then feelingly.*)

Take care!

(*Naozamurai has his right hand in its
sleeve; with a feeling of great coldness,
he walks off slowly, evoking a strong
feeling of desolation. The drum beats out
the sound of the falling snow. Ushimatsu
stands watching Naozamurai exit. Naozamurai walks as if through deep snow.
When he enters the curtain at the end of
the hanamichi the drum beats loudly and
rapidly for a few seconds, then ceases.
Ushimatsu briefly holds his hat up as
protection from the snow. He speaks his
first few lines while holding his hat before him in his right hand.*)

USHIMATSU: Brrr! It's cold, it's cold. The
snow is starting to fall again with flakes as big
as rice-balls. I can't make it to Sōka but it
would be foolish to get captured in all the
confusion tonight. That's my main thought
right now.

(*He puts his left hand in his right sleeve
and poses.*)

Naojirō and I had to split up after that caper
we pulled recently and the cops are now
searching for us. Nao's speed has kept him
out of their clutches thus far and he may
manage to slip away by heading for Minobu
on the Kōshū Road. If he can get across
the Isawa River he should have nothing to
fear. But, on the other hand, if I go to the
authorities and tell them everything, I may be
able to save my neck even though my
crimes weigh as heavily as rocks. At least I
would not be hanged or exiled to Sado Island.
Should I turn traitor and betray him?

(*Walks right a few steps quickly with his left hand in his sleeve before his face, his hat held about a foot above his head. He returns to center.*)

How can I save my skin while turning in my old friend, who has been so good to me?

(*He walks left holding hat high, crosses right a few steps, goes left again, perplexed. At center.*)

Should I forget it and try my luck on the road?

(*Going back and forth, from left to right and right to left*)

Should I tell and save my neck?

(*Pause*)

What the hell should I do?

(*Nihachi is heard at left, opening the door of his shop. Ushimatsu holds his hat overhead with his right hand and goes to the right of the water box where he crouches low. Nihachi enters, takes the sign off his window, and turns to go back in. He stops, noticing something amiss.*)

NIHACHI: Oh! My neighbor's gate is open. I better go and inform him before something is taken.

(*He goes into the shop, closing the door. Ushimatsu comes down to center. There is a sharp crack of the ki. He sees the open fence up center and, taking Nihachi's words as a cue for action, speaks.*)

USHIMATSU: I will inform on him.

(*A song is heard striking the hour. Snow falls, the drum beats. Ushimatsu holds his hat so as to cover his face, places his left hand in his right sleeve, crosses his left leg high over his right one as he moves sideways, facing the audience, puts his leg down slowly, does the same with his right leg, and stealthily slips off, right. Flutes and drums play, there is the sound of the ki being struck again, and the curtain closes. The flutes and drums continue to play for several moments after the curtain closes.*)

CURTAIN

THE ŌGUCHI HOSTEL SCENE

(*Hauta, a popular type of Edo music, begins playing in the geza several moments before the curtain opens. As the ki begin to beat faster, the curtain is pulled open. No one is on stage. The scene revealed is an indoor-outdoor setting. The interior portion represents the formal living room at the hostel where Michitose, the lovesick courtesan, has been recuperating. The room is set on a platform about eighteen inches high. A verandah runs along its downstage edge. A number of pillars*) *support a snow-covered roof. Up center is a set of sliding doors with a weeping willow and a plum tree painted on them. To the left of these is a space about three feet wide with several empty shelves in it. To its left is a* tokonoma, *the formal Japanese alcove found in traditional Japanese rooms; a scroll painting is hung here. Beneath it a free-form arrangement of winter camellias in a vase is placed. Shoji screens form the room's right wall. Steps lead down from here to the stage right portion of the garden. On the stage floor before the center platform is a large stone step also leading to the garden. Round stepping stones lead in a curved line from this center step to both left and right. At the right of the hostel is a straw-thatched gateway, now covered with snow, attached to a fence leading off right. A sort of bamboo clapper* [nariko] *hangs from the gate on its left side. A low bamboo fence runs downstage from this gateway, on its left. In the garden area at left is a snow-covered plum tree and stone lantern. A round paper-covered window is in the wall of the house immediately upstage of this garden. At extreme left is a roofed platform area with a low balustrade running along its length. This is the platform* [yamadai] *upon which the kiyomoto musicians and singers sit. At present they are hidden by a rattan blind hanging across the face of the platform. The stage floor and hanamichi are covered with snow-cloths as in the previous scene. A black curtain hangs at the rear of the stage, signifying the night sky. A tall folding screen stands at left within the room, before the tokonoma. Also in the left area is a round paper lantern, its nonpaper portions being made of red lacquer. Nearby is a beautiful round hibachi of paulonia wood and a red silk pillow. A tobacco box and long Japanese pipes are placed within this area, too. Up right is another folding screen beneath which are utensils for preparing tea. Sandals sit on the top step at right. Three strips of bamboo matting are placed along the floor of the room. A few moments following the opening of the curtain, the blind hiding the kiyomoto musicians rolls up. The singers begin to perform in their clear, high, melancholy tones.)*

KIYOMOTO:

Icy blasts of winter wind,
The silent silver snow.
The clanging of Ueno's gong.

(Gong sound)

Glasslike twisting rivulets
Ending in the River Ta
Beside Iriya Village.

(Gong. Naozamurai enters on the hana-michi, slowly, stepping as if the snow were even higher than before. He is dressed as in the previous scene.)

As he approaches his waiting lover
The white snow rises to

(gong)

His left and right
Along the icy rice field path.

(*As he nears the shichi-san, the drums beat loudly. Naozamurai stumbles, his umbrella falls forward a bit, loose snow on it drops off, he whirls about to his left, buffeted by the wind, and poses with his umbrella over his right shoulder, left leg extended, the weight on his right leg, looking off behind him down the hanamichi. Gong sounds.*)

Relieved that no one yet has seen
  him
The fugitive stops and
Cautiously looks about him.

(*He straightens up and addresses the audience.*)

NAOZAMURAI: I'm sure that Joga, the blind masseur I met before, has delivered my letter to Michitose by now. The gate is probably locked so I'll try knocking on it lightly till someone comes.

KIYOMOTO:

Seeing the familiar gate before him
He approaches it with care.

(*As the kiyomoto sings this passage he half-closes his umbrella and walks to the main stage, stops about six feet from the gate at right, turns front, turns again and moves to the gateway, shakes the snow off his umbrella, closes it, counts the houses on the street, taps his hand at the top of the gate, and accidently knocks*

the clapper hanging there. This makes a loud noise and causes snow piled on the eaves to fall off on his neck and shoulders. The beating of the snow drum in the geza is heard.)

The wind blows the door-clapper
  and
Surprises the maids within
Who come out carrying small
  lanterns.

(*At the noise of the clappers Naozamurai quickly turns front. With the snow on his neck and shoulders he stands holding the closed umbrella in his right hand, his back to the gate, his knees bent, left hand at his breast, and his eyes glaring back over his left shoulder at the clapper. After posing like this for a moment he brushes the snow off his shoulders, stands up straight, his left hand against the gate but his back still to it, a cautious expression on his face. At the sound of the clapper, Michitose's two maids, Chiyoharu and Chiyozuru enter up center, through the sliding doors. Chiyoharu carries a small, cylindrical paper lantern. The maids come to the center of the room.*)

CHIYOHARU: (*As they enter*) I thought I heard the sound of the clapper but I think it may have been the wind.

CHIYOZURU: Perhaps it is Nao-san.

CHIYOHARU: Ah. Then let's be quiet.

(*She gives the lantern to Chiyozuru and crosses right, steps into the clogs on the steps at right of the platform, and goes behind the gate. She bundles her clothes tightly around her to keep warm. Chiyozuru crosses to the room's down right corner, by the beam there, and looks off right, a lantern in her left hand, her right on the beam.)*

KIYOMOTO:

> *Chiyoharu steps carefully and comes
> up to the gate.
> She speaks cautiously.*

CHIYOHARU: Who's there, please?

NAOZAMURAI: That voice must belong to Chiyoharu, eh?

(As he waits to have the gate opened, Naozamurai looks here and there cautiously.)

CHIYOHARU: Nao-san! I'll open the lock so please wait a moment.

CHIYOZURU: I'll hurry and inform the mistress that Nao-san has come.

(She exits up center.)

KIYOMOTO:

> *The clever Chiyozuru
> Goes off to see her mistress
> While Chiyoharu's key
> Opens the gate to Nao-san.*

(As she is opening the gate Naozamurai is whispering, "Quickly, quickly." When the gate is opened he runs in, takes off his clogs on the steps at right, crosses to

the front edge of the platform down right, facing the audience, leans over the edge, removes the scarf from his head, putting it in his breast fold, drops his hitched-up kimono hem, brushes off the knees, and crosses left where he leans on the beam there with his left hand, looking off into the garden. Chiyoharu crosses to the round brazier and sits right of it. Meanwhile, Ushimatsu quickly enters right, stands by the gateway, indicates he is aware of Naozamurai's presence by assuming a pose with his back to the gate, the weight on his left leg, his left hand in his right sleeve, his round hat held before him in his right hand. He then tosses his hat and rainjacket off right into the wings, hitches his kimono at the rear, exposing his legs, and runs off down the hanamichi with broad bouncing steps to suggest his running through the snow. He performs this as the chorus sings.)

KIYOMOTO:

> *At this moment, Ushimatsu
> Appears outside the gate,
> Spies on those inside,
> Nods to himself and hurries off
> Down the snow laden road.*

CHIYOHARU: *(At right of brazier)* Oh, Nao-san, it's so good to see you.

NAOZAMURAI: *(Crosses to pillow by brazier; warms hands over brazier)* I've barely managed to get here at the risk of my life.

CHIYOHARU: You simply don't know how the mistress has been pining for you.

NAOZAMURAI: So I heard. They say Michitose has been sick.

(*Chiyoharu crosses right to the teapot and pours Naozamurai a cup of tea. He dries his right, then left, sleeves over the brazier.*)

CHIYOHARU: Yes, and it's all your fault, you know.

(*She brings him the tea. He holds it in his hands, warming them. He sits on his right knee, his left hand in the fold of his kimono at his chest, his left knee raised. He drinks his tea. The maid returns to the right and warms her hands at a brazier.*)

NAOZAMURAI: Who's next door?

(*Gestures to the left*)

CHIYOHARU: Oh, they're practicing kiyomoto music over there.

(*He puts his teacup down as the chorus begins to sing.*)

KIYOMOTO:

Told by her maid of her lover's
    presence

(*There is a long pause as Naozamurai picks up the brass tongs in the brazier and pokes around vacantly in the ashes. The kiyomoto group sings the word, "Michitose," slowly, extending it over several seconds; the tempo then increases and Michitose opens wide the upstage doors and stands there a moment before coming to Naozamurai. He raises his hand as if to warn her not to speak too loudly.*)

Michitose almost flies out from
    within.
Then tears of joy run
Freely down her cheeks.

(*She sinks to the ground at her lover's right, against him, her long robe trailing out behind her on the floor. Chiyozuru enters behind her, closes the door, goes to the right, and sits. Chiyoharu crosses center and sits. The maids sit with their right knees slightly raised, both hands on the knee.*)

MICHITOSE: Nao-san, oh, I've missed you so badly.

NAOZAMURAI: (*Gestures with right hand and looks upstage*) Shh. Don't speak so loudly.

CHIYOHARU: Oh, don't worry. We can talk as loudly as we like. Yoshibei, the caretaker, knows everything about you

(*she straightens up, right hand at her breast*)

and just before gave me the gate key without a word and went to take a bath. So there's absolutely nothing to worry about.

CHIYOZURU: The only others in the house are the maid, Okome, and her friend, Joga, the masseur. Those two are in the kitchen and have fallen asleep from too much sake so they won't bother you at all. You can talk as freely as you wish.

MICHITOSE: (*Rises to knees, hands at breast*) I thought up so many things to say to you if we met but now that you are here I'm so happy I've forgotten everything and don't know where to start.

NAOZAMURAI: I'll be leaving on a journey and we may not meet again for a year or two. After that we'll have plenty of things to say to each other but as for now, its been only since last month, a mere twenty days, that we haven't met. Not even a month has passed since we last saw each other.

CHIYOHARU: Yes, but up to now we've met so often that even a mere twenty days separation is like a year to a woman in love.

CHIYOZURU: Your absence has meant so much that the mistress has grown quite ill from longing for you.

CHIYOHARU: Your fond words are better medicine than any doctor's prescription.

BOTH: Please cure the mistress quickly, Nao-san.

NAOZAMURAI: (*Slowly, movingly*) I appreciate your concern, ladies, but I'm afraid

(*pause*)

I can't effect the cure.

MAIDS: Please tell us why.

(*Michitose adjusts her kimono with her right hand and puts both hands on her right lap.*)

NAOZAMURAI: (*A bit faster*) If it were only a short time in the past, I would most certainly have stayed on, even for three days in a row

(*pause*)

but seeing the snow out there

(*pause*)

I have no choice

(*pause*)

but to leave tonight as soon as possible.

MICHITOSE: After not coming to see me for so long you say you must leave because of the snowstorm. I don't understand your reasoning at all.

(*She places her left hand down at her side; her right is at her breast.*)

NAOZAMURAI: (*Confidentially; he gestures with his right hand, looking at the maids.*) I can't tell you the reason now.

(*Pause*)

I'll tell you later.

(*The maids look at each other.*)

CHIYOHARU: I think that Yoshibei may be coming back about now...

CHIYOZURU: So we'll just go within and keep an eye out for him...

CHIYOHARU: And you two have a nice...

BOTH: And easy chat.

(*Chiyozuru takes Naozamurai's cup and brings it right while Chiyoharu crosses right and brings a small red tobacco box to the lovers. The maids then leave up center. During this business Michitose raises herself to her knees, watching them. After a long pause she decides to see if they are listening. When Naozamurai starts to speak she gestures for him to be quiet and rises. She crosses to the door, opens it, looks off in both directions, then turns. Meanwhile the kiyomoto has been singing.*)

KIYOMOTO:

*Used to the ways of the licensed
     quarters
The maids discreetly leave the room,
And leave the lovers free to
     converse.
Michitose wipes her tears.*

(*Naozamurai rises and crosses left a step. Michitose steps right in a sweeping movement and looks off right. Naozamurai is looking off left. They step slowly backward to center, their backs touch, and, their downstage hands entwined, they sink slowly to their knees, shoulder to*

shoulder. Michitose's right hand is high on her breast.)

*When they have gone
She looks at Nao-san with
     reproachful eyes.*

(*As they sink she places her right sleeve to her eyes, then replaces it on her breast. A shamisen continues playing softly in the background as the dialogue resumes.*)

MICHITOSE: (*Slowly, sadly*) I want you to tell me why you haven't come to see me for so long

(*pause*)

that I've grown as thin as a reed

(*pause*)

from loneliness.

(*Naozamurai turns front to speak, left knee raised. Michitose adjusts her position to look at him. She is seated in a half-erect position, her right hand in its sleeve, her left on her obi at the right.*)

NAOZAMURAI: The things I've done are known all over and I take my life in my hands by merely appearing in public. I can't go anywhere for fear of being captured and was forced to cease my visits to the pleasure quarters. I had to hide in Manuena like a badger in his den.

MICHITOSE: (*Places both hands on her lap*) Please give me some idea of what you've done that is so bad you can't even show your face in public.

(*As she speaks he places his left hand in his kimono at the breast.*)

NAOZAMURAI: I visited you in the quarters at every opportunity and promised you that we would marry once the New Year had begun but now it seems that, after all, we shall never be as one.

(*He takes out a written vow by bringing his left hand out of his kimono at the breast. He takes this with his right hand and places it on the floor at his right.*)

I am forced to return to you this written vow and must soon depart.

MICHITOSE: (*She moves it near the tobacco box.*) But please, please tell me why!

(*She places her left hand on Naozamurai's right knee, her right hand at her breast.*)

NAOZAMURAI: If I reveal to you the reason why I can no longer look the world in the face, you will cease to love me any longer.

(*His right hand is on his knee, his left out at his breast.*)

MICHITOSE: (*Softly*) What! How could I cease to love you?

NAOZAMURAI: Because what I've concealed from you till now is that

(*strongly, gestures with right hand*)

every penny I so freely gave you

(*pause*)

was dishonestly obtained.

MICHITOSE: Eh?

(*Removes her hand*)

NAOZAMURAI: (*One hand in his sleeve, the other on the brazier*) I dressed in a black silk jacket and even carried two swords as if I were a samurai. Together with a servant at my side I passed myself off in the quarters as a big-shot rice broker. Once I made some inroads I used my false position to practice blackmail.

(*Pause*)

I'm just a common crook. If I return to the pleasure quarters I'll be caught and either get my head chopped off, or, if I'm lucky, be exiled to Sado Island. I can't risk either. As for you and me, we must cut our ties completely and consider our engagement as mere foam upon the sea.

(*As he talks Michitose slowly wipes her tears away with the tip of her right sleeve. Then she puts her right hand in her sleeve at the right side, her left hand on her obi.*)

You didn't know, did you, that I was the kind of man who had committed crimes so serious that he would be forced to flee to some distant region? Did you know that?

MICHITOSE: No matter how stupid I may be, I have known for a long time that you have been engaging in illegal acts.

(*Her right hand is now at her breast, in the fold of her kimono, her left resting on the floor at her side.*)

NAOZAMURAI: What?

(*turning to her a bit*)

You've known all along?

MICHITOSE: Everytime Ichinojo, my wealthy client, came to see me he tried to get me to give you up. He said if you continued to extort money you'd be killed or exiled.

(*She removes her hand from her breast, points off in the distance with her right hand, and wipes her tears with her right sleeve.*)

No matter what, you'd always be an outlaw. He told me to give you up for good but to me his words were little more than a passing breeze. After we pledged our troth I resolved that if we two could not be man and wife in this world

(*brings hands together, then wipes tears with right hand*)

we could be so in the next

(*pause*)

where we would not fear to show our faces openly.

NAOZAMURAI: If what you say is so then I should not throw away my vow. I will soon depart and have no notion of when we might meet again. Since it will be impossible to write you for a long while, you must promise not to hold it against me.

(*As he speaks Michitose places her left hand in her left sleeve, placing her right on her obi at the right side. She leans on her left hand within its sleeve.*)

MICHITOSE: If you aren't able to write for a long time I'd rather have you kill me

(*raises right knee a bit and faces down right*)

and end it all right now.

NAOZAMURAI: What's this?

(*Turning to her a bit*)

Why should I kill you?

MICHITOSE: It's no different from not having you with me.

(*She places her shoulder against his.*)

KĪYOMOTO:

Not seeing you for even one day
Is like 1,000 days without you.

(*Michitose brings her hands together,*
wipes her tears, one eye at a time with the
tip of her right sleeve, first the left then
the right. She then looks at Naozamurai,
pauses, sinks against his side, her right
hand to her breast, takes the red sleeve of
her undergarment out from her right
sleeve using her right hand, puts it in be-
tween her teeth, and pulls on it with her
hand. In this pose her head is looking up
but her eyes are closed in sorrow. Naoza-
murai places his right arm around her
gently. She replaces the red sleeve in her
outer sleeve.)

There are no doctors who can cure
my sickness

(*she lifts a pipe from the floor near the*
brazier, gestures with it off in the dis-
tance, holding it in her right hand, shakes
her head as if weeping, rises to her knees,
points to the strip of paper ["expected*
visitor" or machibito *paper] tied around*
the pipe stem, undoes it and removes it
from the pipe, stretches it between her
hands, lays the pipe down, puts the paper
between her teeth, moves on her knees
closer to Naozamurai, pulls the strip with
her left hand as she sinks against Naoza-
murai and, picking up the pipe and hold-
ing it on her lap, drops her hands to his
lowered right knee; she then fills the pipe
with tobacco from the red box, lights it,

puffs, and offers the pipe to Naozamurai
in her right hand)

Or stop the tears which wet my
pillow.

(*Naozamurai takes the pipe in his right*
hand. He sits facing down left on a diag-
onal. He takes a puff, Michitose rises to
her knees, moves a step or two above
him, takes the wad of paper from the
breast of her kimono, puts it in her
mouth with the folded edge toward the
inside of her mouth, removes a single
sheet, replaces the rest in her right sleeve,
leans against Naozamurai, gestures with
the paper, wipes her tears with it, turns
to him, and picks up the vow. He puts
the pipe down after tapping out its ashes.
They ad-lib about the vow, their voices
being a sort of counterpoint to the slow
and sentimental strains of the kiyomoto
which continues unabated. He tries to
give her the vow and she tries to return it.
She forces him to take it. With his right
hand holding the vow he rises on one
knee, his left hand thrust out at the
breast, holding Michitose's hand as he
towers over her.)

I see you in my dreams each night
My pillow—a mirror of your face.

(*He stands, then crosses to center and*
falls to the floor at right center, his left
hand in his sleeve, held before him at the
breast in the yazō kata, while his left
knee is raised, his right foot on the floor
and turned under his left knee, his face

looking up at Michitose. She has risen and stands facing up right, having swept around to the left, her robe open wide as she holds it with both hands at the lapels and looks down at Naozamurai. Naozamurai sits up on his right knee, his left raised above the ground, his left hand thrust out at the breast. Michitose dabs her tears then moves behind him.)

I cannot live without you
So I beg you to take my life.

(She removes her hairpin; it falls and Naozamurai, still seated, picks it up in his left hand and hands it back to her, making an arclike gesture in doing so. He puts his left hand in its sleeve as using the hairpin Michitose mimes fixing his hair with it a moment of extreme intimacy on the Kabuki stage. Both his hands emerge at the breast of his kimono; he holds the vow and looks at it as Michitose turns gracefully to face upstage and inserts the hairpin in the topknot of her coiffure. Naozamurai folds the vow paper smaller and smaller, as Michitose weeps facing upstage. He rises and they cross left to stand above the brazier. She faces left, he right. She begs him to kill her, ad-libbing, but he tries to change her mind.)

Her tear-filled voice pleads with her
*   lover*
As she clings to him in grief.

(They sit, he in his former one-kneed position, and she sinks against his side,

weeping and wiping her tears with her right hand. He has his right hand on her left arm. She straightens up and he speaks, gesturing with his right hand.)

NAOZAMURAI: That's a terrible idea. And please don't suggest we die together. It's too late to change what's happened so if I should be caught and executed I won't be able to rest my bones near those of my ancestors. I want you to build a tomb for me at Ekoin Temple. This is my last request of you.

(As the kiyomoto begins he clasps his hands before him in supplication and closes his eyes. She rises to her knees and turns away from him a bit, weeping. He bows his head. They ad-lib softly during this sequence. Michitose separates his clasped hands taking his right in her left and his left in her right. They gaze deeply at one another, he rising on one knee to look down on her. They sway from side to side then move into an embrace with Naozamurai on one knee, holding her to him, both arms around her, she with her face against his chest, he facing the audience.)

KIYOMOTO: *(During the above mime-sequence)*

This is my request, he says
And clasps his hands together.
Tears blind the lovers' eyes.

(He rises and crosses to center; she follows and tries to block his way. He sinks to his right knee, she stands above him,

her arms about him from behind. He rises and they debate, ad-libbing, on what to do, he at the left, she at the right, holding hands, her left in his right. They then return to their former positions near the brazier at left. During this the kiyo-moto sings.)

She is bewildered by his request
And at a loss as to what to do.
Just then, the caretaker, old
  Yoshibei,
Who has heard everything
Enters from within.

(Yoshibei, a middle-aged man in simple brown kimono, enters up center. He moves down right and bows low to the couple. Michitose wipes her tears as he talks.)

YOSHIBEI: Naojirō-sama. It's been a long time, hasn't it?

NAOZAMURAI: Ah! It's the caretaker, Yoshibei, isn't it? I'm ashamed to meet you like this.

YOSHIBEI: Please don't be. And since the snow is keeping all our guests away tonight there is no need to worry.

NAOZAMURAI: I suppose you've heard everything, eh?

(Shamisen music begins in the background.)

YOSHIBEI: Yes. I was listening and you must banish from your minds all this talk of killing and dying. You must take advantage of the snowstorm and run away together while there is still time.

NAOZAMURAI: We truly appreciate your advice but if we flee from here you will be held responsible.

YOSHIBEI: I am resolved to bear the blame. During the long period you have been a guest at the Ōguchi I have amassed many obligations to you. My daughter has received great kindnesses from Michitose-sama and my son looks to you, Nao-san, as his personal savior. I needn't go into more details as time is running out so please, the two of you, flee from here quickly.

NAOZAMURAI: If it were a simple journey there would be no reason not to go together but we will be followed by the police and I could never make it through the mountains with a woman at my side.

MICHITOSE: If you won't take me then kill me!

NAOZAMURAI: Why on earth should I kill you?

YOSHIBEI: You don't think she'll commit suicide if you leave her?

NAOZAMURAI: No, I don't, but . . .

MICHITOSE: Please take me with you!

NAOZAMURAI: Well, if I . . .

MICHITOSE: Then kill me!

(A section of kuriage begins as they start out separately and built to a joint climax.)

NAOZAMURAI: Saa

MICHITOSE and YOSHIBEI: Saa, saa

ALL: Saa, saa, saa, saa, saaa.

YOSHIBEI: You must flee together.

(*Yoshibei inches toward center, Michitose tries to get Naozamurai to go. She falls against him, her head hung sadly.*)

KIYOMOTO:

Their sorrow piles higher and higher
Like the snow falling outside.

(*The two police spies from the soba shop scene burst in up center. One rushes to Naozamurai, who quickly throws him down right, off the platform into the garden. Naozamurai rises, tosses off his jacket, and runs down right. Yoshibei has fled to the right. The other policeman holds Michitose for a moment. Naozamurai kicks and trips the first policeman but the other one runs up behind him and seizes him under both arms. Naozamurai poses in a mie, his left foot on the back of the first policeman, his hands up in the air at about shoulder level, the right one slightly higher than the left, palms facing the audience. The tsuke beat to emphasize the pose.*)

MICHITOSE: (*Held back at the center step by Yoshibei, she tries to flee to her beloved.*) Nao-san!

NAOZAMURAI: (*Stretching the vowels for full effect*) Michitose. We shall never in this world meet again.

(*He throws the second policeman off his back. The policeman bumps into his partner who is trying to rise and they both fall to the ground, one behind the other. Naozamurai jumps the low bamboo fence and runs to the shichi-san position on the hanamichi. He performs a powerful mie there as he suddenly stops, whips back the lower half of his kimono on the left with his left hand and holds it back at about chest level from its lower corner while his right hand holds it at a point slightly below the obi, thus exposing his muscular left leg all the way up to the top of the thigh. His right foot is thrust directly before him, bent at the knee, the left leg being extended behind him in a straight line. Yoshibei meanwhile comes to the center step of the platform and holds back Michitose.*)

MICHITOSE: (*Holding the vowels for a feeling of great pathos*) Nao-san!

(*Naozamurai, holding the hem back for freedom of movement, moves off rhythmically down the hanamichi. The policemen run off after him. The curtain closes on the picture of Yoshibei, his knees on the ground and back to the audience, holding back the weeping Michitose, who is standing on the step looking off after Naozamurai.*)

CURTAIN

Figure 77. Ichimura Uzaemon XV as Naozamurai. Nao is about to enter the soba shop.

Figure 78. Joga chats with Nihachi and Okayo as Nao listens from behind his screen (*Naozamurai,* Morita Kanya).

Figure 79.   A close-up of
Joga and Okayo (*Joga,*
Bandō Yoshitarō; *Okayo,*
Ichikawa Masunosuke).

Figure 80.   Nao slurps
his soba (*Naozamurai,*
Ichikawa Ebizō).

Figure 81. Nao disguises his speech by talking to Okayo with his scarf in his mouth (*Okayo,* Ichikawa Masunosuke; *Naozamurai,* Ichikawa Ebizō).

Figure 82. Nao writes his secret letter to Michitose (*Naozamurai,* Ichikawa Ebizō).

Figure 83. Nao waits in the snow for Joga; he stands in the yazō kata of mid-nineteenth century rogues (*Naozamurai,* Ichikawa Ebizō).

Figure 84. Nao asks Joga to deliver his message to Michitose (*Joga,* Bandō Yoshi-tarō; *Naozamurai,* Ichikawa Ebizō).

Figure 85. Nao walks off through the snow on the hana-michi; he lifts his legs high to suggest the presence of deep drifts (*Naozamurai,* Ichikawa Ebizō).

Figure 86. The setting for the hostel scene. The decor was not yet complete when this dress rehearsal picture was taken; however, one can see the kiyomoto musicians seated in their pavilion on the left.

Figure 87. Nao stares up in consternation at the wooden clapper just after a load of snow has fallen on his shoulders; the string that pulls the snow off the eaves can be seen in this photo (*Naozamurai,* Ichikawa Ebizō).

Figure 88. Ushimatsu, aware that Nao is visiting Michitose, prepares to run off to inform the police (*Ushimatsu,* Nakamura Matagorō).

Figure 89. Michitose poses with the machibito string as Nao looks on (*Michitose,* Sawamura Sōjūrō; *Naozamurai,* Kawarazaki Gonjūrō).

Figure 90. Lightly, the lovers back into each other (*Michitose,* Bandō Tamasaburō; *Naozamurai,* Ichikawa Ebizō).

Figure 91. Michitose combs Nao's hair with her hairpin (*Michitose,* Nakamura Jakuemon; *Naozamurai,* Morita Kanya).

Figure 92. Nao looks up at Michitose and she down at him in the famous pose which is said to have inspired the writing of the scene (*Naozamurai,* Morita Kanya; *Michitose,* Nakamura Jakuemon).

Figure 93. Accosted by police spies, Nao yells to Michitose that he will never see her again (*Nao-zamurai,* Ichikawa Ebizō; *Michi-tose,* Onoe Kikugorō).

Figure 94. Escaping on the hanamichi, Nao pulls back his kimono as he strikes a dynamic mie (*Naozamurai,* Ichikawa Ebizō).

Glossary

The glossary lists most of the Japanese terms presented in the text. Some additional Kabuki terms, not previously introduced in the text, are also included. The glossary is by no means comprehensive of all Kabuki terms. Such a glossary would be of encyclopedic proportions (a convenient one-volume reference in Japanese is the *Kabuki Jiten*). The emphasis has been on selecting words pertinent to the plays included in this book. Terms have been assigned to several categories: (1) acting terms, (2) role-type terms, (3) scenic terms, (4) property terms, (5) costume terms, (6) wig terms, (7) makeup terms, (8) playwriting terms, and (9) music terms.

ACTING TERMS

aizariashi	あいざりあし	A kind of rhythmic shuffling step, made by crouching with the knees far apart. It is usually performed at moments of tense confrontation between male adversaries, as in *Pulling the Carriage Apart*. Also called *jirijiri, tsumeyori,* and *nijiri*.
aragoto	荒 事	A term meaning something like "wild style." It refers to the bravura style of acting which evolved in Edo where it was created in the late seventeenth century by Ichikawa Danjūrō I. It is still considered the unique "family art" of the Danjūrō line though other actors may perform it. Aragoto is an exaggerated acting and production style, emphasizing the superhuman prowess of one or more characters. *Pulling the Carriage Apart* is a representative example of an aragoto play.
kamisuki	髪 梳 き	"Hair combing." A convention of many Kabuki love scenes wherein the heroine

dresses or combs her lover's hair. It is thought of as being rather erotic in tone. Kamisuki may be observed in the *Naozamurai* scene between Nao and Michitose.

keshogoe   化 粧 声   "Makeup voice." A rhythmic chant spoken in unison by a band of the hero's opponents in aragoto plays. The chant is usually, "Aaaryya, kooorya," nonsense syllables which cannot be rendered in English. *Pulling the Carriage Apart* contains an example of this convention.

kōken   後 見   A stage assistant, usually dressed in a formal costume with his face visible to the audience. He sits upstage of the actor to whom he is assigned and helps him with his costume and props. He may also prompt him. Kōken are normally the disciples of the actors they assist. When the kōken appears in a black costume and has his face covered with a black hood, he is called *kurogo*. In some instances, the kurogo wears a blue costume or a white one to blend with the scenery; blue for water scenes and white for snow scenes. Kōken means "seeing from behind" while kurogo means "black costume." The kōken in dance plays must be prepared to substitute for the performer should the latter be unable to continue with his performance.

kuchidate   口 立 て   *See* sutezerifu.

kudoki   口 説 き   A scene of lamentation. In the kudoki the heroine sorrowfully gives vent to her deepest feelings. The words are usually divided between the actor and the gidayū chanter as the actor mimes the character's emotions. There is a good example of kudoki in *Shunkan*. In *Naozamurai,* the kudoki is shared by the hero and heroine.

kuriage	くりあげ	A technique often used in disputes between characters when the argument comes to a climax as both parties say *saa, saa, saa* ("well, well, well") simultaneously. There are also other phrases that may be used in the kuriage technique.
kurogo	黒衣	*See* kōken.
ma	間	The element of the pause that is so important to Kabuki acting. Kabuki acting, being built on a strong rhythmical foundation, requires a mastery of expressive pausing. Ma is the essential factor in the Kabuki actor's timing.
mie	見得	A highly theatrical pose that is, perhaps, the most representative of the kata performed by Kabuki actors. Mie are typified by an actor's cessation of movement and glaring expression; often the actor crosses one or both eyes. Most mie are accompanied by the striking of the tsuke clappers. There is a wide variety of mie poses and each is expressive of the style of the play and the character performing the mie. The Japanese use the expression "to cut a mie" (*mie o kiru*) in describing this technique. Almost all mie are performed by male characters though there are a few exceptions. Mie may be "cut" by a single actor or several actors posing in a tableau. They may be done while standing or sitting, with the legs apart or together, and with or without the use of a property. Well-known mie are the *ishi nage no* ("stone-throwing") mie, the *Genroku* mie (named after the Genroku era, 1688-1703), the *soku* ("standing like a sheaf") mie, the *tenchi no* ("heaven and earth") mie, the *hashira maki no* ("wrapped around a pillar") mie, the *Fudō* mie (named because of the resemblance to icons of the god Fudō), the

miarawashi ("revelation") mie, the *Kan'u* mie (named after a famous Chinese general), and so on. Examples of mie may be found in each of the plays in this book.

nori	ノ	リ	Rhythmical acting and speech timed to the playing of a shamisen. Among the various types of scenes in which it is used is the kudoki.
ōmu	鸚	鵡	"Parroting." A technique whereby a serious scene, soon after completion, is parodied by other characters in the play. A famous example is in *The Village School*.
onnagata	女	方	"Female impersonator." Probably the most outstanding example of stylization in Kabuki, the onnagata (also called *oyama*) is a man who typifies the essence of femininity more effectively than would an actress playing the same role. Because of the long tradition behind female impersonation in Kabuki, a set of conventions for representing females has been established which even a female performer would have to follow in playing a Kabuki role.
ōotoshi	大 落 し		The technique whereby a major male character breaks down from an excess of emotion and gives vent to his sorrowful feelings. Matsuomaru has a scene of ōotoshi in *The Village School*.
oyama	お や ま		*See* onnagata.
sawari	さ わ り		*See* kudoki.
serifu	台	詞	The art of stage speech. Kabuki dialogue is spoken in a style suited to the formalistic atmosphere of Kabuki production. Actors must learn to speak in an appropriate rhythmical fashion, often with a musical accompaniment played in the background. The role-classification system used in Kabuki demands

that each role-type be played with the correct vocal pitch. Young men have high-pitched voices as do most female characters; a powerful bass is required for roles such as Matsuomaru. A good voice is a Kabuki actor's most important requisite.

sutezerifu	捨 台 詞	The technique of "ad-libbing." Many plays have brief sections where the actors are permitted to improvise their dialogue within the restrictions of a set scenario. This is especially true of the domestic plays. Another term for improvised dialogue is *kuchidate*.
tachimawari	立 廻 り	Also known as *tate,* the stylized fight scenes of Kabuki. These scenes are composed by a specialist, the *tateshi,* who combines mie poses, somersaults (*tombo*), and classical fighting movements in arranging his effects. There are many famous examples of tachimawari. The fight at the end of *Benten Kozō,* though brief, is a well-known example because of the gorgeous costumes worn in it. In contrast to its large-scale style, the two-man fighting scene in *Shunkan* is less spectacular, though no less interesting.
tate	殺 陣	*See* tachimawari.
tobi roppō	飛 び 六 方	"Flying in six directions." A kind of bold exit on the hanamichi calling for the actor to bound off in powerful leaps from one foot to the other. It is one of several exits classed generically as roppō, most being performed by aragoto characters. Other roppō include the *katate* ("one hand"), the *kitsune* ("fox"), the *keisei* ("courtesan"), and so forth. Umeō in *Pulling the Carriage Apart* performs the tobi roppō.
tsurane	つ ら ね 連 ね	A term usually used with reference to long speeches in which a character identifies him-

		self and his virtues. A variant technique is called *yakuharai.*
wagoto	和 事	A gentle, effeminate, and often comical style of acting used in many popular male roles. It epitomizes the acting technique most admired in the Kyoto-Osaka area where it was created and developed. Sakuramaru in *Pulling the Carriage Apart* and Naritsune in *Shunkan* are among the characters acted in the wagoto style. The term means something like "soft style."
warizerifu	割 台 詞	"Divided dialogue." A technique in which a long speech is divided up between two characters who deliver their words antiphonally. It is also called *kakeaizerifu.* Benten and Nango in *Benten Kozō* participate in this technique.
watarizerifu	渡 り 台 詞	"Pass-along dialogue." A technique similar to warizerifu but in which the dialogue is divided among more than two characters. The Mustering scene in *Benten Kozō* demonstrates the technique. In both the warizerifu and watarizerifu conventions, the last line of the dialogue is shared by the speakers.
yakuharai	厄 払 い	*See* tsurane.

ROLE-TYPES

In the mid-seventeenth century Kabuki actors were required by law to officially register as actors of specific types of roles. This practice led to the stereotyping of Kabuki characters by age, sex, and personality. Though the rigid specialization of Kabuki's early years eventually gave way to the practice, among certain actors, of versatility in playing a large number of role-types, most actors still specialize in playing either male or female roles, with occa-sional attempts at roles of the opposite sex. Few, however, are limited to only one kind of role within the general classifications of male or female roles. Actors of male roles are known as *tachiyaku, tateyaku,* or *otokogata.* Actors of female roles are onnagata or oyama. *Katakiyaku* (villains), tachiyaku (leading men), *dokegata* or sanmaime (comic roles), and *oyajigata* (elderly men) are the main categories of male role-types. Each has a number of subclassifications; some of these are listed in the glossary. Among female roles are *wakaonnagata* (young women), *kashagata* (middle-aged or elderly women), and *fuke* *oyama* (old women). These also contain various subclassifications. The following terms apply to some of the characters in the plays in this book. The list is not exhaustive.

akkatsura	赤　　面	"Red face." Characters with evil traits who wear the fanciful painted lines of kumadori makeup on a red base. Gemba in *The Village School* and Senō in *Shunkan* are examples.
aragotoshi	荒　事　師	Supermen heroes acted in aragoto style. Umeomaru and Matsuomaru in *Pulling the Carriage Apart* are examples.
iro wakashu	色　若　衆	A type of youthful male role or *nimaime*. He is a youth who has not yet shaved his forelock; these characters often have an air of decadent sensuality about them. In *Benten Kozō,* Benten's homosexual background is clearly indicated in the text. Such roles may also be called *wakashugata*.
koyaku	子　　役	Child actors or children's roles. These roles often require considerable acting ability. The koyaku parts go to the children of the more powerful acting families. A child from a lesser family must be content with roles such as those of the pupils in *The Village School;* a star's son will play Kan Shūsai or Kotarō.
kugeaku	公　家　悪	Wicked members of the nobility; a subclass of the katakiyaku category. The kugeaku or "evil prince" is a potent figure, often with superhuman powers. Shihei in *Pulling the Carriage Apart* is a prime example. Such characters wear blue-lined kumadori makeup of the *aiguma* variety.
nimaime	二　枚　目	Handsome young men, such as Nao in *Nao-zamurai.* The term derives from the old custom of publishing the names of actors in these roles on the second of the billboards posted in

front of the theaters. Nimaime means "second flat thing."

sewa nyōbo	世話女房	A commoner's wife in the domestic plays who faithfully serves her husband. Though not a commoner, Tonami in *The Village School* is performed in this tradition.
tedai gataki	手代敵	A subclass of katakiyaku, these are dishonest or rascally clerks in the domestic plays, such as Yokurō in *Benten Kozō*.
wagotoshi	和事師	A role such as Naritsune in *Shunkan,* that is, a young man in love who is acted in wagoto style.
wakadanna	若旦那	"Young master." Sometimes called wakashu, he is a delicate, effeminate young man. One type of wakadanna is the *tsukkorobashi* or "pushover." Sonosuke in *Benten Kozō* fits this description.
wakashu		*See* wakadanna.

SCENIC TERMS

agemaku	揭　幕	*See* toya.
asagimaku	浅黄幕	*See* maku.
fune	船	"Boats." There are basically two types of boats seen on the Kabuki stage, those that are built in three dimensions and those constructed as cutouts. The latter are usually found in dance plays. On occasion a three-dimensional boat will be so large that it occupies most of the stage space. The boat in *Shunkan* only shows its prow but is built in three dimensions.
geza	下　座	The musicians' room located on stage behind a rattan blind, stage right. The room is situated on a diagonal near the downstage right corner. It is also called *kuromisu.* See *geza*

hanamichi   花   道

The raised passageway that runs from stage right on a right angle through the auditorium to the rear of the orchestra. The hanamichi represents a development of the bridgeway (*hashigakari*) used in the Nō theater. Its original uses are unclear but it is thought to have first come into use as an acting area in the Kyōhō era (1716-1735). The hanamichi can serve a wide variety of functions: it can be a riverbank, a city street, a canal, a mountain path, and so on. Two hanamichi are sometimes used, the permanent one on stage right being called the "regular" (hon) hanamichi and another one set up on stage left being known as the "temporary" (kari) hanamichi. In the past, the kari hanamichi was a permanent feature and was called "the eastern walkway." The hanamichi is an extension of the stage proper and many important scenes are acted upon it. It is used for important entrances and exits. In some plays processions of over fifty actors make their way along this unique passageway. Its width is normally about five feet. Lights are set into it flush with its floor; when an entrance or exit is to take place on it these lights are turned on. Each of the plays in this book offers several interesting uses of the hanamichi. In *Benten Kozō,* for example, Benten and Nango have a humorous scene on the rampway as they play "The Priest Holds the Bag." A spectacular employment comes in the Mustering scene of this play as the thieves enter one by one and line up on it in their elaborate robes. In *Pulling the Carriage Apart* Umeomaru makes his exciting tobi roppō exit on the hanamichi. It is used effectively in *The Village School* in several instances, such as when Genzō enters or Chiyo makes her sad departure. In *Shun-*

kan there is a novel use of the passageway when a wave-cloth is pulled along it by invisible strings, forcing Shunkan back to his island. In *Naozamurai* the hanamichi is covered with a white sheet to represent snow. Though none of the plays in this volume utilize it, it should be noted that there is a trapdoor built into the hanamichi at the spot known as the shichi-san. This trap, called the *suppon* ("snapping turtle"), offers exciting possibilities for magical entrances and exits.

jigasuri	地 が す り	The groundcloths that cover many Kabuki stage sets. They represent a variety of ground surfaces. Jigasuri are used in both indoor and outdoor scenes. Indoors versions may show woodgrained floors. In snow scenes such as *Naozamurai* a white snow-cloth (*yuki nuno*) is spread over both the outdoor portion of the setting on the stage proper and all along the hanamichi to the rear of the theater. Other outdoor jigasuri represent waves (as in *Shunkan*) or water.
jōshiki	上　　敷	Thin sheets of straw matting spread over the floor in interiors to represent tatami matting. It is used in *Benten Kozō* and *The Village School*.
kidoguchi	木 戸 口	The free-standing gateway used as an entrance to many Kabuki stage houses. In some plays this gateway is removed before the eyes of the audience by stage assistants when it is no longer needed. *The Village School* is a case in point.
maku	幕	"Curtains." Kabuki makes wide use of many different types of curtains. There is, of course, the striking curtain that is seen at the beginning and end of most Kabuki performances. This billowy curtain of vertical green, persimmon, and black stripes is the standard

curtain (*jōshiki maku;* also called *hiki maku*). It is pulled across the stage from right to left by a stage assistant when the play opens. At the end of the play it is pulled back to its original position. This "pull curtain" or hiki maku is contrasted with the drop curtain (*donchō*) that is the Western-style curtain used in non-Kabuki plays. Among other curtains in Kabuki are the asagimaku, a pale blue curtain that hides the scenery behind it so that it may be dropped suddenly and display the set as if by magic; the *anten maku,* a black curtain that, dropped quickly, gives the effect of a blackout; the *dōgu maku,* a curtain that may have any one of a number of scenes painted on it; the *dandara maku,* a huge, billowy curtain of bold red and white stripes, and others.

| mawari butai | 廻り舞台 | The revolving stage. It is well known that the Japanese invented the revolve long before it came into general use in the West. Used to its fullest advantage, the Kabuki revolve can handle three sets so that scenic changes may be smoothly effected. The first mawari butai is believed to have been invented by the playwright Nakamura Denshichi during the Kyōhō era (1716-1735). Denshichi's revolve consisted of a platform on wheels which had to be pushed to make it revolve. Namiki Shozō went further with his revolve of 1758, which was made by placing an extra stage on top of a wheeled circular platform. An axle at the center allowed it to turn. A later development saw a circle cut in the stage floor with wheels attached to the underside; a framework under the stage received the wheels. Men situated under the circle were responsible for pushing it around. Of course, the modern

mawari butai is electrically operated. *Naoza-murai* and *Shunkan* both employ the revolving stage.

noren	暖	簾	The split curtains often seen hanging in the doorways of traditional Japanese houses. In Kabuki the doorways they hang in are called *norenguchi* (''curtained doorways''). A decorative pattern usually adorns the noren. *The Village School* has such curtains in a norenguchi.
seri	迫	り	Stage traps. Modern Kabuki traps are electrically operated. A Kabuki stage usually has a variety of different-sized traps. Some are large enough for a whole setting to rise on. Traps on which actors or sets appear are called *seridashi* or *seriage* while traps for the reverse process are called *serisage* or *serioroshi*.
shichi-san	七	三	''Seven-three.'' A place located about seven-tenths of the distance from the rear of the hanamichi to the stage. It is the place where the hanamichi trap, the suppon, is situated. Actors often do an important piece of acting here when exiting or entering.
shōji yatai	障子屋台		A part of many interior settings that call for a roomlike enclosure, the walls of which are made of sliding shoji screens. Shōji yatai are found in all kinds of plays, both historical and domestic. *The Village School* makes much use of this little room.
shuro buse	棕櫚伏		The embankment setting used in many plays, such as that at the Mustering scene in *Benten Kozō*. The typical embankment usually depicts a fairly high platform with a flat upper surface running horizontally across the stage. Its front face is covered with scenery flats (called *harimono*) painted to look like earth or grass. Ground rows of grass or weeds may

			be placed in front of the platform and one or more ramps may lead down to the stage floor proper.
toya	鳥	屋	"Chickencoop." The little room at the rear end of the hanamichi from which actors make their entrances or into which they exit. A curtain that, when used, is pulled aside with a swishing noise, hangs in the doorway. This is the agemaku, a name by which the room itself is often called. A black-robed stage assistant is always stationed in this room to aid the actors and pull the curtain open and shut.
tsuri eda	釣	枝	A decorative hanging border of flowering branches which is often seen running across the inner edge of the proscenium arch. The flowers used vary according to the play. In *Benten Kozō*'s Mustering scene they are cherry blossoms but in *Pulling the Carriage Apart* they are plum blossoms.
yamagumi	山	組	The conventional Kabuki stage representation of small hills and mountains. *Shunkan* makes use of this scenic element.
yuki	雪		"Snow." Kabuki snow is made from pieces of paper cut into little pieces (formerly triangles but, more recently, squares). The paper is placed in large bamboo baskets suspended over the stage. When the baskets are gently moved from backstage the snow paper falls through the holes in the baskets to the stage floor. *Naozamurai* contains a famous example of a snow scene.

PROPERTY TERMS

aibiki	合	引	A black lacquered stool on which actors sit in certain Kabuki plays. There are aibiki of several sizes. Some have a compartment for plac-

ing a property or even a cup of tea. Aibiki are never part of the set properties associated with a particular setting; they are always brought on stage by stage assistants just at the point they are needed and removed when no longer required. The audience never sees one on stage unless it is actually being used. The impression given by the actor on a high (*taka*) aibiki is that he is standing, not sitting. As a result, he looks quite impressive.

chūkei	中	啓	A type of fan. Fans are used by most important characters and, consequently, are of many types. The chūkei is a fan that does not fold tightly but in which the rib section always remains slightly open in a triangular shape with the apex at the bottom. It is carried by characters such as Senō and Tanzaemon in *Shunkan* and Gemba in *The Village School*.
jitte	十	手	A weapon carried by Kabuki policemen (*torite* or *yoten*). It is a slim metal rod the handle of which is decorated with red cord and a hanging tassel. A prong protrudes from the upper portion and is used to ward off sword blows. The torite in *Benten Kozō* and those in *The Village School* brandish this weapon.
katana	刀		"Swords." Swords are essential props in almost every play. As with fans, there is a great variety of types. Some plays use trick swords for special effects. In aragoto plays the superheroes usually wear gigantic swords, to emphasize the great strength of their bearers. These swords are the *ōdachi*. Samurai carry two swords, a long one and a shorter one, while commoners carry one or none at all.
kiseru	煙	管	"Pipes." Japanese pipes are long-stemmed with a small bowl which can hold only one or two puffs of tobacco. A considerable amount

of acting is done as the actor skillfully gestures with a pipe. The pipe is held differently for each role-type; from the manner in which a pipe is held, one can tell a great deal about the character. The Hamamatsu-ya in *Benten Kozō* and the love scene in *Naozamurai* contain important moments of acting with kiseru.

kodōgu	小 道 具	The general term for properties used on stage by the actor. There are hand props (*mochidōgu*); set props (*dedōgu*); props used up at each performance (*kiemono*); animal costumes (*nuigurumi;* these are considered props, not costumes); and footwear (also considered props).
kubi	首	"Heads." Kabuki makes frequent dramatic use of decapitated heads. There are two main types: the *dakubi* and the *jōkubi*. The former are roughly made, stuffed-cotton heads with the hair and features painted on crudely. A red cloth is usually attached to the neck part. Aragoto plays make use of them. Jōkubi are the more realistic heads, such as that used in *The Village School*. Some examples still remain from the Meiji era and give a striking impression of the actors after whom they were modeled. Oak or paulonia wood is the main material used in constructing the heads, though papier-mache pasted over a wooden base and called *hariko no kubi* is occasionally used as well. Yet another method uses crepe for material. When the head is brought on stage for a scene of head inspection, it is carried in a paulonia-wood box, the *kubioke*. This box is cylindrical in shape, being one foot in diameter and more than an inch thick.
tenugui	手 拭 い	A small towel used by many characters. It is an extremely helpful hand property for gesturing with but serves many other functions

too. It can be worn as a headband or a scarf or can be used to wipe one's sweat or tears. Good use is made of it in *Benten Kozō, The Village School, Shunkan,* and *Naozamurai.*

COSTUME TERMS

amigasa	編笠	A basket-shaped hat made of pampas leaves which completely hides the face of the wearer. Umeomaru and Sakuramaru wear it in *Pulling the Carriage Apart*. Also called the *kuka-amigasa*.
atsuwata	厚綿	A thickly padded outer kimono (*kitsuke*) designed to make the wearer look larger than he is. It resembles the dotera, a padded dressing gown. Umeomaru in *Pulling the Carriage Apart* wears it.
dōjigōshi	童子格子	The name given the bold checkerboard pattern seen on the costumes of the triplets in *Pulling the Carriage Apart*.
dōnuki	胴抜	An indoors kimono worn by courtesans under an uchikake robe. The upper and lower portions are of different colors and patterns. Michitose wears one in *Naozamurai.*
fukuzōri	ふく草履	Thick-soled straw sandals.
furisode	振り袖	A kimono with long hanging sleeves worn by young women.
geta	下駄	Wooden clogs.
hakama	袴	The culotte-type trousers worn with formal samurai dress.
hanten	半纒	A type of jacket or short coat, similar to the haori but without a means to tie the lapels together.
haori	羽織	A type of jacket or short coat tied in front with a pair of strings.

happi	法 被	A jacket worn over the kimono.
juban	襦 袢	An under-kimono.
kamiko	紙 子	A kimono supposed to be made of paper and signifying the wearer's poverty.
kamishimo	裃	A samurai's formal attire. It is made up of a winglike jumper, the kataginu, and hakama trousers. In addition to dramatic characters who wear it, it is always worn by the gidayū chanter and shamisen player in plays adapted from the puppet theater.
kataginu	肩 衣	The sleeveless winglike jumper worn over the kimono as part of the kamishimo costume.
kataire	肩 入 れ	A costume designed to symbolize its wearer's poverty. Patches are sewn to the shoulder area, but in a conventionalized, not naturalistic, fashion.
kitsuke	着 付	A general term for the outer, as opposed to the under, kimono. An obi is worn over it around the waist.
kokumochi	石 持 ち	A kimono, generally solid in color, with three to five circular white crests (*mon*) sewn on. This simple kimono is usually purple and is worn by certain wives in domestic plays. Tonami in *The Village School* wears it.
mon	紋	"Crests." Mon represent the Japanese tradition of heraldry and assume many different and beautiful patterns, all fixed by tradition. They are worn on the costumes of most Kabuki characters.
montsuki	紋 付	A formal kimono with mon sewn on in the appropriate places.
nikujuban	肉 襦 袢	A garment that is supposed to represent the naked skin. It is tight-fitting and of the same color as the actor's body makeup. Tattoos often adorn it. It may be worn on the torso or on the hips, like shorts.

ryūjin maki	竜 神 巻	A highly exaggerated costume usually worn by Kabuki envoys or Imperial messengers. The right sleeve is tucked behind the actor at his rear where it is folded in an old-fashioned style resembling that in which dried abalone is prepared. The left sleeve is stiffened with splints and held in front of the actor almost like a shield. It has a large mon on it. Another element of the costume is hakama tucked up at the thighs.
sanriate	三里あて	A kneepad-like accessory often worn by samurai or others who wear their hakama tucked up at the thighs.
suo	素 網	A formal costume often worn by male characters in history plays. It consists of a wide-sleeved kimono over which long, trailing hakama (nagabakama) are worn.
tabi	足 袋	The Japanese bifurcated sock. To facilitate the wearing of thonged sandals, the big toe is separated from the other toes.
uchikake	打 掛	A robe worn over the kimono by female characters.
uwagi	上 着	A type of overjacket or coat.
yoten	四 天	A type of kimono worn by policemen and samurai involved in fighting scenes. It is usually worn at shin length and is higher at the sides than in the front. Its color varies according to the character wearing it.
zōri	草 履	Thonged straw sandals.

WIG TERMS

Kabuki actors have worn wigs since the mid-seventeenth century. There are numerous classical wig-types for both male and female roles. Wigs are made from real hair by specialists attached to the theaters. Names of the wigs are complex, often being composed of words for the various parts of the wig, that is, the forelock, sidelocks, topknot, and back-hair. A wig may be known by one or a combination of these elements.

abura tsuki	油 付 け	A male wig that gets its name (''applied oil'') from the fact that its back hair is dressed with oil to give it a high shine. The other main type of male wig back-hair style is the *fukoro tsuki,* which is arranged in a pouchlike manner.
bin	鬢	The sidelocks. Each wig has a distinctive style of sidelocks.
chigomage	稚 児 髷	A type of topknot on the wigs of certain youthful characters. The topknot is tied in a bowlike shape. Sugiomaru in *Pulling the Carriage Apart* wears it.
chikaragami	力 紙	A high-quality paper that is used to tie the base of the topknot on the wigs of powerful samurai characters. Matsuomaru in *The Village School* provides an example. The paper is folded in the shape of two large wings that open to either side of the topknot. In some cases, the size of the bow is highly exaggerated; Matsuomaru's is rather conservative.
daigane	台 金	The copper framework to which hair is sewn in making a wig.
fukuro tsuki	袋 付	The pouchlike arrangement of back hair on many male wigs. This backhair is called the *tabo.* It is usually worn by townsmen in the domestic plays. Nao in *Naozamurai* wears such a back-hair arrangement.
gojūnichi	五 十 日	The ''fifty days'' wig. It has a bushy crown, signifying that its wearer has not shaved his head in a long time because of illness. Matsuomaru in *The Village School* and Nippon Daemon in *Benten Kozō* both wear this wig.
habutae	羽 二 重	The silk cloth worn on the actor's head to represent the shaved portion of his crown. The wig is worn over the habutae.
itabin	板 鬢	A wig with its sidelocks heavily covered with oil. The sidelocks jut out to either side like

		stiff boards. Matsuomaru in *Pulling the Carriage Apart* wears this exaggerated wig.
kuruma bin	車 鬢	A highly stylized wig with several tufts of hair on each sidelock pulled out and thickly pomaded with oil. The pomaded tufts resemble carriage spokes, giving the wig its name (kuruma means carriage). A variation is worn by Umeomaru in *Pulling the Carriage Apart*.
mae chasen	前 茶 筅	A wig with a topknot resembling a teawhisk.
maegami	前 髪	A boy's or young man's wig with the forelock not yet shaved off. One version is the *tsukami tate,* a pom-pom-like forelock worn by Umeomaru in *Pulling the Carriage Apart*. Other maegami wigs are worn by Benten and Sonosuke in *Benten Kozō*.
mage	髷	The topknot. Most wigs have a distinctive topknot style.
megane	目 鏡	A topknot style seen on clerks such as Yokurō in *Benten Kozō*. Its name comes from its resemblance to a single eyeglass (megane).
mushiri	む し り	A wig with the crown hair partly grown in. Masterless samurai such as Tadanobu Rihei in *Benten Kozō* wear it. Another such character is Naozamurai.
sakaguma	逆 熊	*See* mushiri.
shimada	島 田	A female wig worn by single women. Benten Kozō's bunkin takashimada is a variation. The term refers to the style of dressing the topknot.
tsukami tate	摑 み 立 て	*See* maegami.
yahazu bin	矢 筈 鬢	Sidelocks that protrude like arrow feathers (yahazu). It is similar to the itabin. Gemba in *The Village School* wears it.
yamai hachimaki	病 鉢 巻	A purple headband often worn by male characters who are ill (or feigning illness). A knot is normally tied at the left with the ends of the band hanging down.

| yuiwata | 結　綿 | A female topknot style in which a piece of attractive crepe is tied around the topknot. Kikugorō V used to wear it to play Benten Kozō. |

MAKEUP TERMS

aiguma	藍　隈	A kumadori-style makeup of blue lines on a white base. It is worn by such evil members of the nobility as Shihei in *Pulling the Carriage Apart*.
beniguma	紅　隈	A generic term for kumadori styles using the cosmetic known as *abura beni,* a crimson color mixed in a compressed oil . Ipponguma, sujiguma, and nipponguma are among the beniguma types.
hayagane	早　鉄　漿	The tooth blackener used to blacken the teeth of married women, courtesans, waitresses, etc. Some male roles, such as certain members of the nobility, also use hayagane. This usage reflects the actual customs of Edo-period Japan. Hayagane is made of a combination of crude wax, pine resin, lamp black, red pigment, rice honey, and lamp oil, to which perfume is added. It is softened by heating it over a flame. Characters such as Tonami and Chiyo in *The Village School* wear it as does Shihei in *Pulling the Carriage Apart* and Michitose in *Naozamurai.*
ipponguma	一　本　隈	A type of kumadori makeup, using beniguma. Over a white base, a red line is drawn from cheeks to temples.
kaniguma	蟹　隈	"Crab"-style kumadori. An exaggerated makeup worn by the herald in *Pulling the Carriage Apart.*
kumadori	隈　取　り	Kabuki's most elaborate system of makeup styles. It is often compared to the painted

face styles of Peking Opera which some scholars believe influenced its early development. It includes a large number of types, some of which are included in the glossary. Kumadori is distinctly nonnaturalistic. It consists chiefly of curved lines drawn with the finger or a brush on a base of white, red, or brown makeup. These lines may be of several colors though the most common are red and blue. It is thought that Danjūrō I created this approach to makeup when he made his debut in 1673, at the age of thirteen. Kumadori literally means ''taking the shadows'' and may be said to be a means whereby the shadows delineated by the facial musculature are clearly outlined. The two main categories of kumadori are beniguma (those using red lines) and aiguma (those using blue lines). Red is supposed to signify righteousness and physical strength and passion. Blue indicates the negative qualities of evil and hatred. Good examples of several kumadori types may be found in *Pulling the Carriage Apart.*

mebari　　目　張　り　Eyeline styles. Each role-type emphasizes the line of the eyes in a different manner. The eyes are generally made to look larger than normal. Male roles use a black liner or a mixture of black and red to outline the eyes, while red is used by female roles.

mukimiguma　　むくみ隈　An attractive kumadori style worn by both Sugiomaru and Sakuramaru in *Pulling the Carriage Apart.* A soft red line is drawn from below the inside corner of the eye past the eye and upward at the outer corner of the eye where it continues to the outer corner of the eyebrow. Its name is said to come from its resemblance to a shucked trough shell (*bakagai no mukimi*).

nippon (suji) guma	二本（筋）隈	Also pronounced nihonguma; the two-line kumadori style worn by Matsuomaru in *Pulling the Carriage Apart*. It is sometimes called the *Matsuō no guma*. Two oblique lines rise from the eyebrows and are paralleled by two others, one on either side of the eyes.
oshiroi	白　粉	The white makeup made from a ground-flour base mixed with water. Most roles use it to some extent.
seitai	青　黛	The blue cosmetic used to paint on the lines of the aiguma makeup. It is also used to depict the shaved portion of the crown and face.
sujiguma	筋　隈	The kumadori used by Umeomaru in *Pulling the Carriage Apart*. Two red lines sweep upward from the inner corners of the eyebrows where they meet at the upper end of the nose. Curved red lines run from the outside tip of each eyebrow down past the eyes and back to the sides of the face. Another pair of curved red lines runs from the wings to the nose under each cheek.

PLAYWRITING TERMS

ie no gei	家　の　芸	"Family art." The acting style and plays in which a family of actors specializes. The major Kabuki acting families have compiled play groupings in which their predecessors made outstanding successes; these groupings are known as their ie no gei. For instance, the Ichikawa family has its Kabuki Eighteen (Kabuki Jūhachiban), the Onoe its Selection of Ten Plays, Old and New (Shinko Engeki Jūshu), and so on. Similarly, a type of acting such as the Ichikawas' aragoto or the ghost play style of the Onoe may be called ie no gei.

gidayū kyōgen	義太夫狂言	Plays written for the puppet theater, with gidayū style chanting, which have been adapted for Kabuki. Chikamatsu Monzaemon's *Yosaku of Tamba* (*Tamba no Yosaku*), taken over by Kabuki in 1708, is thought to have been the first example of such borrowing. *Pulling the Carriage Apart, The Village School,* and *Shunkan* are all gidayū kyōgen. Such plays are also known as maruhon kyōgen.
jidaimono	時 代 物	The history play genre. These plays generally deal with materials based on the pre-Edo era society of noble princes, monks, and samurai. Central to the repertory are those plays known as ōdai and ōcho mono, which deal with the Nara and Heian periods of medieval Japanese history. Many plays are concerned with Edo era samurai families but are disguised by being placed in earlier periods. This practice stems from the prohibition against dramatizing events occurring to the Edo-period samurai class.
kizewamono	生 世 話 物	Plays which realistically depict the lower stratum of city life during the late Edo period. The plays are probably the most externally naturalistic of Kabuki dramas, though they are performed in a clearly conventionalized manner. Of course, Western naturalism is itself highly conventionalized in its attempts to use artificial means to convince an audience that what it is seeing is actually happening. Kabuki naturalism also approaches the realm of illusionism in its detailed representation of the atmosphere and artifacts of daily life; however, far more than is obvious in the West, such plays make extensive use of techniques that constantly remind the audience that it is watching a play, not real life. Most

predominant of these techniques is the rhythmic foundation of the acting and the presence of a musical accompaniment. *Benten Kozō*'s Hamamatsu-ya scene and the two scenes from *Naozamurai* are examples of the genre. Also called *masewamono*.

ōcho mono	王 朝 物	*See* jidaimono.
ōdai mono	王 代 物	*See* jidaimono.
sewamono	世 話 物	The domestic play genre. Sewamono are based on the daily life of the townsman class during the Edo era. They are often based on actual contemporary events. *The Village School, Benten Kozō,* and *Naozamurai* are sewamono.
shin kabuki	新歌舞伎	New works written for Kabuki since the late Meiji era by playwrights not attached to any specific theater. These writers were usually scholars, critics, or other literary men who hoped to write plays in keeping with the rationalism of the modern age. Their plays are often lacking in precisely those elements that make the classical Kabuki dramas unique. Shin kabuki are normally performed as part of most contemporary Kabuki programs.
shiranami mono	白浪もの	"Bandit plays." A kind of kizewamono that deals with bandits and blackmailers. *Benten Kozō* fits this description, as does *Naozamurai.*

MUSIC TERMS

aikata	合 方	Musical accompaniment. It is usually a shamisen accompaniment that is played in the background as a scene is being acted. Strictly speaking, there is no singing during an aikata

interlude. The aikata is played in the geza at the opening or closing of the curtain, when a character enters, during conversations, and the like. It provides interesting emotional and psychological overtones to the scene.

chobo　　チョボ

The shamisen and chanter combination used in plays taken from the puppet theater. Seated on a platform called the *yuka* or "floor," at stage left, the chobo performs those passages that describe the emotional and mental states of the characters in the play and sometimes speaks their dialogue.

geza ongaku　　下座音楽

The geza is the rattan-screened room situated on a forty-five-degree angle to the audience on the down right corner of the stage. In it are the musicians who perform the background music called geza ongaku. Chief of the instruments used in this music is the shamisen. Geza ongaku also uses singing. Several musicians may be stationed in the geza during the course of a play. They may play any one of a number of drums, the flute, gongs, and other instruments. These musicians are called the *hayashikata* or *narimonoshi,* both of which terms may be translated as "orchestra." All geza musicians belong to the school of music called nagauta. Geza ongaku often includes sound effects among its responsibilities. The sound of waves, snow, and rain are some of the effects that may be beat out on a drum in the geza. Aikata and *narimono* are the two main types of geza music employed. The latter usually uses four instruments, the flute (*fue*), kotsuzumi drum, otsuzumi drum, and taiko drum, but may also use more than thirty instruments.

gidayū bushi　　義太夫節

A narrative musical style created by the chanter Takemoto Gidayū (1651-1714). It is the main style of musical accompaniment in plays adapted from the puppet theater. It involves the chanting of the play's narrative content in time to the playing of a shamisen.

jōruri	浄 瑠 璃	A word usually used to refer to the puppet theater style of presentation. It may be used to denote any Kabuki play that uses a narrative accompaniment with shamisen, no matter what the school of music employed.
ki	木	Also called *hyōshigi* and *tanniki.* Wooden clappers consisting of two rectangular sticks about ten inches in length which are struck against each other. They are usually made from a hardwood, such as oak. The sides that come in contact when struck are carved so that their surface is curved. Almost invariably, the ki are used to signal the opening and closing of an act or scene. A variety of techniques is used in striking them. The man who strikes them is a member of the theater's literary staff (*kyōgen sakusha*); he stands near the lower edge of the proscenium arch, downstage left; the audience normally does not see him. In addition to signaling the opening and closing of the curtain, the ki are also used to cue the backstage personnel that performance time is approaching or to note certain scenic changes, such as the use of the revolving stage.
kiyomoto	清 元 節	A type of narrative music often used in Kabuki dance plays. It involves the use of shamisen playing and singing. A number of dramas use it for effective background music; a famous example is Naozamurai's scene of parting with Michitose in *Naozamurai.* The style was founded in 1814 by Kiyomoto Enjudayū.
nagauta	長 唄	Kabuki's representative musical style. It has evolved a diversity of forms in its long his-

tory. The style developed for Kabuki used to be known as Edo nagauta to distinguish it from Kamigata (the Kyoto-Osaka area) nagauta. Kamigata practitioners frowned upon using nagauta as theater music. Nagauta has had an influence on all forms of Kabuki music. It is a narrative style using a variety of instruments, including shamisen and drums. Its scope is quite broad and may range from one singer and shamisen player to an orchestra of twenty musicians.

tsuke   ツ   ケ

A type of clapper effect. Two rectangular wooden sticks are beaten on a square, flat board placed on the floor near the onstage side of the proscenium arch, downstage left. The tsuke are used to create several interesting sound effects. They emphasize the movements of the actors in stage battles, increase the excitement produced when a character makes a running entrance or exit, and act as an exclamation point to the actor's mie poses. A specialist handles the tsuke; he is called the *tsukeuchi,* and the board he strikes is the *tsukeita.*

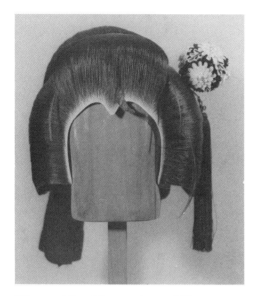

Figure 95. Front view of Benten Kozō's bunkin takashimada wig.

Figure 96. Rear view of Benten Kozō's bunkin takashimada wig.

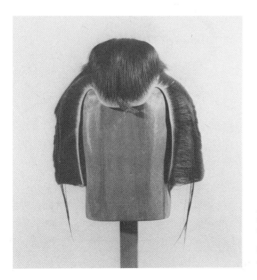

Figure 97. Benten's maegami wig worn in the Mustering scene. Notice the half-moon scar attached to the forehead part of the wig.

Figure 98.   Matsuō's gojūnichi wig, from the side.

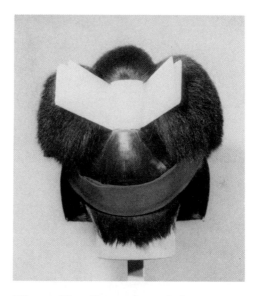

Figure 99.   Rear view of the same. Notice the chikaragami or "strong paper" tied in a bow. The headband denotes that the character is ill.

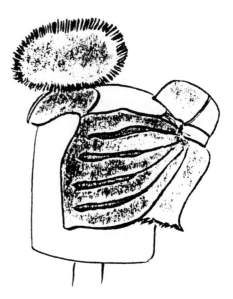

Figure 100.   Umeō's kuruma bin wig.

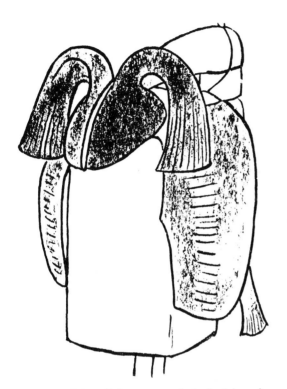

Figure 101.   Sakuramaru's hakobin wig.

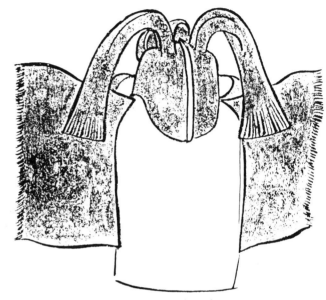

Figure 102.   Matsuo's itabin wig.

Figure 103. The wig worn by Gemba.

Figure 104. The wig and beard worn by Shunkan.

Figure 105. The pony tail or uma no shippo wig worn by Chidori.

Figure 106. Naozamurai's mushiri wig.

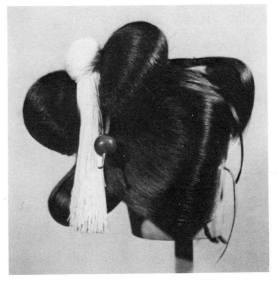

Figure 107. Michitose's hyōgo wig.

Selected Bibliography

Arnott, Peter D. *The Theatres of Japan.* New York, 1969.

Atsumi Seitaro. *Kabuki Kyōgen Ōrai* (*Here and There with Kabuki*). Tokyo, 1927.

Bandō Mitsugorō VIII. *Kabuki no Kumadori* (*Kabuki Makeup*). Tokyo, n.d.

Bowers, Faubion. *Japanese Theatre.* New York, 1952.

Brandon, James R. *Kabuki: Five Classic Plays.* Cambridge, Mass., 1975.

Brandon, James R., with Tamako Niwa. *Kabuki Plays: Kanjinchō and The Zen Substitute.* New York, 1966.

Chikamatsu Monzaemon. Tokyo, 1972 (Vol. 19 in the *Nihon no Koten* [Japanese Classics] series).

Dazai Semon. *Kabuki Geijutsu* (*Kabuki Artistry*). Tokyo, 1942.

Dōmoto Masaki. *Kotengeki to no Taiketsu* (*Confrontation with the Classics*). Tokyo, 1959.

Dunn, Charles J., and Bunzō Torigoe, trans. and ed. *The Actor's Analects* (*Yakusha Rongo*). Tokyo and New York, 1969.

Engeki Hyakka Daijiten (*Encyclopedia of the Theatre*). 6 vols. Tokyo, 1960-1962.

Ernst, Earle. *Three Japanese Plays From the Traditional Theatre.* New York, 1959.

———. *The Kabuki Theatre.* Rev. ed. Honolulu, 1974.

Fujii Yasuo. *Kabuki Hassen* (*Discovery of Kabuki*). Tokyo, 1971.

Fujinami Yohei. *Shibai no Kodōgu: Sōi to Denshō* (*Theatrical Properties: Their Creation and Traditions*). Tokyo, 1974.

Gunji Masakatsu. *Kabuki.* Trans. John Bester. Tokyo, 1968.

———. *Kabuki: Yōshiki to Dentō* (*Kabuki: Style and Tradition*). Tokyo, 1969.

———. *Buyō: The Classical Dance.* Trans. Don Kenny. New York and Tokyo, 1970.

———. *Kabuki Fukuro* (*A Bagful of Kabuki*). Tokyo, 1970.

———. *Kabuki no Bigaku* (*Kabuki Aesthetics*). Tokyo, 1972.

———. *Namari to Suigin* (*Lead and Mercury*). Tokyo, 1975.

Gunji Masakatsu, ed. *Kabuki: Dentō to Gendai* (*Kabuki: Tradition ⁚ ⁺he Modern World*). Vol. 4 in the ⁻ ⁻endai series. Tokyo, 19⁶⁰

Halford, Aubre, ⁝ Halford. *The Kabu⁝ ⁝* ⁹52.

Hamamura Yonezō. ⁝ *ⁱa* (*How to View Kabuki ⁚* 1920.

———. *Jūgose Ichimura Uzaemon Butai Shashinshū* (*Collection of Stage Photographs of Uzaemon XV*). Tokyo, 1951.

———. *Kabuki.* Tokyo, 1956.

Hamamura Yonezo, et al. *Kabuki*. Trans. Fumi Takano. Tokyo, 1956.

Hattori Yukio. *Kabuki no Kozō (Kabuki's Construction)*. Tokyo, 1970.

———. *Zankoku no Bi (The Aesthetic of Cruelty in Traditional Japanese Theatre)*. Tokyo, n.d.

Hattori Yukio, and Gondō Hōichi, eds. *Kabuki: Shibai to Sekai (The World of Kabuki)*. Vol. I in the *Nihon Geinō (Forms of Japanese Theatre)* series. Tokyo, 1971.

Hitta Kanezaburō. *Kabuki Enshutsu Ron (Notes on Kabuki Production)*. Tokyo, 1943.

Hozumi Shigetō. *Kabuki Omoide Banashi (Memories of Kabuki)*. Tokyo, 1948.

Ichikawa Danzō VIII. *Ichikawa Danzō VII*. Tokyo, 1971.

Ichikawa Ennosuke III, ed. *En'ō*. Tokyo, 1969.

Ishida Ichirō. *Kabuki no Mikata (How to View Kabuki)*. Tokyo, 1974.

Itō Kisaku. *Butai no Sōchi (Stage Settings)*. Tokyo, 1949.

Japanese National Commission for UNESCO. *Theatre in Japan*. Tokyo, 1963.

Kagayama Naozō. *Kabuki no Kata (Kata of Kabuki)*. Tokyo, 1957.

———. *Kabuki*. Tokyo, 1968.

Kanazawa Yasutaka. *Haiyū no Shuhen (The Actor's Surroundings)*. Tokyo, 1957.

———. *Kabuki Meisaku Jiten (Dictionary of Kabuki Masterpieces)*. Tokyo, 1971.

Kawajiri Seitan. *Engi no Denshō (Acting Traditions)*. Tokyo, 1956.

Kawatake Mokuami. *The Love of Izayoi and Seishin*. Trans. Frank T. Motofuji. Tokyo, 1966.

Kawatake Shigetoshi. *Nakamura Kichiemon*. Tokyo, 1955.

———. *Nihon Engeki Zuroku (An Illustrated History of Japanese Theatre Arts)*. Tokyo, 1956.

———. *Kabuki: Japanese Drama*. Tokyo, 1958.

———. *Nihon Engeki Zenshū (Complete History of Japanese Theatre)*. Tokyo, 1959.

———. *Kabuki Meibutai (Famous Scenes from Kabuki)*. Tokyo, 1971.

Kawatake Shigetoshi, ed. *Kabuki Meisakushū (Collection of Kabuki Masterpieces)*. 2 vols. Tokyo, 1936.

———. *Sōgo Nippon Gikyoku Jiten (Combined Dictionary of Japanese Drama)*. Tokyo, 1964.

Kawatake Shigetoshi, and Fujino Yoshio, eds., *Sugawara Denju Tenarai Kagami (An Annotated Edition of "Sugawara's Secrets of Calligraphy")*. Tokyo, 1953.

Kawatake Toshio. *A History of Japanese Theatre, II: Bunraku and Kabuki*. Tokyo, 1971.

———. *Kabuki no Sekai (The World of Kabuki)*. Tokyo, 1974.

Keene, Donald. *Major Plays of Chikamatsu*. New York, 1961.

———. *Chūshingura: The Treasury of Loyal Retainers*. New York, 1971.

Kima Hisao. *Kabuki*. Tokyo, 1958.

Kimura Yunosuke. *Katsura (Kabuki Wigs)*. 3 vols. Tokyo, 1974.

Kincaid, Zoe. *Kabuki: The Popular Stage of Japan*. New York, 1925.

Kokuritsu Gekijō Kōen Taihonshū (Collection of National Theatre Production Scripts). 5 vols. Tokyo, 1973-1975.

Komiya Toyotaka, comp. and ed. *Japanese Music and Drama in the Meiji Era.* Trans. and adap. Donald Keene and Edward G. Siedensticker. Tokyo, 1956.

Malm, William P. *Japanese Music and Musical Instruments.* Tokyo, 1959.

———. *Nagauta: The Heart of Kabuki Music.* Tokyo, 1964.

Miyake Saburō. *Kabuki o Mirume (An Eye for Kabuki).* Tokyo, 1956.

Nakamura Kan'emon III. *Engi Jiden (Acting Autobiography).* Tokyo, 1973.

———. *Kabuki no Engi (Kabuki Acting).* Tokyo, 1974.

———. *Omocha Bako (The Toy Box).* Tokyo, 1975.

Nakamura Shikaku. *Yakusha no Sekai (The Actor's World).* 2 vols. Tokyo, 1966-1971.

Noguchi Tatsuji. *Kabuki.* Tokyo, 1965.

Onoe Kikugorō VI. *Gei (Art).* Tokyo, 1947.

Pronko, Leonard. *Theatre East and West: Perspectives Toward a Total Theatre.* Berkeley and Los Angeles, 1967.

———. *Guide to Japanese Drama.* Boston, 1974.

Richie, Donald, and Miyoko Watanabe, trans. *Six Kabuki Plays.* Tokyo, 1963.

Scott, A. C. *The Kabuki Theatre of Japan.* London, 1955.

Scott, A. C., trans. *Kanjinchō: A Japanese Kabuki Play.* Tokyo, 1953.

Segawa Jōkō. *Genyadana: A Japanese Kabuki Play.* Trans. A. C. Scott. Tokyo, 1953.

Shaver, Ruth. *Kabuki Costume.* Tokyo, 1966.

Soma Akira, and Torii Kiyokoto. *Kabuki: Ishō to Funsō (Kabuki Costumes and Makeup).* Tokyo, 1957.

Suzuki Shunbō. *Kabuki no Kata (Kabuki's Kata).* Tokyo, 1927.

Takechi Tetsuji. *Kari no Tayori (Missives).* Tokyo, 1969.

———. *Dentō Engeki no Hassō (The Emergence of Traditional Theatre).* Tokyo, 1972.

Tanaka Ryō. *Kabuki Jōshiki Butai Zushū (An Illustrated Account of Kabuki Stage Sets).* Tokyo, 1958.

Tōbe Ginsaku. *Kabuki no Engi (Kabuki Acting).* Tokyo, 1956.

———. *Kabuki no Mikata (How to View Kabuki).* Tokyo, 1973.

Toita Yasuji. *Kyō no Kabuki (Today's Kabuki).* Tokyo, 1947.

———. *Maruhon Kabuki (Kabuki Versions of Puppet Plays).* Tokyo, 1949.

———. *Waga Kabuki (Our Kabuki).* 2 vols. Tokyo, 1949.

———. *Kabuki: The Popular Stage.* Trans. Don Kenny. Tokyo and New York, 1971.

———. *Kārā Kabuki no Miryoku (The Charm of Kabuki in Color).* Tokyo, 1973.

Toita Yasuji, ed. *Kabuki Kanshō Nyūmon (An Introduction to Kabuki Appreciation).* Tokyo, 1971.

Tsubouchi Shōyō, and Yamamoto Jirō. *History and Characteristics of Kabuki.* Yokohama, 1960.

Waseda Theatre Museum. *Meisaku Kabuki Zenshū (Complete Collection of Kabuki Masterpieces).* Tokyo, 1967-1974.

Waseda Theatre Museum, ed. *Geinō Jiten (Dictionary of Traditional Entertainments).* Tokyo, 1974.

Yamamoto Jirō et al. *Kabuki Jiten (An Encyclopedia of Kabuki).* Tokyo, 1972.

Yoshida Chiaki. *Kabuki.* Tokyo, 1971.

In addition, the following periodicals were of invaluable aid:

Jōen Shiryōshū, a monthly series published by the National Theatre providing many pertinent facts about the play being performed in the month the specific pamphlet is published.

Engekikai, a monthly magazine of Japanese theater arts, with excellent articles and numerous photographs.
Kabuki, a quarterly, each issue of which usually contains an exhaustive account of one famous Kabuki play.
Engei Gahō, no longer published, an old periodical of inestimable value in documenting late nineteenth- and early twentieth-century Kabuki.

Index